THE FATHERS
OF THE CHURCH

MEDIAEVAL CONTINUATION

VOLUME 10

THE FATHERS
OF THE CHURCH

MEDIAEVAL CONTINUATION

LANFRANC
OF CANTERBURY
ON THE BODY AND BLOOD
OF THE LORD
&

GUITMUND OF AVERSA
ON THE TRUTH OF THE BODY
AND BLOOD OF CHRIST IN THE
EUCHARIST

Translated by

MARK G. VAILLANCOURT

THE CATHOLIC UNIVERSITY OF AMERICA PRESS
Washington, D.C.

The paper used in this publication meets the minimum
requirements of the American National Standards for
Information Science—Permanence of Paper for Printed
Library Materials, ANSI z39.48—1984.
∞

LIBRARY OF CONGRESS CATALOGING-IN-PUBLICATION DATA
Lanfranc, Archbishop of Canterbury, 1005?–1089.
[Liber de corpore et sanguine Domini. English]
On the body and blood of the Lord / Lanfranc of Canterbury.
On the truth of the body and blood of Christ in the Eucharist
/ Guitmund of Aversa ; translated by Mark G. Vaillancourt.
p. cm. — (The fathers of the church mediaeval
continuation ; v. 10)
Includes bibliographical references and indexes.
ISBN 978-0-8132-1678-2 (cloth : alk. paper)
1. Transubstantiation.   2. Berengar, of Tours, ca. 1000–
1088.   3. Transubstantiation—History of doctrines—Middle
Ages, 600–1500.   I. Vaillancourt, Mark G., 1959–
II. Guitmund, of Aversa, 11th cent. De corporis et sanguinis
Christi veritate. English.   III. Title.   IV. Series.
BX2220.L36 2009
234'.163088282—dc22
2009002800

Dedicated to
FR. JOSEPH T. LIENHARD, S.J.,
and
FR. JAMES T. O'CONNOR

CONTENTS

LANFRANC, *ON THE BODY AND BLOOD OF THE LORD*

GUITMUND, *ON THE TRUTH OF THE BODY AND BLOOD OF CHRIST*

ACKNOWLEDGMENTS

The inspiration for the translation of Guitmund of Aversa's *De veritate* came from Fr. James T. O'Connor's work *The Hidden Manna*. A long-time friend, Fr. O'Connor offered a great deal of sage theological advice for the commentary, and his critique of the translation of Lanfranc's *De corpore* was most helpful. This volume, developed out of my dissertation for the doctoral program at Fordham University, which contained only Guitmund's work, was guided with the utmost care and patience by Fr. Joseph T. Lienhard, S.J., who proved to be a great mentor and friend. Both Fr. Lienhard and Fr. O'Connor deserve from me not only a special word of thanks, but also of recognition, as scholars, theologians, and priests devoted to Christ in the Eucharist.

I would like to take this opportunity to thank His Eminence, Edward Cardinal Egan, for supporting my studies, and the readers of the dissertation, Fr. Joseph Koterski, S.J., and Dr. George Demacopoulos of Fordham University. I would also like to offer a special commemoration to His Eminence, the late Avery Cardinal Dulles, S.J., who, as an examiner at my defense, urged this publication for the history of the Sacrament.

The many drafts to the manuscript required the assistance of an equal number of proofreaders: the Rev. Msgr. John McCarthy, pastor of St. Patrick's Parish on Staten Island, the Rev. John Wroblewski, pastor of St. Anthony's Parish on Staten Island, Sr. Mary McCaffrey, O.S.F., of Kennedy Catholic High School, and Mrs. Joanne Baranello of St. Charles Parish, Staten Island. I thank them all for their hard work and patience.

I thank for their help the Head of Circulation at the Walsh Library of Fordham University, Mr. John D'Angelo, and Sr. Monica Wood, S.C., Director of the Corrigan Memorial Library at St. Joseph's Seminary.

I also have to thank for their support and encouragement Mr. David DeMartino, President of the parish council of St. Patrick's Parish; the Rev. Msgr. Joseph C. Ansaldi, Principal of St. Joseph-by-the-Sea High School, Staten Island, New York, and his Vice Principal, Fr. Michael P. Reilly; Deacon Alfred Impallemeni of Kennedy Catholic High School, Somers, New York; Fr. Fernando Hernandez, pastor of St. Patrick's Parish in Newburgh, New York; Fr. Kazimierz Kowalski, pastor of the Church of Our Lady of Good Counsel in Manhattan; and Fr. Rees Doughty, the pastor of St. Ann's Church in Nyack, New York.

I also wish to thank Dr. Carole Monica Burnett for the fine job she did in editing the manuscript and Dr. Gregory F. LaNave and Dr. David J. McGonagle for publishing it with the Catholic University of America Press.

I would be remiss if I did not thank in a very special way Peter and Martha Marron of the Marron Foundation, whose generosity to my many projects helped make this one a success. And to my brother David and sister Janice, I am grateful for your ever-present support.

ABBREVIATIONS

ACO	Acta Conciliorum Oecumenicorum
ACW	Ancient Christian Writers
CCCM	Corpus Christianorum Continuatio Mediaevalis
CDM	Chiese del Mezzogiorno
COD	Conciliorum Oecumenicorum Decreta
CPL	Clavis Patrum Latinorum
CSEL	Corpus Scriptorum Ecclesiasticorum Latinorum
CSL	Corpus Christianorum, Series Latina
CT	The Christian Tradition
DC	*De corpore et sanguine Domini*
DS	Denziger Schönmetzer
DTC	*Dictionnaire de théologie catholique*
DV	*De corporis et sanguinis Christi veritate in Eucharistia*
FC	Fathers of the Church
HC	History of the Church
MC	Montclos-Migne Editions
NPNF	Nicene and Post-Nicene Fathers
PG	Patrologia Graeca
PL	Patrologia Latina
SCG	*Summa contra Gentiles*
SCh	Sources chrétiennes
SP	Sanctorum Patrum opuscula selecta
ST	*Summa Theologiae*
Vg	Vulgate
WSA	Works of St. Augustine

SELECT BIBLIOGRAPHY

Sources

Ambrose of Milan. *Saint Ambrose: Theological and Dogmatic Works.* Trans. R. Deferrari. FC 44. Washington, DC: The Catholic University of America Press, 1963.

Anselm of Canterbury. *Why God Became Man.* Trans. J. Colleran. Albany: Magi Books, 1969.

Augustine of Hippo. *Expositions of the Psalms: 33–50.* Trans. M. Boulding. WSA 3/16. Hyde Park, NY: New City Press, 2002.

———. *Expositions of the Psalms: 73–98.* Trans. M. Boulding. WSA 3/18. Hyde Park, NY: New City Press, 2002.

———. *Sermons.* Trans. E. Hill. WSA 3/6. New Rochelle, NY: New City Press, 1995.

———. *St. Augustine: Teaching Christianity.* Trans. E. Hill. WSA 1/11. Hyde Park, NY: New City Press, 1996.

———. *Tractates on the Gospel of John: 11–27.* Trans. J. Rettig. FC 79. Washington, DC: The Catholic University of America Press, 1988.

Berengar of Tours. *De sacra coena: Rescriptum contra Lanfrannum.* CCCM 84. Turnhout: Brepols, 1988.

———. *Serta Mediaevalia Textus varii saeculorum X–XIII.* CCCM 171. Turnhout: Brepols, 2000.

———. *Epistola contra Almannum.* In *Lanfranc et Bérenger.* Edited by J. de Montclos. Pp. 531–38.

Biblia Sacra: Iuxta vulgatam versionem. Edited by R. Weber. 2 vols. Stuttgart: Württembergische Bibelanstalt, 1969.

Cyprian of Carthage. *St. Cyprian: Letters (1–81).* Trans. R. Donna. FC 51. Washington, DC: The Catholic University of America Press, 1964.

Cyril of Alexandria. "Cyril's Third Letter Against Nestorius." Translation from *Creeds, Councils and Controversies: Documents Illustrating the History of the Church AD 337–461.* Cambridge: University Press, 1991.

Durandus of Troarn. *De corpore et sanguine Christi contra Berengarium et ejus sectatores.* PL 149: 1375–1424.

Gregory the Great. *St. Gregory the Great: Dialogues.* Trans. O. J. Zimmerman. FC 39. New York: Fathers of the Church, Inc., 1959.

Guitmund, Archbishop of Aversa. *Confessio de sancta Trinitate, Christi humanitate, corporisque et sanguinis Domini nostri veritate.* PL 149: 1495–1502.

―――. *De corporis et sanguinis Christi veritate in eucharistia libri tres.* PL 149: 1427–94.

―――. *Epistola ad Erfastum.* PL 149: 1502–8.

―――. *Oratio ad Guillelmum I Anglorum regem cum recusaret episcopatum.* PL 149: 1510–12.

―――. *La "Verità" dell' Eucaristia.* Trans. L. Orabano. Naples: Edizioni Scientifiche Italiane, 1995.

Hilary of Poitiers. *Saint Hilary of Poitiers: The Trinity.* Trans. S. McKenna. FC 25. New York: Fathers of the Church, Inc., 1954.

Hurter, H., ed. SP 38. Innsbruck: Libraria Academica Wagneriana, 1879.

Lanfranc of Canterbury. *De corpore et sanguine Domini adversus Berengarium Turonensem.* PL 150: 407–42.

Leclercq, Jean. "Passage authentique inédit de Guitmond d'Aversa." *Revue Bénédictine* 57 (1947): 212–14.

Leo the Great. Sermon 91. *De Jejunio septimi mensis.* PL 54: 452.

Mansi, G. D., ed. *Sacrorum conciliorum nova et amplissima collectio.* Vol. 19. Paris and Leipzig: H. Welter, 1902.

Paschasius Radbertus. *De corpore et sanguine Domini: cum appendice epistola ad Fredugardum.* CCCM 16. Turnhout: Brepols, 1969.

Ratramnus. *De corpore et sanguine Domini.* PL 121: 103–222.

Studies

Bareille, G. "Eucharistie d'après les pères." *Dictionnaire de théologie catholique* 5, 1134–81. Paris: Letouzey et Ané, 1913.

Benoit, Pierre. "The Ascension." *Jesus and the Gospel.* Vol. 1. New York: Seabury, 1973. Pp. 209–53.

Cowdrey, H. *Lanfranc: Scholar, Monk, and Archbishop.* Oxford: Oxford University Press, 2003.

Gaudel, A. "Stercorianisme." *Dictionnaire de théologie catholique* 14, 2590–2612. Paris: Letouzey et Ané, 1941.

Geiselmann, Joseph. *Die Eucharistielehre der Vorscholastik.* Paderborn: F. Schonigh, 1926.

Gibson, Margaret. *Lanfranc of Bec.* Oxford: Oxford University Press, 2002.

Grabmann, Martin. *Die Geschichte der scholastischen Methode nach den gedruckten und ungedruckten Quellen dargestellt.* Freiburg: Herdersche Verlagshandlung, 1909.

Jungmann, Joseph. *The Mass of the Roman Rite: Its Origins and Development.* Trans. F. Brunner. 2 vols. New York: Benziger Bros., 1949.

Kempf, Friedrich. *The Church in the Age of Feudalism.* Trans. A. Biggs. HC 3. New York: Crossroad Publishing Co., 1982.

Lienhard, Joseph T. Contra Marcellum: *Marcellus of Ancyra and Fourth-Century Theology.* Washington, DC: The Catholic University of America Press, 1999.

Loofs, F. "The Lord's Supper." *Schaff-Herzog Encyclopedia of Religious Knowledge.* Edited by S. Jackson and L. Loetschen, vol. 7. Grand Rapids: Baker Book House, 1955. Pp. 24–37.

Lubac, Henri de. *Corpus Mysticum.* Paris: Aubier, 1949.

Macdonald, A. J. *Berengar and the Reform of Sacramental Doctrine.* New York: Longman's, Green and Co., 1930.

———. *Lanfranc: A Study of his Life, Work and Writing.* Oxford: Oxford University Press, 1926.

Macy, Gary. *The Theologies of the Eucharist in the Early Scholastic Period.* Oxford: Clarendon Press, 1984.

———. *Treasures from the Storeroom: Medieval Religion and the Eucharist.* Collegeville, MN: The Liturgical Press, 1999.

Moloney, Raymond. *Problems in Theology: The Eucharist.* Collegeville, MN: The Liturgical Press, 1995.

Montclos, Jean de. *Lanfranc et Bérenger: La controverse Eucharistique du XIe siècle.* Louvain: Spicilegium Sacrum Lovaniense, 1971.

O'Connor, James T. *The Hidden Manna: A Theology of the Eucharist.* San Francisco: Ignatius Press, 2005.

Pelikan, Jaroslav. *The Growth of Medieval Theology (600–1300).* CT 3. Chicago: University of Chicago Press, 1978.

Radding, Charles, and Francis Newton. *Theology, Rhetoric, and Politics in the Eucharistic Controversy, 1078–1079: Alberic of Monte Cassino against Berengar of Tours.* New York: Columbia University Press, 2003.

Rahner, Karl. "The Duration of the Presence of Christ after Communion." *Theological Investigations* 4, 312–20. Baltimore: Helicon Press, 1966.

Sasse, Hermann. *This Is My Body.* Minneapolis: Augsburg Publishing House, 1959.

Shaughnessy, Patrick. "The Eucharistic Doctrine of Guitmund of Aversa: A Dissertation Submitted to the Theological Faculty of the Pontifical Academical Institution of St. Anselm." Rome: Scuola Salesiana del Libro, 1939.

Sheedy, Charles. "The Eucharistic Controversy of the Eleventh Century against the Background of Pre-Scholastic Theology: A Dissertation Submitted to the Faculty of Sacred Theology of the Catholic University of America in Partial Fulfillment of the Requirements for the Degree of Doctor of Sacred Theology." Washington, DC: The Catholic University of America Press, 1947.

Somerville, Robert. "The Case Against Berengar of Tours: A New Text." *Studi Gregoriani* 9 (1972): 55–75.

———. *Pope Urban II: The* Collectio Britannica *and the Council of Melfi (1089).* Oxford: Clarendon Press, 1996.

Stone, Darwell. *A History of the Doctrine of the Holy Eucharist.* 2 vols. New York: Longmans, Green and Co., 1909.

Vaillancourt, Mark. "The Role of Guitmund of Aversa in the Developing Theology of the Eucharist: A Dissertation Submitted in Partial Fulfillment of the Requirements for the Degree of Doctor of Philosophy

in the Department of Theology at Fordham University." New York:
Fordham University, May 2004.

———. "Guitmund of Aversa and Aquinas's Eucharistic Theology." *The Thomist* 68, 4 (October 2004).

———. "The Eucharistic Vision of Guitmund of Aversa." *Homiletic and Pastoral Review* 106 (January 2006): 46–52.

Vernet, F. "Eucharistie du IX à la fin du XI siècle." *Dictionnaire de théologie catholique* 5, 1209–33. Paris: Letouzey et Ané, 1913.

INTRODUCTION

INTRODUCTION

Next to Berengarius of Tours, Lanfranc of Canterbury stands out as one of the most significant figures in the eucharistic crisis of the eleventh century. Although he was only prior of Bec at the onset of the controversy, his theological acumen and forensic abilities were a significant factor in the literary warfare which marked the period of time immediately following the Council of Rome in 1059. The situation is much different, however, with Guitmund of Aversa. A student of Lanfranc and future Archbishop of Aversa, Guitmund's name surfaces very little in the literary cross-fire of the period, and unlike Lanfranc, is someone whom Berengarius never mentions by name. Yet despite the great difference in popularity, Guitmund's contribution to the development of eucharistic theology far outweighs that of his former master. Lacking all the polemical color that marks Lanfranc's *De corpore et sanguine Domini*, Guitmund's *De corporis et sanguinis Christi veritate in eucharistia* is a far more profound document, in both its depth of theological reflection and its breadth of doctrinal expression—a fact that readily explains why his work, unlike Lanfranc's, had a very real impact on the theological issues of the time.

I. THE EUCHARISTIC THEOLOGIES
OF LANFRANC AND GUITMUND

The two poles in the debate over the presence of Christ in the Eucharist are the professions of faith of the Roman councils in 1059 and 1079,[1] and taken together, they make a strong affirmation of the two doctrines that Berengarius consistently de-

1. See chapter 2 of Lanfranc's *De corpore* for the full text of each profession of faith.

nied: the Real Presence and the doctrine later to be defined as Transubstantiation. Whereas the former asserted the fact of Christ's presence, the latter defined exactly what that presence was and how it came about, for the profession of 1079 made it clear that the Real Presence of Christ in the Eucharist was none other than the same body born of the Virgin, made present on the altar by a substantial conversion [*substantialiter converti*] of the elements at the consecration.

The council of 1059, on the other hand, said that this same body was broken by the hands of the priest and chewed by the teeth of the faithful—not just sacramentally but physically [*sensualiter*]. And it will be Lanfranc's great task to prosecute Berengarius's misrepresentation of the events of the 1059 council, and Guitmund's even greater one to prove that what the council taught was not only the Church's tradition, but the reasonable faith of every Catholic as well. Let us turn, then, first to the mentor, Lanfranc, and after that we shall assess the faithful student, Guitmund, and see how both together articulated the Church's faith against the criticisms of Berengarian rationalism.

A. Lanfranc of Bec

The general consensus is that the *De corpore et sanguine domini* was written by Lanfranc at the request of a former student, Theodoric of Paderborn, shortly after the deaths of Humbert and Leo in the year 1061. This places the date around 1062, while he was still prior at Bec and just before he became the abbot at Caen.[2] The tract was written ostensibly to refute Berengarius's polemical pamphlet the *Scriptum contra synodum,* a literary attack on the council of 1059, written soon after the council itself. All that survives of the document today is the fragment made up of twenty-three excerpts found in Lanfranc's work.[3] It is safe to

2. See Margaret Gibson, *Lanfranc of Bec* (Oxford: Clarendon Press, 2002), 103; Jean de Montclos, *Lanfranc et Bérenger: La controverse eucharistique du XIe siècle* (Louvain: Spicilegium Sacrum Lovaniense, 1971), 196.

3. H. E. Cowdrey, *Lanfranc: Scholar, Monk and Archbishop* (Oxford: Oxford University Press, 2003), 64. Macdonald cites an alternative tradition that the work of Berengarius was received by Lanfranc "for destruction," and holds the view that Berengarius's work could not have been written before 1059 or later

hold, then, that it was started sometime in 1062, finished in 1063, and edited by Lanfranc himself after 1079 to include the second profession of faith of the Roman council.[4]

Although the twentieth-century literature on the period is extensive, there is no study of the events and doctrine that can compare with Jean de Montclos's monograph *Lanfranc et Bérenger: La controverse eucharistique du XIe siècle.* In this work Montclos does for the eucharistic doctrine of Lanfranc what I have tried to do for the doctrine of Guitmund in my own.[5] I will give a brief summary of his assessment[6] and then refer the interested reader to his work for a more detailed study of the subject. For the sake of brevity, however, I will restrict my analysis to Lanfranc's doctrine on the Real Presence, and when the time comes to treat the doctrine of Guitmund, I shall limit myself to the same—for that was what Berengarius really challenged, and what Lanfranc and Guitmund faithfully defended.

1. The Real Presence of Christ in the Eucharist

Central to any discussion of Lanfranc's theology of the Real Presence is the confession contained in chapter eighteen, the first of five chapters that offer an exposé of his faith:

We believe, therefore, that the earthly substances, which on the table of the Lord are divinely sanctified by the priestly ministry, are ineffably, incomprehensibly, miraculously converted by the workings of heavenly power into the essence of the Lord's body. The species and whatever other certain qualities of the earthly substances themselves, however, are preserved, so that those who see it may not be horrified at the sight of flesh and blood, and believers may have a greater reward for their faith at the sight. It is, nonetheless, the body of the Lord himself exist-

---

than 1061; see A. J. Macdonald, *Lanfranc: A Study of his Life, Work and Writing* (Oxford: Oxford University Press, 1926), 52.

4. Montclos, *Lanfranc et Bérenger,* 261.

5. See my dissertation entitled, "The Role of Guitmund of Aversa in the Developing Theology of the Eucharist: A Dissertation Submitted in Partial Fulfillment of the Requirements for the Degree of Doctor of Philosophy in the Department of Theology at Fordham University" (New York: Fordham University, May 2004), and my article "Guitmund of Aversa and Aquinas's Eucharistic Theology," *The Thomist* 68, 4 (October, 2004).

6. I have in effect summarized Montclos's thought as it can be found in chap. 18, "Veritas Carnis ac Sanguinis," of his work *Lanfranc et Bérenger,* 346–91.

ing in heaven at the right side of the Father, immortal, inviolate, whole, uncontaminated, and unharmed.[7]

From this confession, one can see three points of doctrine in Lanfranc's understanding of the nature of the Real Presence:

(1) The earthly substances of bread and wine that are placed on the altar to be consecrated in the Mass are miraculously changed, through the ministry of the priest, by a divine power, at the consecration.

(2) These substances are changed in "essence" into the body of the Lord, while the former appearances of bread and wine, along with the other certain qualities of the things which they once were, are retained.

(3) This body of the Lord is the same body of the Savior born of the Virgin, who exists at the right hand of the Father: immortal, inviolate, whole, entire, and intact in heaven, while at the same time essentially on the altar under the forms of bread and wine.

Let us now turn our attention to each of these three points in particular, and expound at length how Lanfranc understands them.

a. The Substantial Change in the Elements of Bread and Wine

Lanfranc's view of the transformation of the elements can be summed up in these words: "We believe, therefore, that the earthly substances, which on the table of the Lord are divinely sanctified by the priestly ministry, are ineffably, incomprehensibly, miraculously converted by the workings of heavenly power into the essence of the Lord's body."[8]

For Lanfranc, the consecration effects a miraculous transformation of the elements of bread and wine on the altar such that they become in "essence" the flesh and blood of Christ. This consecration takes place through the ministry of the priest, and is an action that Lanfranc describes as a benediction [*benedictio*].[9] This conversion of the elements, which effects the Real Presence of Christ upon the altar, is supernatural, beyond the

7. *DC* 18, PL 150: 430B–C.   8. Ibid.
9. *DC* 9, PL 150: 420A.

ability of the human mind to comprehend, and is accessible to the mind only by faith. The words that describe this change are as follows: *converti*,[10] *mutari*,[11] *conversio*,[12] *commutari*,[13] *materialis mutatio*,[14] *transferri*,[15] *transire*,[16] and *fieri*.[17]

The Eucharist itself is realized on the part of the bread and the wine—material realities both visible and corruptible, which, after the consecration, become the invisible and incorruptible flesh and blood of Christ. The bread and wine placed on the altar are transformed *essentially* in substance into the body and blood of the Lord, where the *nature* of the bread and wine themselves are replaced by the *nature* of the flesh and the blood of Christ. It is a miraculous work of divine power that supplants the reality of the bread and wine with the flesh and blood of Christ.

The words that Lanfranc uses to express this new reality are as follows: Christ,[18] the Lord Jesus Christ,[19] the Eucharist,[20] the mystery of faith,[21] the divine mystery,[22] the Host and the Blood,[23] the sacrifice of Christians,[24] the sacrifice of the Church.[25]

In the *De corpore*, Lanfranc insists that this change brings about an authentic presence of Christ in the Eucharist. It is a change that affects the very essence of the bread and wine by transforming their natures in such a way that the bread and wine essentially, or really, change into the body and blood of Christ. The Eucharist, then, because of this change, really and truly becomes the body and blood of the Lord. It is a realism which holds that the flesh of Christ present on the altar is the same as that which came forth from the Virgin Mary, and the body of Christ is the same historical body that trod upon the earth, suffered under the hands of sinful men, died, rose again, and is now seated at the right hand of the Father in heaven.[26] It is the same body, and

---

10. *DC* 4, PL 150: 414B.

11. *DC* 7, PL 150: 417B.

12. *DC* 9, PL 150: 420A.

13. *DC* 8, PL 150: 419A.

14. *DC* 5, PL 150: 415B.

15. *DC* 6, PL 150: 416A.

16. *DC* 10, PL 150: 420C.

17. *DC* 20, PL 150: 438A.

18. *DC* 11, PL 150: 422A.

19. *DC* 17, PL 150: 427C.

20. *DC* 4, PL 150: 413B–C.

21. *DC* 7, PL 150: 416D.

22. *DC* 1, PL 150: 409A.

23. *DC* 13, PL 150: 423A.

24. *DC* 9, PL 150: 419D.

25. *DC* 10, PL 150: 421B.

26. The eucharistic theology of both Lanfranc and Guitmund derives from the theology of Paschasius Radbertus, the ninth-century abbot of Corbie and

yet not the same body, for unlike the glorified body in heaven, the body of Christ on the altar appears under the forms of bread and wine.

b. The Species of Bread and Wine

For Lanfranc, after the consecration, although there has been a substantial change in the elements, "the species and whatever other certain qualities of the earthly substances themselves, however, are preserved, so that those who see it may not be horrified at the sight of flesh and blood, and believers may have a greater reward for their faith at the sight."[27]

A consideration of the eucharistic species themselves draws one's attention to how that which is visible and palpable—the appearances of bread and wine—relates to that which is invisible and impalpable—the true body and the blood of Christ. This distinction between the hidden reality of the body and the blood and the outward appearances of bread and wine is the point of doctrine which Lanfranc insists upon throughout the whole of his involvement in the argument with Berengarius. For the Christian, Lanfranc says, is called to contemplate not those things which are seen, but those which are unseen.[28] Such an activity calls for a humble attitude of faith before the "mystery" of the Eucharist, which is a sacrament of the Lord's body and blood and a reality of the same:

The sacrament of the body of Christ, as much as it looks to the Lord Christ himself who was immolated upon the cross, is his flesh, which we receive in the sacrament covered in the form of bread, and is his blood, which we drink under the taste and appearance of wine. The flesh is the sacrament of the flesh, and the blood is the sacrament of the blood. In the flesh and the blood, both of which are invisible, intelligible, spiritual, there is signified the body of the Redeemer, which is visible, palpable, manifestly full of every grace and virtue and the divine majesty. When the first is broken and divided up unto the salvation of the people, and the other is poured from the chalice and received by the mouth of the faithful, his death upon the cross and the blood flowing from his side are symbolized.[29]

---

the author of the first monograph on the Eucharist, *De corpore et sanguine domini*, CCCM 16.

27. *DC* 17, PL 150: 430A.   28. *DC* 1, PL 150: 409A.
29. *DC* 14, PL 150: 424A.

The sacramentality of the Eucharist, therefore, resides primarily with the external appearances and secondarily with the inner reality. The Eucharist, then, is constituted in two principles—the visible and the invisible—for "the sacrifice of the Church exists in two realities and is confected in two things, that is, in the visible appearance of the elements, and in the invisible flesh and blood of the Lord Jesus Christ, namely, in the sacrament and in the reality of the sacrament."[30] That which is symbolized, then, is conveyed to the senses by way of the appearances, but what is communicated to the soul is not a mere symbol but reality in truth:

Yet the Church salubriously believes and truly recognizes that it is a sacrament of the Lord's Passion, a sacrament of divine propitiation, a sacrament of concord and unity, and finally, a sacrament of the flesh and blood assumed each in its own distinct and unique way from the Virgin.[31]

The elements of bread and wine on the altar he calls the "visible species," which cover or envelop the invisible realities of the flesh and blood of the Lord.[32] They are called the "body and blood" of Christ, because they are essentially the same, yet significantly different in the qualities: "Indeed, it is the same body as far as it concerns its essence, true nature, and its own excellence. It is not the same body in its appearance, however, if one is considering the species of bread and wine and the rest of the qualities mentioned above."[33]

It is significant to note, that, unlike Guitmund, Lanfranc never uses the word "accidents" to describe these qualities, nor does he attempt to distinguish the appearance of bread and wine from the "substance" of the flesh and the blood in an Aristotelian substance-accident composite. Instead, he uses the substantive noun *essentia* seven times, and the adverb *essentialiter* three times to maintain the distinction between the bread and the wine on the altar and the body and the blood of the Lord. In

30. *DC* 9, PL 150: 421C.
31. *DC* 5, PL 150: 415A.
32. *DC* 14, PL 150: 424A. Lanfranc uses the word *opertim* of the bread in relation to the Lord's body.
33. *DC* 18, PL 150: 430C.

the Eucharist, the interior "essence" is the body and blood of the Lord, while that which is visible is only the "appearance" of bread and wine. Thus the conversion in the elements, because of the power of the consecration, brings about a real change in the inner reality which leaves the outward appearances and sensual qualities unaffected.

The first reason for the retention of the external species of bread and wine is for the exercise of faith. For the great mystery of the Eucharist is that it hides the glory of the risen Christ behind the veil of terrestrial substances. The second reason is to shelter the faithful on earth from the horror at the sight of eating the flesh and drinking the blood of Christ, who remains "immortal, inviolate, whole, uncontaminated, and unharmed" in heaven.

c. The Relationship Between the Flesh and Blood on the Altar and the Body of Christ in Heaven

Lanfranc expresses the relationship between the body of Christ in heaven and the body of Christ on the altar in these words: "It is, nonetheless, the body of the Lord himself existing in heaven at the right side of the Father, immortal, inviolate, whole, uncontaminated, and unharmed."[34]

The main point of the Berengarian argument was the impossibility of eating the flesh and drinking the blood of Christ on the altar, the same Christ who is now whole and entire in heaven, seated at the right hand of the Father, and will not leave there until the end of the world. To counter this point, Lanfranc adds a level of precision to his understanding of the Real Presence by holding for a nuanced presence of Christ on the altar. "Truly" he says, "it is possible to say, therefore, that it is the same body that was assumed from the Virgin, and also not the same body, which we receive."[35] It is the same body, because the consecrated elements are essentially the same as the body which is glorified in heaven, and it is not the same body, because one beholds it under the appearances of bread and wine. "For both the body and the blood are real, and both are those which have

34. Ibid.
35. Ibid.

been taken from the Virgin. Indeed, the flesh is received by way of the flesh itself, and the blood is received by way of the blood itself, but not without a certain amount of mystery."[36]

Lanfranc supports this distinction verbally by referring to the realities on the altar as "the flesh and the blood" which relate to the "body" of Christ in heaven. Thus the flesh and blood of Christ are on the altar, but the body of Christ, that is, Christ's own proper body, is in heaven. The bread and the wine on the altar, which are essentially the same reality as the body of Christ, retain their former appearances to veil this mystery. This appearance Montclos calls a "secondary essence" in an Aristotelian sense; that is, they are incomplete in themselves. The principal essence, from which they receive their existence, is Christ's own flesh and blood: "For we do indeed believe that the Lord Jesus is truly and salubriously eaten on earth by worthy recipients, and we most certainly hold that he exists in heaven uncontaminated, incorrupt, and unharmed."[37]

This distinction within Lanfranc's understanding of the Real Presence, though incomplete, will receive a far more expanded treatment in the work of one of his former students from Bec: Guitmund of Aversa.

B. Guitmund of Aversa

Written ostensibly to address questions on the Eucharist by a certain monk named Roger, it is apparent from internal evidence that the *De corporis et sanguinis Christi veritate in eucharistia* of Guitmund of Aversa could not have been written before Hildebrand became pope,[38] or after the Roman council of 1079. It was probably written while Guitmund was still in Normandy, before he left for Rome, and very possibly before the council of Poitiers in 1075. It is safe, then, to date the publication of the *De veritate* around the end of the Berengarian controversy between the years 1073 and 1075.

It is clear from the text that the work is a theological defense

36. *DC* 15, PL 150: 425C.
37. *DC* 17, PL 150: 427C.
38. See *De veritate* 3.42. Numeration refers to the SP 38 edition of Hurter; see embedded notation for cross-reference to PL 149.

of the "Ego Berengarius" confession of faith of 1059, because it contains language characterized by some theologians as "grossly material"[39] or "carnalist,"[40] that is, statements that the body of Christ is chewed by the teeth in Holy Communion, not just sacramentally [*sacramentaliter*] but sensibly [*sensualiter*]. To defend this definition, Guitmund uses two words, both verbs that appear as passive infinitives in the Latin text, which serve as points of departure for Guitmund's doctrinal exposition on the Real Presence: *atteri* and *dissipari*,[41] and an analysis of both will clearly illustrate Guitmund's understanding of the same.

1. The Body of Christ is Chewed by the Teeth: Atteri

Guitmund begins his treatise with a certain Augustinian boldness when he asks: "Why is it not right for Christ to be chewed by the teeth?"[42] For him, the objection can admit of only two prospects: either it is not possible for God to will such a thing, or, even if he could, it would be beneath his dignity to do so. To the first, Guitmund adduces the all-powerful will of God. If God has willed it, there is nothing on the part of created reality that can resist it,[43] for, to quote the psalmist, "whatever God has willed to do, he has done, both in heaven and on earth" (Ps 134.6, Vg). For as Author of creation, God can will a relationship between Christ's body in heaven and the faithful on earth, in such a way that it can be touched by them today just as physically as it could then, that is, when Christ was still on this earth.

Guitmund then asks: "Just what do they mean by *atteri*?"[44] If by *atteri,* he says, they mean "to touch more closely" or "more forcefully," then why cannot Christ be touched? Was not Christ touched by Thomas and the holy women after his Resurrection? "If, therefore, after the Resurrection the body of the Lord could

---

39. A. J. Macdonald, *Berengar and the Reform of Sacramental Doctrine* (New York: Longmans, Green and Co., 1930), 131.

40. J. de Montclos, *Lanfranc et Bérenger,* 25.

41. Thomas, in his commentary on the 1059 oath (*ST* 3, 77, a. 7 ad 3), uses the word *masticari* instead of *atteri* and *dissipari,* but the sense is the same: that is, these two words taken together mean the one process of mastication during Holy Communion.

42. *DV* 1.10.   43. Ibid.

44. Ibid.

be touched by the hands of the Apostle Thomas and the holy women, why can it not be touched either lightly or more forcefully by the teeth of the faithful today, that is, be chewed [*atteri*]? There seems to be no reason to prevent it."[45] *Atteri*, therefore, is no more than an extension of the sense of touch—something proper to physical bodies. Since the Eucharist is truly the body of Christ, and Christ's resurrected body has retained its physical nature, it must be possible, then, to touch Christ in the Eucharist—either with the teeth, or the hand, or any other part of the body.

The first argument in the *atteri* discourse was from possibility, and the second is from suitability. One might consider it unseemly to chew Christ with the teeth. But if Christ was "irreligiously crushed [*atteri*] by the unfaithful for the salvation of the faithful, by their rods, the crown of thorns, the cross, the nails, the lance,"[46] would this same Christ refuse, for the sake of the same faithful, to endure that which was less worthy, namely, to be crushed by their teeth? Certainly if Christ subjected himself to the extreme humiliation of the Passion, Guitmund says, which caused his body to be crushed by sinful men, then it stands to reason that he would also allow it to be touched by his faithful today.

Guitmund continues the *atteri* discourse—meant to address the Berengarian objections to 1059—by asking yet another rhetorical question: does "to press more forcefully" mean the same thing as "to wound"? The former, he says, pertains to the sense of touch, which is natural to human flesh, but the latter belongs to the infirm character of our mortal human nature. "The flesh of the resurrected Lord," he says, "retained what was of its nature, and lost what belonged to its infirmity." Christ, therefore, can be pressed by the teeth of the faithful with all the strength that is in them, and they can never harm or wound him, for his resurrected flesh, characterized by impassibility, is now impervious to any form of injury or suffering.[47]

After a lengthy treatise on these Berengarian objections, Guitmund concludes:

45. Ibid.   46. *DV* 1.11.
47. *DV* 1.13.

Therefore, since there exists no impossibility, nor does the humility of Christ shun it (if it is necessary for our life), and since there is no possibility of bringing uncleanness to the Savior in this, or wounding him bodily, then there is no reason why it would be unlawful for Christ to be chewed [*atteri*] with the teeth. Therefore, if *atteri* means "to be touched more forcefully," then what they arrogantly say, that is, "It is not right for Christ to be chewed [*atteri*] by teeth," has no value as an argument against us.[48]

But if the body of Christ can be chewed by teeth in a way that is both doctrinally defensible and reasonably understandable, one could also ask about its logical consequence: Is that same body also "broken into pieces [*dissipari*], just like those things that teeth chew and break into pieces?"[49] As in the case with *atteri*, so it is with *dissipari:* a close examination reveals a great deal about Guitmund's conception of the Real Presence.

2. *The Body of Christ is Undivided:* Dissipari

No sooner does Guitmund affirm the appropriateness of *atteri*, than he qualifies its logical consequence, *dissipari:* "This then is what we confess: that it is certainly not right for Christ to be ground up into pieces [*dissipari*] by any form of violence, either by the teeth or in any other way."[50] It is this notion of *dissipari*, construed in the context of "bodily division" and applied to the Eucharist, that brings the reader to some of Guitmund's most difficult thought. It is helpful to keep in mind, however, that the principal object under Guitmund's consideration is the Eucharist, which for him *is* the body of Christ. On the level of *presence*, therefore, no distinction is to be made between the body of Christ in heaven, and the body of Christ on the altar, except in the manner of *appearance*. This then leads to a paradox: although the eucharistic body of Christ is broken at the *fractio* at Mass, the glorified body in heaven must be unbroken:

For although the priest seems to divide these [sacraments] because of the great mystery, nevertheless, we should believe that when the venerable body of our Lord and Savior is distributed to the faithful, he has not divided himself up among the individual recipients, but rather, we ought to believe that it is by way of participation that he comes into the diverse members of his faithful.[51]

48. *DV* 1.14.   49. *DV* 1.7.
50. *DV* 1.15.   51. *DV* 1.16.

Here one encounters an important theological principle, drawn from the tradition, articulated by Guitmund, and now a standard in eucharistic theology:

We are also able to say that he is as much in one little portion of the Host as he is in the whole Host. It is as when one reads about the manna, that neither he who gathered more had more, nor he who gathered less had less. Thus the whole Host is the body of Christ in such a way that each and every separate particle is the whole body of Christ. Three separate particles are not three bodies, but only one body. Nor do the particles themselves differ among each other as if they were a plurality, since the one particle is of the whole body as the rest of them are that same body. Therefore, they must not now be called many particles, but rather, one Host, intact and undivided, even though it seems to be divided by the priestly ministry, because of the great mystery, as I have said, which must be celebrated in this way. In a like manner, if the Host seems to be broken by the teeth or in some other way, we understand it to be unbroken, because we believe that the whole body is contained in each single part.[52]

For Guitmund, then, the whole Christ is present entirely under each part of the Host, whether the Host remains whole or is fractioned during Mass, and the whole Christ is entirely present under the whole Host as he is under each fractioned portion of it. None of the different portions of the fractured Host differ among themselves, for they are the one and the same Christ. The same would be true of a thousand Masses offered at the same time, for in each Mass the whole Christ would be present, that is, in each Mass individually, so that Christ himself would not be divided by either the different places or the individual priests, for "at one and the same time in a thousand places the one and the same body of Christ can be whole and undivided."[53]

If Christ is present whole and entire in the Host, as well as in its subsequent divisions, and even present in a thousand Masses at once, how can this certain manner of faith be reasonably possible? By way of explanation, Guitmund resorts to the example of the voice and the soul to illustrate Christ's presence in the Eucharist. For just as the human voice can make known the thoughts of the human heart to many ears at once without be-

52. Ibid.
53. *DV* 1.18.

ing divided in any way, so in the same way does the body of
Christ, one in heaven, come to the many without suffering any
division in himself.[54] Also in a similar way, just as the soul is not
divided among the many members of the body, but is wholly
present entirely to each, so the flesh of Christ is present to his
body, which is the Church, without being divided up in any way:

Why would he who has bestowed such power upon our soul, so that it
is simultaneously one and the same, and indivisible in each and every
portion of its own body, not also be able to give that same dignity to his
own flesh if he wished? Is not his flesh just as powerful, so that it also
could be whole and entire in the diverse portions of his body, which
is the Church, since, just as the soul is the life of our body, so also is
the flesh of the Savior (by all means many times better than our soul
through the grace of God) in a similar way the life of the Church?[55]

In *dissipari*, then, just as in *atteri*, one finds another of Guitmund's important theological principles, namely, the ability of
Christ to be whole and entire in every portion of the Host as
well as to each of the faithful at one and the same time. Because
that body cannot be divided, it cannot be harmed, nor is a
breaking of the Host a cause of division in Christ's body, since,
as many times as it undergoes division, it is not diminished, but
instead remains a means of multiplying the one for the sake of
the many, and at the same time rendering a richly symbolic commemoration of the Lord's Passion.

Should one object that the testimony of the eyes is contrary
to all that he has asserted, Guitmund replies that the senses can
be deceived, often in little things, and always in this one.[56] What
is absolutely essential on the part of the believer, then, is faith.[57]

Next comes a most interesting query: "Is there any difference
in the way that the eyes of the faithful are deceived today, from
the way that the disciples were betrayed by their eyes with the
different appearances of our Lord while he was still upon this
earth?" And it is just this consideration that leads us to perceive
the bread and wine of the Eucharist as just another appearance
of the Lord, or a *species domini*.

54. *DV* 1.19.   55. Ibid.
56. *DV* 1.22.   57. Ibid.

3. The Eucharistic Species

One of the most fascinating aspects of Guitmund's eucharistic theology is his understanding of the sacraments of the altar as another post-Resurrection appearance of the Lord, that is, of a genre like those various appearances of Christ recorded in Scripture where he went unrecognized by his disciples. The notion of the *species domini*[58] has its origin in the theology of Paschasius, but has been expanded in its scope by Guitmund. For in Guitmund's theology, the Real Presence is simply a sacramental continuation of Christ's earthly presence. According to Guitmund, Christ "is wholly in heaven while his whole body is truly eaten upon the earth."[59] What one sees on the altar, therefore, is merely another of the many appearances that Christ assumed while he was in this world, that is, when the disciples, although looking at him, did not recognize him:

> For when Mary Magdalene, weeping at the tomb of the Lord, saw the Lord himself, was it not most certainly Jesus, although, deceived by the eyes, she thought instead that she was looking at a gardener? Or, when the Lord himself, on the day of his own Resurrection, as if he were a pilgrim, explained the Scriptures to two of his disciples while they were walking along the way, was it anyone other than Jesus? For it is written: "Their eyes were held lest they recognize him"?[60]

If the eyes could see the true reality of the sacrament, then one would see the Lord Jesus in his own proper form in the glory of heaven.

In the tradition first articulated by Paschasius, after the consecration the appearances of bread and wine cease to have their own proper reality, but instead, owing to the miracle of transubstantiation, they derive their new reality directly from Christ himself. Viewed in this way, the "sacraments of the Lord's Body and Blood" have lost all of their natural nutritive capacity. Hence in addressing the issue of stercorianism,[61] Guitmund emphatically

---

58. A term that I have coined to classify the scriptural accounts of Christ's being unrecognized by his disciples. Guitmund clearly sees the Eucharist as a mere extension of those events in the life of Christ.

59. *DV* 2.51.

60. *DV* 1.23.

61. The term, which derives its name from the Latin term *stercus,* or "dung,"

denies that "these sacraments" are subject to the same laws of bodily digestion as normal bread and wine.[62] In fact, so direct is the relationship between Christ and the "sacraments of the altar" that Guitmund absolutely rejects any notion that they can corrupt or decay. Christ can never know corruption, and the Eucharist is Christ, the food of eternal life:

> But to us, however, that Eucharist, that divine manna, is the heavenly bread from God. For truly we receive from the sacred altars the flesh of the immaculate Lamb rendered incapable of suffering, through which we both live and are healed from corruption; this flesh can never be corrupted, nor perish, because, although from day to day it renews us, it itself never grows old.[63]

This notion of the absolute impossibility of these "divine sacraments" undergoing any form of corruption, either from being reserved too long or from any other natural process, can be found in Ambrose, but Guitmund's interpretation of it will bring strong criticism upon him. For in Guitmund's theology, the species of the sacrament derive their existence directly from Christ, and hence are completely subject to his will, just as he manifested his glory in the Transfiguration, or disguised his identity in the post-Resurrection appearances:

> [T]he Lord himself is reported to have shown himself to his disciples in different appearances [*species*]. At one time he showed himself to them in the customary color, at another in the transfigured splendor of the sun and snow; at one time he showed himself as a pilgrim, another time he looked like a gardener.[64]

The sacraments of the altar, therefore, are a species of Christ (that is, not his proper, or natural one), and as such are a manifestation of his presence—a presence brought about by transubstantiation.

4. The Substantial Change of the Eucharistic Elements

Towards the end of the first book of the *De veritate,* Guitmund admits that the type of substantial change that one finds in the

---

denotes a doctrine that applies to the objective nature of the eucharistic species themselves, and their subjection to the usual laws of bodily digestion.

62. *DV* 2.13.   63. *DV* 2.2.
64. *DV* 3.29.

Eucharist poses a certain difficulty for some. For in the normal course of events, "when one thing is substantially changed into another [*substantialiter transmutatur*], it is usually changed into that which did not exist before."[65] Nevertheless, in the Eucharist the change involves one reality being transferred into another [*in unum aliud transferatur*],[66] or, to be more specific, "bread and wine . . . change into [*transire*] the body and blood of Christ."[67] It is a type of change "where that which exists passes [*transit*] into that which is no less existing," that is, the one whereby "bread and wine are changed [*commutari*] by a certain unique power into Christ's own body [and blood]."[68]

Guitmund makes it clear that "when . . . we say that the bread is changed, it is not changed into that which had not been flesh, but we confess that it is changed into the flesh which was already the flesh of Christ, without any increase in the flesh of the Lord himself."[69] This last type can be known only by faith;[70] it is reserved by God himself for his own body,[71] and has no equal in the created order.[72] It is singular and unique, open only to the eyes of faith, yet it can be understood from other types of change experienced in nature, and is very similar to that which occurs to accidents inhering in a substance:

[A]bout the singular accidents that depart when other accidents supervene, it would appear that someone cannot say that they become completely nothing. Indeed, if they were something, they would be in a subject. But with contrary ones supervening, they cannot remain in their subject, nor pass over [*transmeare*] into another one. Therefore, they become completely nothing, unless perchance someone could say that they are changed [*transmutari*] into those accidents which supervene. But if this is so, then innumerable examples occur to us of those things which are essentially changed [*essentialiter transmutantur*] into those things which exist in like manner.[73]

In Guitmund's mind, this understanding of accidental change is one that offers an insight into the change that the substances of bread and wine undergo at the consecration, for "just as we

65. *DV* 1.31.
67. *DV* 2.18.
69. *DV* 1.31.
71. *DV* 1.37.
73. *DV* 1.38.

66. *DV* 1.9.
68. *DV* 1.39.
70. Ibid.
72. *DV* 1.34.

have said: the accidents having receded, either they become absolutely nothing, or, if they are changed [*permutantur*], then they are changed into the supervening accidents, which in no small way approaches the matter we are investigating."[74] On the basis of this analogy, the eucharistic change is one where the substance of the bread, by means of a change in the order of substance, becomes the preexisting reality of the body of Christ.

Articulated in this way, the substantial change in the Eucharist parallels that of an accidental change observed in nature, that is, the change whereby accidents that inhere in a substance are changed into those accidents which are coming down upon the subject, the substance itself remaining the same. So for Guitmund, transubstantiation involves accidental change in reverse; in other words, substances change while the accidents remain. Thus in Guitmund's doctrine, as in later Scholastic theology, the substantial change in the Eucharist is a change that takes place in the order of reality, where the reality of the bread gives way to the higher reality of Christ's body, and the reality of the wine gives way to the higher reality of Christ's blood. What remains are only the "appearances" of bread and wine, which have retained their "likeness" to the former reality that they once were, for "the substances [*substantiae*] of things are changed, but, on account of horror, the prior taste, color, and the other accidents [*accidentia*], in so far as they pertain to the senses, are retained."[75]

C. Conclusions: Lanfranc and Guitmund

Certainly both Lanfranc and Guitmund made a contribution to the Church's understanding of the nature of the Real Presence by responding to the questions that arose out of the eucharistic crisis of the eleventh century; from the standpoint of theological development, however, Guitmund added far more than Lanfranc. This is because Guitmund's doctrine contributed to the magisterial deliberations of the period. If one accepts the position that Gregory VII himself insisted that the adverb [*substantialiter*] be included in the profession of faith of 1079, then, as far as it concerns the history of eucharistic doctrine, Guit-

---

74. Ibid.
75. *DV* 3.28.

mund is to be credited with that innovation. Guitmund uses the word *substantialiter* twenty-four times in his work, and when it modifies a verb that describes the change in the eucharistic elements, he speaks of *substantialiter transmutari* (two times) and *substantialiter commutari* (two times). Considering the period of time and the circumstances of the publication of Guitmund's work, it is safe to conclude, therefore, that the *substantialiter converti* of 1079 originated from, and means the same thing as, the *substantialiter transmutari* found in Guitmund's *De veritate*—an important first step toward final formulation of the doctrine of transubstantiation.

II. THE LIVES OF LANFRANC AND GUITMUND

Of our two authors, Lanfranc is certainly the better known and the subject of far more study than Guitmund. Born in Pavia, Italy, around 1010, there is strong evidence that Lanfranc was well trained in the liberal arts and law in the tradition of the Northern Italian schools. It is surmised that he left Italy for France somewhere around 1030. It was about that time that he encountered Berengarius for the first time as a teacher of the *trivium*. One finds that by the year 1042, Lanfranc has become a mature scholar, and, after a religious conversion of sorts, has decided to enter the monastery. To that end, he arrives at Bec in 1042 and becomes the prior within three years, and the instructor of his fellow monks almost immediately. In the year 1063, he was made the abbot at St. Etienne in Caen, where he presided until 1070. Soon after the Norman conquest of England, Lanfranc became the Archbishop of Canterbury, where he remained until his death in 1089.

Guitmund was born sometime during the first quarter of the eleventh century in Normandy, and joined the Order of St. Benedict at the Abbey of the Cross in St. Leufroy.[76] Around the year 1060 he began his theological studies at the monastery of Bec, where he fell under the influence and became the faithful disciple of Lanfranc. We know from his own correspondence that around the year 1070 William the Conqueror ordered him

76. See *Notitia historica et litteraria*, PL 149: 1425A–1426B.

to leave France and travel to England, where William offered him a diocese, but Guitmund rejected the offer because of William's brutality and the Norman hegemony over the British people.[77] He then left England and returned to France. After his return to Normandy there was a movement to have Guitmund fill the see of Rouen, but the attempt was blocked by his enemies. Subsequent to his episcopal rejection, Guitmund sought permission from his abbot to leave Normandy and reside at a monastery in Rome, where he assumed the name of "Christian."[78] Upon his arrival, "Pope Gregory VII received him with joy and made him a cardinal."[79] In February of 1077, the same Pope Gregory appointed him to a papal legation north of the Alps.[80] It appears that Guitmund continued to reside in Rome after the death of Gregory VII, and was elevated to the see of Aversa in southern Italy by Pope Urban II at the council of Melfi in 1089,[81] where he remained until his death around 1095.

III. WORKS AND CRITICAL EDITIONS

Lanfranc's works can be broken down into seven categories: (1) liberal arts, (2) patristic studies, (3) biblical commentaries, (4) the *De corpore et sanguine Domini*, (5) letters, (6) monastic constitutions, and (7) verses on the "Quattuor Tempora."[82] Compared with the rest of Lanfranc's literary corpus, the *De corpore* stands out as something distinct from, yet developed out of, a long and scholarly career.

Lanfranc's *De corpore*[83] was edited for the first time in 1528 by

77. See Guitmund, *Oratio ad Guillelmum I Anglorum regem cum recusaret episcopatum*, PL 149: 1509A–1512A.

78. See the anonymous *De Berengarii haeresiarcha damnatione multiplici*, PL 145: 8B. See also Theodoric Ruinart, *Vita beati Urbani II papae*, PL 151: 78A.

79. See excerpt from *Historia ecclesiastica* 5.17, by Oderic, appended to the end of Guitmund's *Oratio*, PL 149: 1512D.

80. See Paul Bernrieden, *Vita S. Gregorii VII*, PL 148: 81D.

81. Robert Somerville, *Pope Urban II: The* Collectio Britannica *and the Council of Melfi (1089)* (Oxford: Clarendon Press, 1996), 53–57.

82. Margaret Gibson, *Lanfranc of Bec* (Oxford: Oxford University Press, 2002), 239–41.

83. See R. Huygens, "Berengariana," 4, CCCM 171, 225–38, for an extensive manuscript history of the text.

John Bale, using a manuscript from the diocese of Treves. A second edition was made in 1540 at Rouen by Guillaume Le Rat. The next two editions were made at Louvain: 1551 by John Coster and 1561 by John Vlimmerius. The edition of Dom L. d'Archery,[84] according to Montclos, corrected many of the textual errors in the Rouen edition of 1540.[85] The next edition, by J. Giles,[86] used the d'Archery version. J.-P. Migne's *Patrologiae cursus completus*[87] also used the d'Archery edition.

No modern critical edition of the work has been produced to date. Although J. de Montclos intended to produce one for the series *Sources chrétiennes*,[88] it was never finished.[89] The historical matter in the beginning of the *De corpore* was critically edited by Huygens, but constitutes only a very small part of the entire work.[90] There is, however, a list of corrections prepared by Montclos to the Migne edition, which he developed from three different manuscript traditions.[91] In preparing this translation, I have used the Migne version corrected to reflect the Montclos editions,[92] with the PL numeration embedded in the text.

Guitmund of Aversa, in a sharp contrast with the rather large literary corpus of Lanfranc, has authored only four works: (1) *Confessio de sancta Trinitate, Christi humanitate, corporisque et sanguinis Domini nostri veritate,* (2) *Oratio ad Guillelmum I,* (3) *Epistola ad Erfastum,* and (4) *De corporis et sanguinis veritate Christi in Eucharistia libri tres.*[93]

The first edition of Guitmund's *De veritate* was published by Ioannes Faber at Freiburg in 1529.[94] Erasmus produced the

---

84. In *Lanfranci opera omnia* (Paris, 1648).

85. J. de Montclos, *Lanfranc et Bérenger,* 259.

86. See vol. 2 of his *Opera omnia Lanfranci* (Oxford and Paris, 1844).

87. PL 150: 407–42 (Paris, 1854).

88. J. de Montclos, *Lanfranc et Bérenger,* 250.

89. See R. Huygens, "Berengariana," 4, CCCM 171, 159, n. 9.

90. Ibid., 239–46.

91. J. de Montclos, *Lanfranc et Bérenger,* 540–45.

92. These corrections are noted by the abbreviation "MC" in the translation.

93. See also J. Leclerq's "Passage authentique inédit de Guitmund D'Aversa," *Revue Bénédictine* 57 (1947): 213–14.

94. The text is incomplete, however, and is missing a portion of the third book. This version is significant nonetheless, because it contains the profession of faith of the council of Rome in 1059, of which the *De veritate* is an explicit defense.

next edition at Antwerp in 1530. Like Lanfranc's *De corpore,* Guitmund's *De veritate* was edited by John Vlimmerius at Louvain in 1561. Migne's *Patrologiae cursus completus,* however, uses the Erasmus edition.[95] The work has since been republished by the Jesuit theologian Hugo von Hurter. Hurter, who taught dogmatic theology at the University of Innsbruck, published the *De veritate* in his series *Sanctorum Patrum* as a patristic exposition of eucharistic doctrine.[96] This translation uses Hurter's text and paragraph notation, cross-referenced with the Migne column numeration, embedded in the text.

[handwritten: Study of the Eucharist — 1909]

[handwritten in margin: Lanfranc]

IV. MODERN STUDIES ON LANFRANC AND GUITMUND

Darwell Stone's landmark work, *A History of the Doctrine of the Holy Eucharist,* studies both Lanfranc's and Guitmund's theology at length in a developmental context.[97] The next major study of both Lanfranc and Guitmund comes from the German historian Joseph Geiselmann; his approach, however, is not so much a history of doctrine as it is a neo-Scholastic analysis.[98] In 1930, the Anglican scholar A. J. Macdonald studied both Lanfranc and Guitmund in the context of the Berengarian crisis of the eleventh century. Jean de Montclos has done an exhaustive treatment of the Berengarian crisis and Lanfranc's involvement in it, but has treated Guitmund only in an incidental fashion.[99] J. T. O'Connor in *The Hidden Manna* studies the works of both Lanfranc and Guitmund.[100] Charles Sheedy, in his dissertation on the pre-Scholastic movement, studies the theological methods of Lanfranc and Guitmund as members of the eleventh-century pre-Scholastic movement.[101]

95. PL 149: 1427–94 (Paris, 1853).

96. *Sanctorum Patrum opuscula selecta* 38 (Innsbruck: Libreria Academica Wagneriana, 1879).

97. 2 vols. (New York: Longmans, Green and Co., 1909).

98. *Die Eucharistielehre der Vorscholastik* (Paderborn: F. Schönigh, 1926).

99. For Macdonald, see n. 39, above; for Montclos, see n. 2.

100. *The Hidden Manna: A Theology of the Eucharist* (San Francisco: Ignatius Press, 2005).

101. "The Eucharistic Controversy of the Eleventh Century Against the Background of Pre-Scholastic Theology: A Dissertation Submitted to the Faculty of

Twentieth-century scholars who have contributed works devoted solely to Lanfranc are A. J. Macdonald, Margaret Gibson, and H. Cowdrey;[102] studies of Guitmund *per se,* however, are fewer in number. Before my own dissertation, "The Role of Guitmund of Aversa in the Developing Theology of the Eucharist,"[103] the only work dedicated solely to the eucharistic theology of Guitmund was Patrick Shaughnessy's doctoral dissertation, "The Eucharistic Doctrine of Guitmund of Aversa."[104]

To date there has been no translation of Lanfranc's *De corpore* into a modern language. There is, however, one other translation of the *De veritate* into a modern language, and that is Italian.[105] Orabona's translation was done to commemorate the 900th anniversary of Guitmund's death and to study the Norman influence on the Church in southern Italy. This effort by Professor Orabona developed into a symposium held in Aversa, sponsored by the University of Cassino in the fall of 1997, the proceedings of which have been published.[106]

Sacred Theology of the Catholic University of America in Partial Fulfillment of the Requirements for the Degree of Doctor of Sacred Theology" (Washington, DC: The Catholic University of America Press, 1947).

102. For Macdonald's *Lanfranc,* see n. 3, above; for Gibson's *Lanfranc of Bec,* see n. 2; for Cowdrey's *Lanfranc,* see n. 3.

103. See n. 5, above.

104. "The Eucharistic Doctrine of Guitmund of Aversa: A Dissertation Submitted to the Theological Faculty of the Pontifical Academical Institution of St. Anselm" (Rome: Scuola Salesiana del Libro, 1939).

105. Lorenzo Orabona, *Guitmundo di Aversa, La "verità" dell' Eucaristia* (Naples: Edizioni Scientifiche Italiane, 1995).

106. *Guitmundo di Aversa: La cultura europea e la riforma Gregoriana nel Mezzogiorno: Atti del Convegno Internazionale di Studi Cassino-Aversa, 13-14-15 novembre 1997,* CDM 13, 14, and 15 (Naples: Edizioni Scientifiche Italiane, 2000).

LANFRANC

ON THE BODY AND BLOOD
OF THE LORD
AGAINST BERENGARIUS OF TOURS
IN ONE BOOK

ON THE BODY AND BLOOD OF THE LORD

CHAPTER ONE

LANFRANC, [407 A] CATHOLIC by the mercy of God, to Berengarius, adversary of the Catholic Church.

If divine piety had deigned to breathe into your heart the desire to speak with me, since it is a matter of great concern to both God's honor and your soul, then you would have chosen an opportune place where the matter could have been discussed competently and with salutary deliberation. Such a meeting would have been very beneficial for you, but it would undoubtedly have benefited very many[1] of those whom you deceive since, truly deceived and liable to death, you send them into eternal punishment.

With the cooperation of the Spirit, who blows where he wills, one of two things might have happened. On the one hand, having set aside that haughtiness of pride which, being full of, you began to think contrary to the whole world, you might have assented to the authority of the entire Holy Church and the right exposition of Sacred Scripture. This [407 B] would have rescued both you and your followers from the darkness of error and the depth of iniquity. On the other, should you have persisted in your obstinacy, your followers at least, by the mercy of God, would have recovered their senses, having heard the arguments, [408 A] and would have returned better informed to the true faith which Holy Church has never ceased to preach.

But because you chose to defend the error, once you had imbibed it, by secret discussions with the unlearned, and chose openly, however, to confess the orthodox faith in the hearing of the holy council, not out of a love of truth but out of fear of

1. MC adds *plurimum*.

death, you therefore avoid me and you avoid religious persons who can pass judgment between your words and mine. And I would have preferred in the presence of such persons to hear you and confer with you about no other matter than the opinions that, with an audacity that should be punished, you pretend are compatible with your own opinions, and attribute them, either from a desire to do harm, or from an ignorance of the truth, to the holy doctors, saying this or that is found in that one, or Augustine testifies to it in this work, or Gregory, or Jerome, or whoever of those men whom the Church of Christ significantly venerates as having been placed on the pinnacle of authority.

For then, every shrewd evasion would come to rest, when the sacred codices would be read in your hearing, or given over to your hands to be read, and a light more splendid than a celestial lamp would shine upon those things which you frequently say that you draw from Sacred Scripture; then, as the reasoning of your business would demand, it would be seen as either completely false, or [409 A] depraved in some part. By what diabolical fallacy do you attack, deceive, and undermine minds that are ignorant of the divine mystery and that trust in you? The more tenacious you are in your evil purpose of subverting and scandalizing those who are your brothers in Christ, the more injurious you are, little considering the words of the Lord as he threatens anyone who scandalizes one of his little ones,[2] nor fearing sufficiently the injunction of the Apostle as he writes to the proud people of the Corinthians and says: "Therefore, when you sin in this way against your brothers, and wound their consciences, weak as they are, you sin against Christ."[3] By this sin, you hold back very many from faith and subvert those who, not knowing enough to resist you, contemplate those things which are seen, and not those things which are not seen. But the firm foundation of God stands immovable, [409 B] having the seal which separates it from iniquity, because it calls upon the Name of the Lord; and you, acting as you do, and not without grave scandal, are not content, as a perverse man, just to say perverse things, but you also transmit perverse writings through diverse regions

2. Mt 18.6.
3. 1 Cor 8.12.

by way of your perverse disciples. And indeed other writings were heard, examined, and condemned by Nicholas of happy memory, who, among all Christians, bears the name of Sovereign Pontiff, and by one hundred and thirteen bishops at Rome. You also, with body bowed but not with a humble heart, enkindled a fire and threw these books of perverse teachings into it in the midst of the holy synod, swearing, by that which is incomparably greater than all things, that you would hold intact the confession of faith which had been handed to you by the fathers who were present, and that you would not preach from that day forward your old doctrine on the body and blood of the Lord. [409 C]

You are a sacrilegious violator of this oath, and afterwards composed a document against the aforementioned synod, against Catholic truth, and against the opinion of the entire Church, to which, trusting in the mercy of Christ, I am disposed to respond in this little work. And so that what you say may appear more clearly, and what I shall respond, I shall distinguish the alternate opinions by placing our names alternately.

Nor am I going to respond to everything; since you have spread roses among the thorns, and have painted your phantasm in black and white colors, you even say certain things which do not pertain to the proposition of the question. I will, then, make the work as brief as possible. For in such inanities I do not wish to waste my life, if you permit the People of God [409 D] to return to their former peace.

CHAPTER TWO

Berengarius: "The document of Humbert of Burgundy, whom the Romans had made a cardinal bishop, was written against Catholic truth, as it will be shown below; and Berengarius was forced to profess[4] the same error as that of the most inept Burgundian."

Lanfranc: Humbert, according to all who knew him either directly or by way of reputation, was acknowledged to be a religious man, adorned with Christian faith, most constant in the

---

4. MC adds *legere.*

performance of most holy works, whose treatises on the divine
sciences and secular letters were recognized to be of the highest
erudition. St. Leo brought him to Rome—not from Burgundy,
but from Lotharingia—and ordained him an archbishop to
preach the word of God to the Sicularians. Afterwards, the Holy
Roman Church made him cardinal to preside over her.

From this position Cardinal Humbert lived and taught, both
the faith and doctrine in such a way that not even the slightest
report of evil suspicion ever arose against him. Almost the whole
Latin Church attests to this fact, nor could it ignore him in his
counsels and advice which were present and preeminent for the
good of the Apostolic See. Yet, even if he were a Burgundian
(and you foolishly and arrogantly call the Burgundians an infamous people), does not the Spirit of the Lord blow where he
wills,[5] and upon whom he wills? Is not the earth the Lord's, and
all those who dwell upon it?[6] And was it not the Prince of the
Apostles who said: "In truth, I see that God shows no partiality,
[410 B] but rather, in every nation, whoever fears him and acts up-
rightly is acceptable to him"?[7] Again, was it not the Doctor of the
Gentiles who said to the Galatians: "God shows no partiality"?[8]

Thus when you attack Cardinal Humbert in this way, and assert that he has written against Catholic truth, you attack not only
him, but also the Roman Pontiffs, the Roman Church, and many
of the Holy Fathers as well. And when you attack these men, you
also attack that which the blessed doctors have formulated in
agreement with them, if not in the same words, nevertheless by
the same thoughts in many places, [namely,] that every man is a
heretic who disagrees with the Roman and Universal Church in
the teaching of the faith. Yet, in the just judgment of God, that is
exactly what has happened to you: for as you strive to brand others heretics, you yourself have fallen into heresy and been con-
victed of it.

5. Jn 3.8.
6. Cf. Ps 23.1. The numeration of the Psalms follows the Septuagint/Vulgate
sequence.
7. Acts 10.34–35.
8. Gal 2.6.

Berengarius: "I condemn all heresy, especially the one which attempts to assert that the bread and wine placed on the altar are, after the consecration, only a sacrament and not the true Body and Blood of Christ."

Lanfranc: It seems to me that you have omitted the first part of your oath, with the result that your readers think that these words are not yours but the words of the venerable Bishop Humbert. That does not hurt our case, however, for—although you tenaciously strive to prove the words of the oath heretical—should you openly proclaim your own doctrine, it would be you who would be shown to be a heretic. But lest anyone in ignorance may report indiscriminately the decree of the Roman Council on this matter,[9] I shall forthwith present it in its entirety—beginning, middle, and end.

I, Berengarius, unworthy deacon of the Church of St. Maurice at Angers, [410 D] knowing the true, Catholic, and apostolic Faith, condemn all heresy, especially that of which I have hitherto been guilty, and attempts to assert that the bread and wine that are placed on the altar are, after the Consecration, only a sacrament [*solomodo sacramentum*] and not the true Body and Blood of Our Lord Jesus Christ and that they are not able to be touched or broken by the hands of the priests or chewed by the teeth of the faithful [*dentibus atteri*] sensibly, but rather only sacramentally [*sensualiter nisi solo in sacramento*]. Moreover, I assent to the holy Roman and apostolic See and, concerning the sacraments of the Lord's table, I profess with mouth and heart that I hold that Faith that the lord and venerable Pope Nicholas and this holy Synod, resting on the authority of the [411 A] Gospels and the Apostles, have handed on to be held and have confirmed for me: namely, that the bread and wine that are placed on the altar are, after the Consecration, not only the Sacrament but the true Body and Blood of Our Lord Jesus Christ, and that they are in truth [*in veritate*] sensibly and not only sacramentally touched by the hands of the priests and are broken and chewed by the teeth of the faithful. I swear this by the holy and consubstantial Trinity and by these holy Gospels [of Christ]. I pronounce that those who will come forward against this Faith with their own doctrines and followers are worthy of eternal damnation. But if I myself should at some point presume to think or preach anything against these things, I submit myself to the severity of canon law. I have read and reread this and sign it willingly.[10]

9. Rome 1059.
10. Trans. J. T. O'Connor, *Manna*, 178. Some of the bracketed Latin words

In the time of Gregory VII,[11] when the teaching on these matters was kept in the Church of the Savior, you, pressed upon by a host of men similar to you, persevered as a teacher of error. [411 B] Then, after you returned, and your soul was breathed upon by the Spirit of the Heavenly Father, you obtained the hoped-for pardon by the pope's clemency, swearing the things that follow:

I Berengarius believe in my heart and confess with my mouth that the bread and wine which are placed upon the altar, through the mystery of the sacred prayer and the words of our Redeemer, are substantially converted [*substantialiter converti*] into our Lord Jesus Christ's very own life-giving flesh, which, after the consecration, is the true body of Christ, born of the Virgin, offered for the salvation of the world, hung upon the cross, [411 C] that sits at the right hand of the Father; and into the true blood of Christ, which poured forth from his side, not only through the sign and power of the sacrament, but in the reality of nature and the truth of substance. Just as it is contained in this brief, and I have read and you have understood, so I believe and will not teach against this faith again—so help me God and these holy Gospels.

Afterwards, this same pope ordered you, Berengarius, by the authority of God and the holy Apostles Peter and Paul, not to presume to dispute any further with anyone about the body and blood of the Lord, save to lead back to this same faith those who had left it because of your teachings.

When you had come to Rome in the time of Nicholas, however, it was a very different matter. You sensed beforehand that your confidence in those who had promised you support was more from the [411 D] favors you bestowed than from hearing the things you had to say. You did not dare, therefore, to defend your opinions at the council. Instead, you requested of both Pope Nicholas and his council that, since this was a matter of the faith, the words of the oath should be given to you and confirmed in writing. This injunction was carried out by Bishop Humbert. And so he wrote and recited[12] the profession of faith

---

were inserted by O'Connor, and others have been added by the translator of the present volume. The bracketed phrase "of Christ" does not appear in the O'Connor translation.

11. MC omits the 1079 profession of faith, citing older manuscript history. See MC 261.

12. MC adds *recitavit.*

comprised of the words cited above. With the agreement of all [the council fathers], he handed them to you to be read and confessed. You received them without protest. You read them, and then, having confessed them, confirmed by an oath that you believed them, and by your own hand you subscribed to them.

Pope Nicholas, [412 A] rejoicing over your conversion, sent the written document containing your oath to cities in Italy, France, and Germany, and wherever else a report of your depravity could have arrived earlier. And just as the scandalized churches previously grieved over your departure from the truth, so afterwards they rejoiced and gave thanks to God at your conversion and return. Why then do you attribute this document to Bishop Humbert rather than to yourself, to Pope Nicholas, to his council, and, finally, to all the churches that received it with due reverence and gave thanks to God for your conversion? Why, I ask, save for the fact that it is easier to persuade the unlearned that one man could err rather than so many persons and so many churches? If you were to attribute it to yourself, however, to destroy it would be seen as perjury. But let us see how you argue.

CHAPTER THREE

Berengarius: "The light appears and [412 B] shines in the darkness, and the darkness has not grasped it."[13]

Lanfranc: This can undoubtedly be turned against you. For the light of faith shines in the darkness of this world, as a mystery through a looking-glass, yet with God's revelation we can behold it. Your darkened mind cannot grasp this true light; having despised the rest of men, and thinking that you are the only wise one, and languishing in your own thought, you have become foolish in the eyes of God.

Berengarius: "Because an enemy of the truth willy-nilly asserts the truth."

Lanfranc: You seem to pay little attention to what you say as long as you drag into contempt the servant of God by your op-

13. Cf. Jn 1.5.

probrious charges. For you make the one who asserts the truth willingly and the one who asserts it unwillingly equally an enemy of the truth. [412 C] For whoever asserts the truth does it either willingly or unwillingly. There can be no middle position. Every defender of truth, however, by your own testimony is an enemy of the truth. But heaven forbid. For Truth itself would call his own defenders by a far different name in the Gospel, saying: "Now I do not call you slaves but my friends,"[14] and elsewhere: "You will be my friends."[15] It is false, therefore, to make someone who asserts the truth, whether willingly or unwillingly, an enemy of the truth.

Berengarius: "Therefore, as did Goliath, so also shall the Burgundian perish by his own sword."[16]

Lanfranc: To disparage others, to proclaim yourself, [412 D] to boast about yourself, to think great things about yourself—that is your way! Indeed, you call yourself David, and Humbert, Goliath. Yet it would have been more correct to call yourself Goliath, because you are a most arrogant man, who thinks, writes, and speaks the very things by which you cut your own throat using your own sword. Humbert, on the other hand, is David, who has lived and taught humbly as a member of the Church, fighting for the Church, taking up the shield of faith and the sword of the Spirit, which is none other than the word of God.[17]

CHAPTER FOUR

Berengarius: "The Burgundian, however, was of the same base opinion as that of the common crowd, Paschasius and Lanfranc, that is, that none of the substance of the bread and wine remain on the altar after the consecration."

Lanfranc: [413 A] Your heresy was reported to the Apostolic See in the time of Pope St. Leo. This was the same Pope Leo who, when he presided at the synod,[18] and had gathered around himself no small number of bishops, abbots, and religious persons

---

14. Jn 15.15.

16. Cf. 1 Sm 17.51.

18. First synod of Rome in 1050.

15. Jn 15.14.

17. Eph 6.17.

of diverse congregations from various regions, ordered, within the hearing of all, that those letters which you sent to me concerning the body and blood of the Lord be read aloud. Indeed, the one who carried them was your agent, for they were not on my person in Normandy. He was the one who then gave them to certain clerics who, when they read them, noted that they were contrary to the customary faith of the Church. They, then, on fire with the zeal for God, gave them to others to be read, who in turn exposed the opinions of those letters in many words. A suspicion thus arose that was just as unfavorable to me as it was to you, [413 B] since I was obviously the one for whom you had destined the letters, and many people thought that the things that you said in them were very favorable and flattering to me. Indeed, they could not determine whether I favored you, or held the true faith. When, therefore, the reader read to the Roman council the accusations from a certain cleric of Rheims—which made clear to all that you extolled John the Scot, condemned Paschasius, held an opinion contrary to the customary faith of the Church about the Eucharist—a sentence of condemnation was promulgated against you, depriving you of the communion of Holy Church—a holy communion that you endeavored to deprive her of.

After these proceedings, the pope commanded that I should rise, cleanse the stain of this depraved rumor from myself, articulate my faith, and that I should demonstrate it by expounding more from the sacred authors than by argumentation. I arose and said what I thought, proved what I said, and what I proved was pleasing to all and displeasing to none. [413 C] After that, the synod of Vercelli was called and convened the following September with the same pope presiding. To that synod you were summoned and did not come. I, however, by the command and entreaties of the aforementioned pontiff, remained with him up until the synod. At that synod, within the hearing of all present who had gathered there from diverse parts of this world, the book of John the Scot *De eucharistia* was read and condemned. Your ideas were also discussed and condemned. The faith of Holy Church, on the other hand, which I hold and which I assert must be held, was heard and confirmed by the unanimous consent of all. Two clerics who identified themselves as your agents, wishing to defend you, at first attempted to withdraw from the council, but were then restrained from leaving.[19]

From this sentence holy Leo never departed in all his councils, which he demonstrated either by a personal presence at his own councils, [413D] or by the presence he established by way of his legates in the councils he convened in various provinces. His successor, Pope Victor of happy memory, also did not back away from this sentence. In fact, Pope Victor aligned himself in this matter in every way possible with other councils, and ordered by his own authority that the teaching of the Roman synod should stand. Furthermore, he confirmed its teaching by the authority of every one of his own councils. Then, in the council of Tours,[20] which his legates mediated and presided over, you were given the option of defending your case. When you did not dare to take up a defense, you swore to the common faith of the Church, confessing before everyone that from that very hour you would believe what you confessed in the Roman synod which took place in the time of Nicholas and which I have already made [414A] known above.

I have digressed and gone over these matters, however, simply because you said: "The Burgundian was of the same base opinion as that of the common crowd, Paschasius and Lanfranc." The Catholic Church, however, is divided up into the clerical order and the lay state. The order of clerics, on the other hand, consists of the bishops and the rest of the priests of Christ and other ecclesiastical persons of diverse dignities. All those clerics, nonetheless, except for a small number of schismatics, most openly hold this faith. You could have more rightly said, therefore, that: "The Burgundian held the opinion of the Catholic Church, but not mine and my followers. For we have

19. According to Macdonald, "He was arrested by the Pope's order, to save him from ill-treatment." *Lanfranc*, 45.

20. Council of Tours, 1054. Both Lanfranc and Bernold of Constance (see Huygens, "Bernold," *Serta Mediaevalla Textus varii saeculorum X–XIII in unum collecti*, CCCM 171, 248–49) were mistaken on this point. Hildebrand was the legate of Leo (†April 19, 1054), not of Victor (March 1055–February 1057), and Berengarius was quick to point out Lanfranc's error (see *De Sacra Coena*, CCCM 84, 52).

chosen to separate ourselves from the Church by pride and make a schism against it unto our own destruction, instead of humbly being its members, and hold with it the common faith unto our own salvation." This is what you would have said if you were a lover of truth [414C] and preserver of justice, that is, if, after having put aside your appetite for empty glory, you had chosen to confess your sins rather than defend them.

That teaching, however, by which we believe bread is converted into the true flesh of Christ, and wine into the true blood of Christ, you call nonsense. I will respond to you on this matter at a more opportune time. Then, by the authority of God, divine authorities, and clear reasoning, I shall have demonstrated this to be the true faith. Furthermore, as far as it concerns what you said above about me, namely, that the "Burgundian held the opinion of the common crowd, of Paschasius, and of Lanfranc": when you identify me as one of the common crowd, [414C] be most certain of the fact that my friends believe without doubts, and the Church of Christ believes. Even if[21] I were lacking authority and reason by which I might defend my faith, I would nevertheless prefer to be a rustic and an illiterate Catholic with the common herd than to be a literate and witty heretic with you. But should the Lord God deign to bring us both together in the hearing of a holy counsel, I would trust in his mercy because you change your words and your opinions.

Berengarius: "Humbert himself rejects this opinion in the words recorded above, and does not pay attention to it."

Lanfranc: While pursuing Humbert with insatiable hatred, you are not ashamed to disgrace yourself. For whoever swears to contraries must themselves incur the crime of perjury when they swear to the one proposition which contradicts it. When you assert, then, that the words handed on to you for the purposes of swearing an oath contradicted one another, you impudently proclaimed yourself openly [414 D] to be a perjurer. O unhappy man! O most miserable soul! Why did you swear that you believed things which you understood to contradict each other to

21. MC: *quia si* substituted for *quasi.*

such a great extent? Would it not be preferable, if you thought that your faith was the true faith, to end your life by an honest death rather than to perjure yourself, order treachery, and abjure your faith? But far be it that any writings of the holy council should contradict themselves, as if a reader who studied them with diligence should exercise caution lest he be scandalized by them. And this fact will also be demonstrated later.

CHAPTER FIVE

Berengarius: "For the one who says that the bread and wine of the altar are only sacraments, or the bread and wine of the altar are only the true body and blood of Christ, proves that in every way it is still bread and wine that remains upon the altar."

Lanfranc: None of the above was decreed by the Roman synod [415 A] for belief, nor did Bishop Humbert present to you anything of the kind for you either to confess or to swear to. In fact, the first part of the above statement, where it says that "the bread and the wine of the altar are only sacraments," is your opinion and that of your followers. The latter, however, which says that "the bread and the wine of the altar are only the true body and blood of Christ," is in fact no one's opinion. For you deny the truth of the flesh and blood, where the Church of Christ, on the other hand, believes that bread is converted into flesh, and wine is converted into blood. Yet the Church salubriously believes and truly recognizes that it is a sacrament of the Lord's Passion, a sacrament of divine propitiation, a sacrament of concord and unity, and finally, a sacrament of the flesh and blood assumed each in its own distinct and unique way from the Virgin—a matter which shall be discussed forthrightly in a more appropriate time and place.

For the present, however, [415 B] I have only undertaken to show that the words of the Roman council—which you swore by an oath that you were going to uphold—in no way contradict themselves. For while your friends and dependents argue that you should not swear oaths that you do not intend to keep, or that you should not keep the oaths that you swore, you are accustomed to defame Pope Nicholas and the remaining fathers of the Roman council by saying that they taught and wrote[22] contrary things, which were the cause of your perjury. And this I will also destroy in this little work, for almost everywhere you struggle to make this point, joining your words to those of the council fathers.

For Pope Nicholas, concluding that you taught that the bread and wine of the altar, after the consecration, remain in their former essences without a change of reality, granted you permission, just as it has been said above, to respond. When you did not dare to offer any defense on your part, the pope, moved by compassion toward your entreaties, ordered that the written statement be handed to you which I have cited above, and which begins as follows: "I Berengarius anathematize the heresy, for which until now I have been infamous, that tried to assert that the bread and wine, which are placed on the altar, are, after the consecration, only a sacrament and not the true body and blood of our Lord Jesus Christ."

Most rightly did the pope command this statement, most rightly did the synod agree to it, and most rightly would you have properly executed it, that is, if the lying tongue of your heart had not spoken from the heart, [415 D] and you had not afterwards returned as a miserable perjurer to your former vomit and pig-trough of mud![23] For we have been instructed by the authority of the sacred canons that no one returning from a heresy is to be allowed to partake of ecclesiastical communion until he first repudiates the perverse doctrine [he once held], and that same doctrine is then bound by the chain of an anathema. Yet in these words [of Pope Nicholas and the council] cannot be found either your words recorded above, or any of the statements of your followers. It should be clear, then, that it is you who pervert and subvert the holy writings, and from depraved and fictitious teachings send out clouds of error for the unlearned—for that which is based on a false principle is false.

perjurer returning to former vomit

---

22. MC: *scribentes* substituted for *scientes*.
23. Cf. 2 Pt 2.22; Prv 26.11.

CHAPTER SIX

Berengarius: "For just as when someone says: 'Christ is the chief cornerstone,'[24] he is not removing Christ, nor is he establishing absolutely [what] Christ is: so it is that, in a similar fashion, when someone says: 'The bread of the altar [416 A] is only a sacrament,' or: 'The bread of the altar is only the true body of Christ,' he does not deny that it is bread on the altar, and he confirms the fact that it is indeed bread and wine on the table of the Lord."

Lanfranc: You could add, further, that anyone who is ignorant of the truth would agree to the first part of the proposition, unless perchance he would prefer to use the word in a figurative way of speaking. Indeed, we are accustomed to call things by the names of that from which they have been made, although having been changed into another nature, it can be proven that they are not that from which they have been made. For example, St. Augustine in the end of the *Enarrationes in psalmos* calls "crystal" the "snow hardened by the passing of many years, and the succession of ages."[25] The nature of snow, however, is liquid and moist, [416 B] and that of a crystal, hard and dry. Therefore, since these natures are so disparate from one another, it is not proper to call "snow" a "crystal" in the strict sense, except as a figure of speech—where one is accustomed to call a thing by the name of the material from which it has been made. And the Creator, in the creation of the first man from the dust, says to man in Genesis: "You are dust, and unto dust you shall return."[26] It is as if God were to say: "Because you have been made from dust, you will someday become dust, and you will turn back into the dust [from which you were made]."

Furthermore, as I have said, no Catholic accepts the doctrines stated above, and the Christian religion does not allow them. For there is no one who doubts that the first part is your assertion alone—and your sect's.[27] The latter part of the proposition, how-

---

24. Eph 2.20.
25. Augustine, *Enarrationes in psalmos* 147, PL 37: 1915.
26. Gn 3.19.
27. That is, "the bread of the altar is only a sacrament"; see above.

ever, you do not accept—for it is you who deny the existence of the body and blood. Nor do we, on the other hand, who confess both, [416 C] deny in any way that they are a figure and sacrament of many and lofty realities. The similitude which you have posited about our Lord Jesus Christ and the cornerstone, then, only hinders you and benefits us. For he who says: "Christ is the cornerstone," has not established that Christ is a stone, but people apply the name to him because of some similitude which they bear to each other. So in the same way, when the divine page calls the body of the Lord "bread," this is done in a sacred and mystical way of speaking, either because it is confected from bread and it retains some of its qualities or because it incomprehensibly satisfies the soul in feeding it and supplies to it the substance of eternal life; or because it is the body of the Son of God who is the bread of angels, and "upon whom," [416 D] just as the prince of apostles says, "the angels desire to look";[28] or in some other way that can be understood by the Church doctors, yet not by us.

CHAPTER SEVEN

Berengarius: "Not every affirmation is able to stand when part of it has been overturned; and this, St. Augustine also says in the book *De doctrina christiana:* 'In the very truth of eternity which God is, it stands indissolubly.'"[29]

Lanfranc: Having abandoned the sacred authors, you take refuge in dialectics. And since the matter that you will hear and respond to involves a mystery of faith, I prefer that you hear and respond from the sacred authors rather than dialectical reasoning. Indeed, it will also be our effort to respond to these things [417 A] lest you think that, because of the lack of the art, I am lacking in this matter. It might seem bragging to some, and it will be imputed to ostentation rather than necessity, but as God is my witness, and my conscience, I would rather not propose nor respond to proposed dialectical questions and their solu-

28. 1 Pt 1.2.

29. Lanfranc is correct when he says at the end of this chapter that "St. Augustine never mentions this proposition" in the *De doctrina christiana.*

tions, when treating of divine matters. When, however, the matter itself necessitates such a disputation, so that only by way of the rules of its own art can it be explained in a clear and pristine manner, then and only then, shall I, to the best of my ability, address them by such dialectical means.

In so doing, I shall defend my position by that same art with propositions equally as powerful as the ones that you advance. By acting in such a fashion, however, I do not wish to seem as if I confide more in the art of disputation than in the truth and the authority of the holy Fathers. St. Augustine, indeed, in certain of his writings, especially in the book *De doctrina christiana,* most amply praises this discipline,[30] [417 B] and many times confirms that it is of great value for [understanding and solving] all questions that appear in the holy writings. For when he contended with the Arian heretic Felicianus, he so bested him by this same art, that the heretic himself, unable to address the points and syllogistic reasoning with its implied logical connections, openly exclaimed: "With Aristotelian subtlety you contend with me, and everything that is said by me, you destroy in the manner of a torrent."[31]

Therefore, wishing to conclude from the above statement that the bread and the wine of the altar at the consecration [*inter sacrandum*] are not essentially changed, you have assumed that the argument is predicated on two points instead of only one. For the first proposition is yours, and the latter, as I have already proven, clearly belongs to no one. In the above argument, therefore, you have introduced a grave flaw. [417 C] For what was yours was in question. Indeed, from that we seek to overturn and destroy it with a mountain of arguments, and we are busying ourselves with the attack. For no question can be the point of an argument. Indeed, the point of the argument must be something certain *per se,* or must be proven by irrefutable logic. That which was yours alone should by no means be assumed to prove a doubtful matter, and what remains is held by no one—

30. MC: *ad omnia* omitted.
31. *Contra Felicianum Arianum de unitate Trinitatis* 4, PL 42: 1159. This work is listed as dubious by the *Clavis Patrum Latinorum* under Vigilius (n. 808), and attributed to Ps. Augustine.

and no one should, for any reason, make a matter of faith out of a doubtful matter.

For who could judge that something which everyone denies and no one confesses is certain, or can certainly come about? Therefore, there was no great reason to your argument. You have, indeed, posited each proposition poorly. From these two most flawed principles you have constructed your whole argument by repeating it over and over again in its entirety. Therefore, it is necessarily flawed, and whatever comes from such flaws should be neither conceded nor acknowledged as emanating from accepted principles. [417 D]

Consequently, you have tried, up until now, to prove by another argument that the bread and wine after the consecration remain in their prior essences, by saying that: "*Not every* affirmation is able to stand when part of it has been overturned." To prove this it is not necessary to bring in or infer a particular negation, which proves nothing in the present question, but rather to bring in a universal negation, which says, "*No* affirmation is able to stand when part has been overturned." Pay attention. Your negation is particular when it says: "*Not every* affirmation is able to stand when part has been overturned." Remember, [418 A] your affirmation is that: "The bread and wine of the altar are only a sacrament," or, "The bread and wine of the altar are only the true body and blood of Christ," and each is affirmed. From these two preceding particular statements, it is enunciated that no affirmation is able to stand when part is overturned. You will not be able to conclude properly, will you, from these two particular propositions, that with one part overturned the statement falls? Far be it! Indeed, no type of syllogism can be set up from these two preceding particular propositions by means of which a conclusion can be properly drawn. Therefore, you have set up the argument badly.

Furthermore, it is by no means a waste of time to revisit the aforementioned proposition, where you have maintained that the truth of your stated proposition stands indissolubly in the eternal truth itself, which is God, and have defended this by the authority of St. Augustine's *De doctrina christiana*. And indeed, the proposition itself is true, and it holds the force of a true

proposition when it is placed in its own context—but you have
advanced it badly and ineffectually. The truth of it is not greater
than the truth of all things and of all propositions, all things
which exist in the truth of God, who knows and foreknows all
things eternally [418 B] and who has established the realities
themselves in their primary and secondary essences and disposed and ordained that they be the causes of both true and
false propositions. Nevertheless, in his work *De doctrina christiana,* St. Augustine never mentions this proposition anywhere,
nor any like it—a fact that anyone would easily come to know if
he bothered to read the book itself, if he has never read it, or to
reread it, if perchance he has read it already. In this matter I
marvel exceedingly at either your error or your foolishness. An
error indeed, if you do not know the evidence brought forth in
sacred codices is other than what you say it is or you do not
know it thoroughly. Foolishness, indeed, if you deem everyone
else so foolish, that they readily believe your words against the
ancient faith [418 C] of the Church, and, as it were, ignore the
unbreakable holy faith.

CHAPTER EIGHT

Berengarius: "This is the assertion, standing in its most notable
parts, in predicate and subject, which on the one hand declares:
'The bread and wine, which are placed on the altar, are only sacraments'; yet on the other hand is professed as: 'The bread and
the wine, which are placed on the altar, after the consecration
are only the true body and blood of Christ.'"

Lanfranc: Since it does not embarrass you to repeat the same
thing over again, I must now reproduce the same argument I
posited above. As I have already said, the first opinion is yours
alone, the second is no one's, [418 D] as I have established above
by clear argumentation. For you deny the flesh and blood, holding that the whole reality exists solely as a sacrament. And we
confess that it is a sacrament, and yet we faithfully and truthfully
confess the reality of each as well. Because you labor to introduce dialectical words, assertion, predicate, subject, and the like
in this way, in a treatise on so weighty a matter, it is obvious that

you do so for no other reason than to take the opportunity to demonstrate your experience in disputation to the unlearned. For without these names you are not able to assert that which you construct, while we are able to abolish the things said by you by the sacred witnesses alone.

Berengarius: "The Burgundian undertook to deny that bread and wine remained on the table of the Lord, but he in fact does not deny it, [419 A] but rather completely confirms that it is bread and wine on the table of the Lord."[32]

Lanfranc: A member of the Church should not dissent from the Church. For the Church, spread over the whole earth, confesses that bread and wine are placed on the altar to be consecrated, but within the consecration, they are incomprehensibly and ineffably changed [*commutari*] into the substance of the body and the blood. That it is his most sacred body about which we speak, with his help, and that it cannot be otherwise, will be demonstrated in its proper place from the diverse testimonies of various fathers. The Church does not deny that it is bread; rather, she confirms it. But it is the bread which descends from heaven, and gives life to the world—the bread that Ambrose and Augustine with the same words call *epiousion,* that is, "super-substantial," because the flesh of Christ exists as something greater than all other created substances; [419 B] it surpasses all other creatures with the most excelling dignity. Likewise, the wine is not like any other, for it is one that gives joy to the hearts of men—not all men, but rather, only to the servants of God, for it inebriates their souls and purges them from sin.

Berengarius: "While at the same time he declares that: 'The bread and wine, which are placed on the altar, are, after the consecration, only the true body and blood of Christ.'"

Lanfranc: Someone full of the Spirit of God said: "The lying mouth kills the soul."[33] If you feared this dreadful sentence, you would not falsely calumniate a servant of God. For the rest of

32. MC: *ad mensam dominicam* added.
33. Wis 1.2.

the statement he said—the adverb "only" he did not. Whatever can be gathered from your lie and your false constructions, therefore, whatever can be inferred, [419 C] will necessarily be thoroughly disparaged, disproved, and brought to nothing. With such things, however, I have sufficiently dealt above, and the many things that could be said here, I have, therefore, spared myself the trouble of saying and will now move on to other matters.

CHAPTER NINE

Berengarius: "Through the consecration the bread and wine of the altar become the sacrament of religion—not that they would cease to be what they were, but rather, that they would still be those things which they were, yet changed into something else, which is what St. Ambrose says in his book *De sacramentis.*"

Lanfranc: O mindless mind! O man impudently lying! O impertinence that should be punished! You presume to call upon the testimony of Ambrose, who you claim says that the bread and wine of the altar by way of the consecration do not cease to be what they were, but are changed into something which they were not. [419 D] Yet in fact, whether it be about the sacraments, or anything else about which Ambrose has written, if you inspect all the books that the Church now has in use, you will never find any such saying or explanation from him. For if he had said such a thing, it would have greatly detracted from his distinguished reputation. For then he would have contradicted himself and advanced something for belief which is in fact unbelievable. Could anyone in possession of his mental faculties believe that one reality can be converted into another without the former reality ceasing to be? But truth itself, who is God above, is ever watchful to ensure that testimony to the truth does not contradict the truth of a testimony. Take, for instance, what Ambrose says in the book *De mysteriis sive initiandis.* For wishing to show the difference between the manna of the Jews and the sacrifice of the Christians, he remarked that one should see in the manna a shadow and figure, [420 A] but in the sacrifice of the Chris-

[handwritten marginalia: manna is from heaven but this is the body of the Lord of heaven]

tians, light and truth—for the manna was from heaven, but this is the body of the Lord of heaven. Lest the mind refuse to believe in such a great conversion of such great elements, he adds further: "To what extent should we use examples to prove that this is not what nature has formed but what the benediction has consecrated, and that the greater force is in the benediction and not in nature—for by the benediction nature itself is changed."[34] And just as no one should be hesitant about, nor ignorant of, the fact that bread and wine are formed by nature, so in a similar vein, no one should have any doubt about the true conversion of the bread into the true body of the Lord. For Ambrose clearly demonstrates this by fitting examples, and affirms it in an equally powerful way by cogent arguments. First he cites the conversion of Moses' staff into a serpent, followed by the conversion of the serpent back into the staff. Then he relates the story of how the waters were changed into blood, and how that same blood [420 B] was turned back again into waters. And he cites many more examples in a similar fashion. Finally, he advances the great and singular miracle of the Virgin Birth, saying: "And that which we confect is the body from the Virgin."[35] And so that you should not place the power of nature over that of the divine, as if God could not change nature in any way that he pleases, or that seems proper to him, he adds: "Why do you seek the order of nature in the body of Christ, when the Lord Jesus himself was born from the Virgin beyond the order of nature?"[36] Also, in the sixth book of the *De sacramentis,* in which work you falsely asserted that Ambrose uttered the aforementioned lie, he in fact begins like this: "Just as our Lord Jesus Christ is the true Son of God, not by way of some grace like the rest of men but by way of nature, so it is his true flesh which we receive, and his true blood which we drink."[37] It is sufficient that I have cited these few examples from among many, [420 C] so that the readers of your opinions and mine may clearly discern with what fraud you have fabricated things that are not found, and

34. Ambrose, *De mysteriis* 9.53, PL 16: 407A.
35. Ibid.
36. Ibid.
37. Ambrose, *De sacramentis* 6.1, PL 16: 453C–454D.

with what skill you have distorted things that are found, and with what lies you try to twist into something else whatever you have left unmutilated. Almost no heretical depravity is similar to your evil from the time of the heretics Lucian and Ischius,[38] both of whom distorted the prophetic, evangelical, and apostolic Scriptures to suit their own purpose.

And each of these heresies, indeed, misunderstood the sacred writings, but nevertheless allowed them to remain in their own state without any change or perversion.[39] Indeed, the aforementioned doctor strove to prove, in the fourth sermon *De sacramentis,* that one should not be surprised if by a divine power [420 D] one thing were to be changed into another, since all things themselves have been made from nothing and continue to subsist by his command. He then added: "If, then, there is so great a force in the word of the Lord Jesus, that those things begin to be which were not, how much more creative is it that those things be which were, and be changed into something else?"[40] Indeed, he testifies that those things which once were still exist according to the visible species, yet are changed into the nature of those things that they were not before, that is, according to their interior essence. Indeed, before and after he explains himself in this way by using different words, but not different opinions. And so it is my judgment that you have brought forth the above teaching of Ambrose in such a way that you accepted that part which you could allow to be said, while at the same time explaining it in an unacceptable manner.

The fact of the matter is that in certain codices the aforementioned opinions can be found written in another way, that is, like this: "If then there is so great a force in the word of the Lord Jesus, [421 A] that those things begin to be which were not, how much more creative is it, that those things which were, are

38. Lucian, fourth-century priest of Antioch and source of Arius's doctrine, published an edition of the Septuagint, as did Hesychius, a bishop of Alexandria who was a contemporary of Lucian.

39. MC: *vel perversione in* added.

40. Ambrose, *De sacramentis* 4.15, PL 16: 441A. Cf. Ambrose, *St. Ambrose: Theological and Dogmatic Works,* trans. R. Deferrari, FC 44 (Washington, DC: The Catholic University of America Press, 1963), 302.

changed into something else?"[41] This writing agrees completely furthermore with those ideas found in the book *De mysteriis sive initiandis* by the same author, which I have cited above this way: "Therefore the word of Christ, which was able to make out of nothing those things which were not, is it not able to change those things that are, into what they were not?"[42]

CHAPTER TEN

Berengarius: "The sacrifice of the Church is made up of two realities; just as the person of Christ is comprised of the divine and the human, so in a similar way the body of Christ is comprised of two realities: one visible, the other invisible. It is also confected in a twofold manner: the sacrament and the reality of the sacrament. The reality, that is, the body of Christ, if it were before the eyes, would be visible, but since it has been raised up into heaven and is seated at the right hand of the Father until the time of the restitution of all things, as the [421 B] Apostle Peter writes,[43] it cannot be called down from heaven until the time of the restitution of all things."

Lanfranc: Caiaphas, when he was high priest that year, unknowingly prophesied the truth about the Savior, saying that it was more expedient for one man to die on behalf of the world than for all the men of the entire world to perish.[44] Indeed, he spoke the truth, yet he did not know the way in which his word would come true. So you also, wishing to speak against our case—which defense we have openly taken up—have in fact taken our part. For this is what we most certainly say, and will thoroughly contend that we can prove in every way against you and your followers, namely, that the sacrifice of the Church exists in two realities and is confected in two things, that is, in the visible appearance of the elements, [421 C] and in the invisible flesh and blood of the Lord Jesus Christ, namely, in the sacrament and in the reality of the sacrament. This reality [*res*] (if I might use

41. Ibid.
42. Ambrose, *De mysteriis* 9.52, PL 16: 406C; FC 44: 25.
43. Cf. 1 Pt 3.22.
44. Jn 11.49–51.

your words) is the body of Christ; just as the person of Christ
(also by your authority) is established and brought together in
God and man, since Christ himself is true God and true man,
because the entire reality contains in itself the nature and the
truth of things from which it has been made. The sacrifice of
the Church, on the other hand, as even you testify, is brought
about in sacrament and in the reality of the sacrament, that is,
in the body of Christ. It is, therefore, both the sacrament and
the reality of the sacrament, that is, the body of Christ. Christ,
however, "rising from the dead dies no more, for death no longer has power over him."[45] But, just as Andrew the apostle[46] says,
although on earth they truly eat his flesh and truly drink his
blood, he himself, however, abides whole and alive in the heavens at the right hand of the Father [421 D] until the time of the
restitution of all things. If you seek the way in which that comes
about, I will now give you a brief answer: The mystery of faith
can be salubriously believed, but is not able to be investigated
usefully.

faith is
a mystery

CHAPTER ELEVEN

Berengarius: "St. Augustine commenting on the Gospel says:
'When Christ is eaten, life is eaten. And when we eat, we do not
break him up into pieces.'"[47]

Lanfranc: St. Augustine never said a thing on the Gospel that
went beyond what the Lord and the Evangelists said and what
those persons who are cited by the writers of the Gospel said in
the Gospel according to the reality and the events at that time.
For he wrote a large work [422 A] historically expounding the
Gospel of the Lord according to John. In this work, the above-
mentioned opinion can be found, which we receive devoutly and
honor with due reverence because he did it for us, and it is consonant with the truth, when he says: "'He who eats my flesh and

---

45. Rm 6.9.

46. Lanfranc cites here a fifth-century apocryphal work entitled *Passio sancti
Andreae apostoli.* See Montclos, p. 295, n. 3.

47. Quotation attributed to Augustine is actually from Bede. See *Aliquot ques-
tionum liber,* ques. 15, "De redemptione humana," PL 93: 473B.

drinks my blood, remains in me and I in him.' When we eat of
him, we do not break him up into parts." For far be it that we
should understand that Christ is eaten in the way that they who
heard the Lord saying: "Unless you eat the flesh of the Son of
Man and drink his blood, you will not have life in you"[48] understood it, and responded to it in these words, saying: "This is a difficult saying; who can endure it?"[49] For they thought, just as the
aforementioned author says in many places, that at the end of
the Lord's life on earth, [422B] his flesh would be cut up into
pieces, and would either be boiled in a kettle or roasted on a spit
to be eaten; and if they did not like this, they could no longer be
his disciples. Because of this, they chose to leave him and walk
with him no longer. May God turn his Church far from any such
belief! For we eat and drink the immolated Christ on earth, in
such a way that he always exists whole and alive at the right hand
of the Father in heaven.

CHAPTER TWELVE

Berengarius: "St. Augustine, in the book *De civitate Dei*, says: 'A
sacrament is a sacred sign.' A sign, however, is defined in the
book *De doctrina christiana* as follows: 'A sign is a thing which
causes us to think beyond the impression which the thing itself
[422 C] makes on the senses."[50]

Lanfranc: We believe the sacrament about which we are talking
to be a sacred sign, and urge that it be believed as such. In this
sign, beyond the appearance which impresses itself on the eyes
of those who are looking, something far other and very different
salubriously comes to the thought of those who perceive it. What
that reality would be, however, or furthermore, what those things
are which I have briefly called to mind above, I will give a more
expanded explanation on a little later. Indeed, St. Augustine, in
his book *De civitate Dei*, defines a sacrament to be a sacred sign,
but not as simply as you say, however. For he says nothing in that

48. Jn 6.54.
49. Augustine, *In Ioannis Evangelium* 27, PL 35: 1616–21. Cf. Jn 6.60.
50. *De civitate Dei* 10.5: "Sacrificium ergo visibile invisibilis sacrificii sacramentum, id est, sacrum signum est." Cf. *De doctrina christiana* 2.1.

place about the body and blood of the Lord, but rather, he is treating of the rite of the Jewish sacrifices, by which, through the sacrifices that are seen, invisible realities are signified, realities through which [422 D] those things in human society that pertain to the love of God and neighbor are called to mind. A little further on, he concludes his approved teaching by saying: "Therefore, the visible sacrifice is a sign [*sacramentum*] of the invisible sacrifice, that is, it is a sacred sign."[51] What is visible, what he will have called an invisible sacrifice, he explains later on in these words: "God does not want a sacrifice of slaughtered animals, but the sacrifice of a contrite heart."[52] And a little later on: "The true sacrifice, however, is mercy."[53]

Sacred
Sign

CHAPTER THIRTEEN

Berengarius: "Augustine in the letter to the bishop Boniface says: 'If the signs of things of which they are signs did not have a similarity, they would not be a sign at all.'[54] The same can be found in the work *De catechizandis rudibus:* 'Indeed, even though the signs of divine realities are visible, nonetheless it is the invisible realities within them that are honored; and the appearance that has been sanctified by the benediction must not be held as if it is in any type of common usage.'"[55]

Lanfranc: Anyone who would ignore this text, whoever they are, has devoted little study to the sacred letters. For the sacraments always bear a likeness to those things of which they are sacraments, just as in this sacrament, that is, the sacrament which we are now discussing. When the Host is broken, when the blood from the chalice is poured into the mouths of the faithful, what other is designated than the immolation on the cross of the body of the Lord and the effusion of blood from his side? Otherwise, it would not be a sacrament, that is, if by this understanding the name of sacrament is understood in the way in which we now un-

---

51. Augustine, *De civitate Dei* 10.5, PL 41: 282. See n. 50.
52. Ibid.
53. Ibid.
54. *Epistle* 98, *Augustinus episcopo Bonifico,* PL 33: 364.
55. *De catechizandis rudibus* 26, PL 40: 345.

derstand it, [423 B] and in which we also think that it is understood by readers or hearers. For even an oath is called a sacrament, not because of a likeness that it has to the thing itself, but
because of an affirmation or denial upon sacred things about
something. This is what St. Gregory meant in his letter to Justin,
when he said: "We made him swear an oath [*sacramenta*] from
the heart over the body of most holy St. Peter."[56] Furthermore, a
consecration of something is also called a sacrament, in the way
that supporting testimony upholds a case in a doubtful matter.

That which you have construed from *De catechizandis rudibus,*
however, asserting that in visible realities invisible ones should be
honored, and thus that the appearance that has been sanctified
by the benediction must not be held as if it has not been sanctified—how this profits you I plainly do not see. [423 C] In fact, it
seems to be more the case that it militates against your opinion
and defends our own. For in the appearance of bread and wine
that we see, we honor invisible realities, namely, the body and
blood of Christ. Nor do we consider these two appearances [*species*] from which the Lord's body is consecrated to be what we
once thought them to be before the consecration, because we
faithfully confess that before the consecration they were bread
and wine, that is, those realities which nature formed. Within the
consecration, however, they are converted into the flesh and
blood of Christ, and these two realities have been consecrated by
the benediction, although St. Augustine in that book is not
speaking specifically about this sacrament, but rather the sacraments in general which Christians are ordered to perform by
custom, and do solemnly perform, [423 D] thus instructing a certain deacon of the Carthaginian Church about the way in which
he himself should instruct the un-catechized about these and
other matters.

Ag. speaks abt sacraments in general

CHAPTER FOURTEEN

Berengarius: "St. Augustine in his letter to Boniface says: 'Just
as the sacrament of the body of Christ in a certain way is the

56. Gregory the Great, "Ad Justinum Praetorem," *Epistulae* 2.33, PL 77:
572A.

body of Christ, and the sacrament of the blood of Christ in a certain way is the blood of Christ, so also the sacrament of faith is faith.'"[57]

Lanfranc: The sacrament of the body of Christ, as much as it looks to the Lord Christ himself who was immolated upon the cross, is his flesh, which we receive in the sacrament covered in the form of bread, and is his blood, which we drink under the taste and appearance of wine. The flesh [424 A] is the sacrament of the flesh, and the blood is the sacrament of the blood. In the flesh and the blood, both of which are invisible, intelligible, spiritual, there is signified the body of the Redeemer, which is visible, palpable, manifestly full of every grace and virtue and the divine majesty. When the first is broken and divided up unto the salvation of the people, and the other is poured from the chalice and received by the mouth of the faithful, his death upon the cross and the blood flowing from his side are symbolized. And this St. Gregory adroitly understands and clearly explains in the fourth book of the *Dialogi* saying: "Where his flesh is eaten, his blood no longer stains the hands of the godless, but flows into the hearts of his faithful followers. Therefore, we must think what type of sacrifice this is, in which for our absolution the death of the only-begotten Son is always imitated."[58] "Imitated," he said, not "performed," because Christ, "rising from the dead, dies no more, for death no longer has power over him."[59] The flesh and blood, by which the mercy of God is besought for our sins, nourishes us daily. They are called the body and blood of Christ, not only because they are essentially the same although differing greatly in the qualities, but also because of the way of speaking in which the signifier is usually called by the name of the reality that is being signified. Nor will anyone have a reason to be disturbed if the same flesh and the same blood exist as sacraments of themselves according to the sense where one thing is received for another, since the Lord Jesus himself after his Resurrection, in his own day, bore a type or figure of himself even though it was for a different reason, suited to the occasion. For while appearing to the

57. *Epistle* 98, *Augustinus episcopo Bonifico*, PL 33: 364.
58. Gregory the Great, *Dialogi* 4.58, PL 77: 425D.
59. Rm 6.9.

two disciples, he spoke to them, and as much as it can be sufficiently judged, [424 C] he made as if he were going to travel farther on.[60] Acting in this way, St. Augustine says, he signified that he was going to ascend into heaven after a few days. That journey, which was far removed from the customary experience of men, was prefigured[61] by Christ to these two disciples. Christ, therefore, is a sacrament of Christ. It is obvious that in acting as if he were going farther on, what was further away would be the time of his ascension into heaven. It is the same figure of the same Christ, although he is not the same in every respect. For he is true God and true man acting and ascending. The one, however, is the figure of the earthly journey; the other is the truth of the heavenly ascension. Nor should anyone be so foolish and presumptuous as to deny that he is the true Christ because he seems to act as if he were traveling farther on, because in the very appearance of a longer journey, the true Christ signified that he would ascend into heaven. Furthermore, St. Augustine calls baptism the sacrament of faith in that same letter to Boniface. True baptism, however, is established to be not so much an ablution of the body as faith in the heart. Such the apostolic teaching hands down saying: "Cleansing their hearts by faith."[62] And elsewhere: "Baptism saves you also, not the removal of dirt from the body, but the pledge of a good conscience before God."[63] One thing is signified through the other. For through the ablution which is applied extrinsically to the body, the cleansing of the soul is expressed—a cleansing accomplished by interior faith. And baptism is called faith according to a manner of speaking in which the mystery of a reality, whose mystery it is, is customarily denoted by that name. The likeness is the cause of this reality, [425 A] a likeness which must always be found between the sacrament and the reality of the sacrament, just as it is in baptism and faith. For both wash, purge, and purify—the former the flesh, the latter the soul.

Therefore, just as the heavenly bread—which is the true flesh of Christ—is in its own way called the body of Christ, namely,

60. Lk 24.13–28.
61. MC: *est* substituted for *et.*
62. Acts 15.9.
63. 1 Pt 3.21.

the body which is visible, palpable, mortal, and hung upon the cross, so the same can be said of the immolation of his flesh as well, that which by the hands of the priest comes about as the passion, death, and crucifixion of Christ, not in the truth of the reality, but in the signifying mystery; so the sacrament of faith— which is baptism—is faith.

CHAPTER FIFTEEN

Berengarius: "St. Augustine in the letter to Boniface says: [425 B] 'Christ has been immolated once in himself.'[64] Christ, however, is immolated in the sacrament, not only in every solemnity of the Pasch, but also on every day for the people."

Lanfranc: Christ has indeed been immolated once in his own body, because in the manifestation of his body, in a distension of its members, true God and true man hung only once upon the cross, offering himself to the Father as a living, suffering, passible, mortal victim, who is efficacious for the redemption of the living and the dead, that is, for those who he judged should be redeemed, whom, in the depth of his divine counsel,[65] he foreknew, predestined, and called in the ways and times he deemed it suitable to come about.[66] In the sacrament which the Church repeats for the memory of this reality, the flesh of the Lord is daily immolated, divided, [425 C] and eaten, and his blood is drunk from the chalice by the mouth of the faithful. For both the body and the blood are real, and both are those which have been taken from the Virgin. Indeed, the flesh is received by way of the flesh itself, and the blood is received by way of the blood itself, but not without a certain amount of mystery. In another manner of speaking, however, it should be believed, and it can be said, that the whole Christ is eaten—when eternal life, which he is, is longed for with a spiritual desire, when the memory of his commands is held in the mind as sweeter than honey from the comb, when fraternal charity, of which this sacrament is the sign, is chosen for the love of Christ, when sweetly and salubri-

64. *Epistle* 98, PL 33: 364.
65. MC: *consilii* substituted for *concilii*.
66. Cf. Rom 8.29–30.

ously stored in the memory is the fact that, for the salvation of contumacious men, this has been brought about by hanging upon the cross, by being fastened by nails and wounded by the lance. Both types of eating are necessary, [425 D] and both are fruitful. The one depends upon the other for any good to be accomplished. For if the first one should be lacking, the second one would not only fail to purge sins, but would even increase sin in, and judgment upon, those who presume to receive it. "For he who eats and drinks unworthily, eats and drinks unto his own judgment."[67] The latter cannot and should not be without the former. For this is called "daily bread" by the Lord, just as St. Ambrose and St. Cyprian explain, and is read in the Gospel: "Unless you eat the flesh of the Son of Man and drink his blood, you will not have life within you."[68] The sacred canons order that no one should be numbered among those who are Catholics who do not communicate with the sacrament of the body of Christ—unless perchance by the practice of penance and episcopal judgment they [426 A] abstain because of capital sins. In vain, therefore, do you offer the argument: "If Christ has suffered once in himself, he also suffered once in his own body, because his own body cannot be separated from himself." Such an argument does not follow. Indeed, there are many things in reality which cannot be equated with their parts. Since the Lord Jesus himself is true God and true man, and since every man is made up of a rational soul and a body, yet neither the soul alone nor the body alone can rightly be called man or God.

CHAPTER SIXTEEN

Berengarius: "The Burgundian said: 'I agree with the Holy Roman Church.' His truth is found not in the Holy Church, but the Church of the evil ones, the worthless council, not in the Apostolic See, but rather the See of Satan."

Lanfranc: You should not say: "The Burgundian said, 'I agree,'" but instead, "'I Berengarius agree.'" For these were your words which you falsely professed to believe in the holy council. You af-

67. 1 Cor 11.29.   68. Jn 6.54.

firmed by way of an oath that you would keep them. The venerable Humbert, whom you name "the Burgundian" by way of a reproach, as if it were not possible for God to have servants in Burgundy, did nothing other than that which had been ordered in the synod by the same rescript handed to you personally. Truly, O miserable soul, you passed first from heresy to perjury, then from perjury back to heresy, and because this has been handed down by way of a reproof, you call the Holy Roman Church the "Church of the evil ones, the worthless council, the See of Satan." And you babble [426 C] with an impious mouth things that no one has been recorded as ever having babbled—not heretic, schismatic, or any false Christian. For however many there have been who from the beginning of the Christian Church until now have gloried in the dignity of the name Christian, although some who, having abandoned the way of truth, have preferred to walk in the way of error, nevertheless, magnificently have they honored the See of the blessed Apostle Peter, and none ever presumed to speak or write such a blasphemy of this type against it. This is undeniable, as anyone knows who has read their writings which the Apostolic See at various times and for various reasons has received from them either as sent to others [via Rome] or as a direct communication. The Lord himself even spoke of this See with honor in the Gospel when he says: "You are Peter, and upon this rock I will build [426 D] my Church, and the gates of hell will not prevail against it. And I will give to you the keys of the Kingdom of Heaven. And whatever you bind on earth will be bound in heaven. And whatever you loose on earth will be loosed in heaven."[69] Although these words are believed to have been spoken about the pastors of the Holy Church, and are thus explained by certain Catholics, nevertheless the sacred canons and pontifical decrees attest that [these words] must be understood specifically to refer to the Roman Church.

CHAPTER SEVENTEEN

Berengarius: "Who could conceive with reason, or who will concede that it is capable of happening by a miracle, that the bread

69. Mt 16.18, 19.

broken is the body of Christ, since after the Resurrection it enjoys total incorruptibility, and remains incapable of being called
down from heaven until the time of the restitution of all things?"

Lanfranc: How the bread is converted into flesh, and the wine
is converted into blood, and how the nature of each has essentially [*essentialiter*] changed, the just man who lives by faith does
not seek to scrutinize by argumentation and grasp by reason.
The man of faith chooses to adhere to that same faith in the
heavenly mysteries, so that at some point he may arrive at the rewards of faith. And when he arrives at the rewards of faith (for
when the faith is lacking, he labors in vain to understand those
things which cannot be understood), he knows that which has
been written: "You should not seek after things higher than you,
nor should you scrutinize that which is greater than you, but instead, that which God has commanded you, meditate always on
that, and do not be curious of his many works."[70] For it is not
necessary to see with your eyes those things which are hidden
from them. The man of faith grants, however, that it can be
done marvelously by the working of the divine power. Nor are
worthy miracles wanting for some who entertain doubts—[427 B]
miracles by which the veil of visible and corruptible realities is
removed, and Christ can be seen as he truly is—his flesh and
blood appearing to bodily eyes. In these miracles, by the omni-
potence of God, the weakness of the infirm is mercifully healed,
and the detestable depravity of all heretics is awesomely damned
and overturned. For Christ perfects the praise of those who take
upon themselves the simplicity of a child and a nursing infant.[71]
Their faith is ridiculed, however, by those who choose to understand all things by way of reason alone, those, that is, who consider themselves experts by their reasoning. Instead, those make
themselves, because of their arrogance and emptiness, just like
a horse or a mule in which there is no understanding.[72] And
about the incorruptibility of the Lord's body, and the fact that it
cannot be called down from heaven until the day of judgment:
[427 C] we believe in our faith which also proclaims that he himself is truly eaten by the faithful. Yet you say that this is imposs-

---

70. Cf. Sir 3.21–22.   71. Ps 8.3; Mt 21.16.
72. Ps 31.9.

ible—either because you do not understand our faith or because you struggle to distort what is badly understood by
explaining it perniciously. For we do indeed believe that the
Lord Jesus is truly and salubriously eaten on earth by worthy recipients, and we most certainly hold that he exists in heaven uncontaminated, incorrupt, and unharmed. You would be inept if
you were to say that the widow of Zarephath could not partake
of the oil of which her jar was full, because the testimony in sacred history was that the amount of oil in the jar was not diminished in any way, for the same Scripture says: "She went away
and returned to Elijah, and he ate, as well as she and her
household."[73] It would be a similar madness if you should try to
assert [427 D] that the Church cannot feed on the flesh and blood
of its Redeemer because the Apostle says: "Christ rising from the
dead dies no more, for death no longer has power over him";[74]
since the Lord himself, speaking to his disciples, testified and
said: "Take and eat; this is my body which is handed over for
you,"[75] and, "This is the cup of my blood, the mystery of faith,
which is poured out for you and the many."[76] And, "The bread
which I shall give is my flesh for the life of the world," and, "Unless you eat the flesh of the Son of Man and drink his blood, you
will not have life within you."[77] From these very words of the
Lord [428 A] two heresies arose in ancient times. In both of them,
all the heretics agreed that bread and wine would be converted
into the true flesh and true blood of the Son of Man, but there
was a disparity in opinion as to just who the "Son of Man" was—
for not all of these heretics held the same opinion. Some
thought that this must be understood as pertaining to a certain
man, either a just person or a sinner, whose earthly substance,
having been turned into his flesh and blood, has been received
unto the remission of sins. Another group of these heretics
judged that this is not about merely any man among many, but
about a just man, sanctified, set apart from the common life of
men by the high quality of his life, who would be the temple of
God, who would possess most truly the divine indwelling in him-

---

73. 1 Kgs 17.15.   74. Rom 6.9.
75. Mt 26.26; Mk 14.22.   76. Lk 22.20.
77. Jn 6.52.

self. And this is the way that they thought with delirious heretical stubbornness [428 B] that the bread and wine of the altar
would be changed into flesh and blood. This happened a few
years after the death of St. Augustine, in the time of Pope Celestine and of Cyril the Bishop of Alexandria, whose injunctions
and prescriptions have been published and celebrated in the
synod of Ephesus—one of the four which St. Gregory[78] in a letter to the patriarchs confesses that he has received, embraced,
and venerated, on a level with the four holy Gospels of our Lord
Jesus Christ. In this synod each of the lethal infections explained
above was condemned, and the faith that we believe was affirmed, namely, that the bread is converted into the same flesh
that hung upon the cross, and the wine into the same blood
which poured from the side of the one who hung upon [that
same] cross. Finally, those two hundred bishops who were present at the same council, among other things, wrote in this way
about the sacrament, and sent a copy of it to Bishop Nestorius,
[428 C] as if to the leader of the heretics:

We approach the spiritual blessings and are sanctified, having been
made sharers in the holy body and precious blood of Christ the Redeemer of us all: receiving it, not as ordinary flesh, God forbid, nor
as the flesh of a man sanctified and joined to the Word according to a
unity of dignity or as one possessing a divine indwelling, but rather as
vivifying and made the very own body of the Word himself. For he is by
nature life as he exists as God, because he who has united himself to
his own flesh is confessed to be vivifying. Therefore, although he says:
"Amen, Amen, I say to you, unless you eat the flesh of the Son of Man
and drink his blood" [Jn 6:54], we should not think of it as one man
from among ourselves (for how could the flesh of a man be vivifying
by its own nature?), but as his very own it has been truly made, who for
our sake has been made and is called the Son of Man.[79]

And around the end of the council:

If someone does not confess the flesh of the Lord to be vivifying, and
the very flesh of the Word of the Father, but flesh other than his own,
joined to him by way of dignity, as if it were a divine indwelling and not

---

78. Gregory the Great, "Ad Joannem episcopum Constantinopolitanum et
ceteros patriarchas," *Epistulae* 1.25, PL 77: 478A.

79. "Cyril's Third Letter Against Nestorius," *Ep. Synodica* (ed. E. Schwartz,
Concilium Universale Ephesinum, V/1, 240, lines 8–18).

vivifying, since it has been made the very flesh of the Word so that it might have the ability to vivify, let such a one be an anathema.[80]

Why would you desire to hear anything clearer, when, if in a serious study of new controversy, you omit the study of the ancient treatises that brought about peace to the Church? This flesh is not, as the ancient synod defines it, the flesh of just any common man, nor of a justified and sanctified man, but rather it is the flesh that God has united to himself, that is, that flesh of the incarnate God-man. What he calls "mystic benedictions," one should take as if he says, "secrets." For just as St. Augustine says in his work *De catechizandis rudibus*, "mystery" comes from the word that means "secret." For what is more secret than to see the appearance of bread and wine, to taste the flavor, to sense the touch, and nevertheless to believe that by God's wondrous work true flesh is eaten and true blood is drunk? If you were reading humbly, for the sake of eternal life, these things and the like teachings that pervade the entire corpus of divine letters, if you had thrown off this appetite for empty ostentation, and if perchance while reading them you should implore the Lord in prayer that you might come to understand by divine grace those things that are to be taken literally and those things that must be understood spiritually, you would distinguish with Christian caution and would believe without doubt what the universal Church believes, and you would preach that which the apostolic doctrine has established to be professed throughout the entire world, namely, that the flesh and blood of our Lord Jesus Christ is both eaten and drunk by the mouth of the body and the mouth of the heart, that is, corporally and spiritually. Indeed we eat and drink corporally with the mouth of the body, as often as we receive the body of the Lord himself from the altar of the Lord at the hand of the priest. We eat and drink spiritually by the spiritual mouth of the heart, when we sweetly and usefully hold in [429 C] memory, just as St. Augustine says, that the Only-Begotten Son of God, for the salvation of the world, took flesh, hung upon the cross, rose again, appeared, ascend-

---

80. "Cyril's Third Letter Against Nestorius," *12 Anathemata*, 11 (ibid., 244, lines 8–12).

ed, is going to come again on the day of judgment to pay a worthy wage to each for his works. This banquet, then, is beneficial to the poor ones of Christ, if those who are seated at the great table of such a rich man eat so that they might be satisfied, and call it to mind so that they might imitate and always be prepared to die for the sake of Christ, constantly mortifying their members which are on earth, crucifying their flesh with its vices and sinful desires, just as Scripture says: "When you are seated at the table of a great man, know that it is needful to prepare for such things."[81] Concerning the eating of the body, the disciples were told by the Lord: "Take, eat and [429 D] drink, this is my body which is to be handed over for you."[82] And: "This is the cup of my blood, which is poured out for you."[83] And the Apostle to the Corinthians: "He who eats and drinks unworthily, eats and drinks unto his own judgment when he does not recognize the body of the Lord."[84] St. Augustine carefully explains the spiritual eating, however, in Homily Twenty-Six on the Gospel of John, when he says: "Eat the heavenly bread spiritually, and bring innocence to the altar."[85] And a little later on: "This is the bread, therefore, that comes down from heaven, so that he who eats of it, may not die. But that pertains to the reality of the sacrament, not to what is visible in the sacrament; that is, he who eats what is within, not just what is without, that is, he who eats in his heart, [430 A] not who presses with his teeth."[86] What the reality of the sacrament is, he explains a little later on, saying: "The faithful recognize the body of Christ, if they do not fail to be the body of Christ. They become the body of Christ, if they choose to live by the spirit of Christ."[87] And some time later on: "What this bread is to us the Apostle Paul explains, 'We the many,' he says, 'are one bread, one body.'[88] O sacrament of piety! O sign of unity! O bond of charity!"[89]

---

81. Sir 31.12.   82. Mt 26.26.
83. Lk 22.20.   84. 1 Cor 11.29.
85. Augustine, *In Ioannis Evangelium* 26.6, PL 35: 1611.
86. Ibid.   87. Ibid.
88. 1 Cor 10.17.
89. Augustine, *In Ioannis Evangelium* 26.6, PL 35: 1611.

CHAPTER EIGHTEEN

Having repulsed, as much as it has seemed sufficient, the calumnies which you have rashly argued, written, and published in a contumacious manner against Bishop Humbert and the Holy Roman Church, it is left for us to explain briefly the faith of the Holy Church and the views of your sect. [430 B] Having advanced both the Church's faith and the opinions of your sect by a few authorities and succinct reasons, let us prove the one and disprove the other. For neither many long testimonies from the Scriptures nor well-argued disputations can be inserted into a brief letter such as this one, nor does reason or necessity require it. For the depraved insist upon the twisted defense of their own twisted teachings, but not the faithful. Rather, for them, having understood the authorities and heard the reasons, they humbly desire to return to the way of truth, and for them, a few words from a few authorities can satisfy. Those, however, who decide to abandon the way of truth by contentious arguments and to persist in their infidelities could not be satisfied even if they were opposed by many words from many authorities.

We believe, therefore, that the earthly substances, which on the table of the Lord are divinely sanctified [430 C] by the priestly ministry,[90] are ineffably, incomprehensibly, miraculously converted by the workings of heavenly power into the essence of the Lord's body. The species and whatever other certain qualities of the earthly substances themselves, however, are preserved, so that those who see it may not be horrified at the sight of flesh and blood, and believers may have a greater reward for their faith at the sight. It is, nonetheless, the body of the Lord himself existing in heaven at the right side of the Father, immortal, inviolate, whole, uncontaminated, and unharmed. Truly it is possible to say, therefore, that it is the same body that was assumed from the Virgin, and also not the same body, which we receive. Indeed, it is the same body as far as it concerns its essence, true nature, and its own excellence. It is not the same body in its appearance, however, if one is considering the species of bread and wine and the rest of the qualities mentioned above. [430 D]

90. MC: *ministerium* substituted for *mysterium*.

This is the faith held from ancient times, and is the one that the Church which is now diffused throughout the whole world, and is called Catholic, now holds. Whence, just as it has been said above, the Lord in the Gospel said: "Take and eat; this is my body, which is handed over for you," and, "This is the cup of my blood, the mystery of faith, which, for you and for many, is poured out for the remission of sins." St. Ambrose, distinguishing between the sacrament of the Christians and the sacrament of the Jews, in a sermon about the mysteries delivered to the neophytes, spoke thus:

Consider now whether the bread of angels is more excellent or the flesh of Christ, which indeed is the body of life. That manna was from heaven, this is above the heavens; that was of heaven, this of the Lord of the heavens; that was subject to corruption if it were kept for a second day, this is foreign to every corruption, because whosoever shall taste in a holy manner [431 A] shall not be able to feel corruption. For them water flowed from the rock, for you blood [flowed] from Christ; water satisfied them for the hour, blood satiates you for eternity. The Jew drinks and is thirsty; when you drink, you will not be able to be thirsty; that was in a shadow, this is in truth. If that which you admire is a shadow, how great is that whose shadow you admire.[91]

And a little later on:

You recognize the more excellent things; for the light is more powerful than the shade, truth than figure, the body of its author than manna from heaven. Perhaps you may say: "I see something else; how do you tell me that I receive the Body of Christ?" This still remains for us to prove. Therefore, we make use of examples great enough to prove that this is not what nature formed but what benediction consecrated, and that the power of benediction is greater than that of nature, because even nature itself is changed by the benediction. Moses held a rod; he cast it down and it became a serpent; again, he took hold of the tail of the serpent and it returned to the nature of a rod. You see then that by the grace of the Prophet the nature of the serpent and that of the rod were changed. The rivers of Egypt were flowing with a pure stream of water; suddenly, from the veins of the springs blood began to burst forth; there was no drinking water in the rivers. Again at the voice of the Prophet the blood of the rivers ceased; the nature of waters returned.[92]

91. Ambrose, *De mysteriis* 8.48, 49, PL 16: 404ff. Translation FC 44: 23.
92. Ibid., 8.49–51. FC 44: 23–24, trans. Roy J. Deferrari, slightly modified.

Having narrated these and other like miracles which have
been brought about by [ineffable divine operation] after a little
while he adds:

So we notice that grace is capable of accomplishing more than is nature, and yet thus far we have mentioned only the benediction of the
prophet. But if the benediction of man had such power as to change
nature, what do we say of the [divine consecration itself, in which the
very words of our Lord and Savior function? For that sacrament, which
you receive, is effected by the words of Christ. But if the words of Elias
had such power as to call down fire from heaven, will not the words of
Christ have the power enough to change the nature of the elements?
You have read about the work of the world: "that he spoke and they
were done, he commanded and they were created." So cannot the
words of Christ, which were able to make what was out of nothing,
change those things that are into the things that were not? For it is not
of less importance to give things new natures than to change natures.
[431 D] But why do we use arguments? Let us use his own examples,
and [by the mysteries of the Incarnation let us establish the truth of
the mysteries.] Did the process of nature precede when the Lord Jesus
was born of Mary? If we seek the usual course, a woman after mingling
with a man usually conceives. It is clear then that the Virgin conceived
contrary to the course of nature. And this body which we make is from
the Virgin. Why do you seek here the course of nature in the body of
Christ, when the Lord Jesus himself was born of the Virgin contrary to
nature?[93]

Again, in the fourth book *De sacramentis:* "You perhaps will
say: 'My bread is ordinary bread.' But that bread is bread before
the words of the sacraments; when the consecration has been
added, from bread it becomes the body of Christ."[94]

And a little later:

The heaven was not, the sea was not, the earth was not, but hear David as he says: "He spoke and they were made, he commanded and
they were created." Therefore, to reply to you, there was no body of
Christ before the [432 A] consecration, but after the consecration I say
to you that now there is the body of Christ. "He himself spoke and it
was made; he himself commanded and it was created."[95]

93. Ibid., 8.52, 53. FC 44: 25–26.
94. Ambrose, *De sacramentis* 4.4, 14, PL 16: 439B. FC 44: 302.
95. Ibid., 4.4, 15–16. FC 44: 302–3.

Christ's words are added —

And a little while later:

Before it is consecrated it is bread; but when Christ's words have been added, it is the body of Christ. Finally, hear him as he says: "Take and eat of this all of you; for this is my body." And before [the words of Christ, the chalice is full of wine and water; when the words of Christ have been added, then blood is effected, which redeemed the people. So behold in what great respects the expression of Christ is able to change all things. Then the Lord Jesus himself testified to us that we receive his body and blood. Should we doubt at all about his faith and testification?[96]

Christ change element into his body

Again, in the sixth book *De sacramentis,* as [432 B] was said above:

Just as our Lord Jesus Christ is the true Son of God, not as man through grace, but as the true Son of God from the substance of the Father, thus he is true flesh as he himself said, which we receive, and is his true blood which we drink. But perchance you say that the disciples of Christ also said at that time when they heard him say: "Unless one eat my flesh and drink my blood, he will not abide in me, and will not have eternal life"—perchance you say: "How true [flesh]? Certainly I see a likeness, I do not see true blood." First of all, I told you about the words of Christ which operate so as to be able to change and transform the established orders of nature. Then, when his disciples did not tolerate the words of Christ, but hearing that he gave his flesh to eat and his blood to drink, [432 C] went back, and yet Peter alone said: "You have words of eternal life, and whither shall I go back from you?"—lest, then, more might say that they go, as if there were a kind of horror of the blood, but as if the grace of redemption did abide, thus indeed in likeness you receive the sacraments, but obtain the grace and virtue of true nature. "I am the living bread," he says, "which came down from heaven." But flesh did not come down from heaven, that is, he took on flesh on earth from a virgin. How, then, did bread come down from heaven and living bread? Because our same Lord Jesus Christ is a sharer of both divinity and body, and you who receive the flesh participate in that nourishment of his divine substance.[97]

X takes on flesh here

Again, in an epistle to Irenaeus: [432 D]

You ask me, why did the Lord God rain down manna upon the people of the patriarchs, and now it does not rain down? If you knew, it does rain, and he rains down manna daily upon his servants. And this corporeal manna is found in many places today, but now it is not a matter

96. Ibid., 4.5, 23, PL16: 444A. FC 44: 305.
97. Ibid., 6.1.1–4, PL 16: 454B. FC 44: 320.

(handwritten margin note, top right) bread from heaven (manna) / body (for Virgin) (Eucharist)

of so great a miracle because that which is perfect comes. The perfect bread from heaven, the body from the Virgin, is the one the Gospel teaches satisfies you. How much more excellent is this one than the former![98]   *(handwritten)* AMBROSE

(handwritten margin note) AUGUSTINE

Augustine in his second Homily on the Thirty-Third Psalm: "The Jews drew near to Christ to crucify him; we draw near to him to receive his body and blood. They were plunged into darkness[99] in the presence of the Crucified; we are illumined by eating and drinking the Crucified."[100] [433 A] And a little later: "Truly it is the great Lord who, in his great mercy, has given us his body to eat, in which he has suffered so much, and his blood to drink."[101] Again, in the Homily on the Forty-Fifth Psalm, speaking to the Jews: "In the name of him whom you have killed, you are baptized, and your sins are forgiven you. After you have recognized the Physician, then drink in safety the blood of him whose blood you have shed."[102] Again, in the Homily on Psalm Sixty-Five: "By way of homicide the gift is given, and the blood of the innocent one is poured out, and the blood itself, which they shed through madness, they drink by grace."[103]

(handwritten margin note) the Lord has given us his body to eat & blood to drink

Again, in a homily on Psalm Ninety-Eight:

I ask what his footstool is, and Scripture tells me: "The earth is my footstool." Hesitatingly I turn to Christ, since it is here that I am seeking him, and I discover how one might worship the earth without sacrilege, how one might worship his footstool without sacrilege. For he took upon himself earth from the earth; because flesh is from the earth, and he received flesh from the flesh of Mary. And because he walked here in true flesh, and gave us that true flesh for us to eat for our salvation—and no one eats that flesh unless he has first worshipped—we have found out in just what sense one may worship the footstool of our Lord, and that we not only do not sin in worshipping it, but rather, that we sin in not worshipping."[104]

And a little while later:

Then, when the Lord commended this, he spoke about his flesh and said: "Unless anyone eats my flesh, he will not have eternal life in him"

98. Ambrose,"Ad Irenaeum," *Epistulae* 64, PL 16: 1219B.
99. MC: *tenebrati* substituted for *tenebrat*.
100. Augustine, *Enarrationes in psalmos* 33.2.10, PL 36: 314.
101. Ibid., 33.2.25, PL 36: 322.   102. Ibid., 45.5, PL 36: 516.
103. Ibid., 65.5, PL 36: 791.   104. Ibid., 98.9, PL 37: 1264.

[Jn 6:54]. Some of his disciples were scandalized—nearly seventy of them—and said: "This is a hard saying; who can understand it?" And they departed from him and no longer walked with him. It seemed hard to them because he said: "Unless anyone eats my flesh, he will not have eternal life" [Jn 6:54]. They understood it foolishly; they were thinking carnally and thought that the Lord would give them some cut-up particles from his body, and so they said: "This is a hard saying," but they were hard, not the saying.[105]

And a little later he says: "Understand spiritually what I have said: you are not to eat this body which you see, nor drink that blood which they will have shed who crucify me."[106]

You rejoice in these last words of St. Augustine. [433 D] In these words above, you boast that you have conquered and are superior, and you rejoice that you have found here the firm foundation of your defense. In what way, you say, do you try to persuade us that we receive true flesh and true blood in this sacrament, when you hear in a manifest way that the body that the disciples see is not the body that they will eat, or the blood that those who crucify him will shed is not the blood that they will drink? Indeed, this objection is a calumny. For since he testified above that the flesh which he took from the Virgin Mother, and in which he walked upon the earth, has been salubriously given us to eat—how could he place contrary opinions in the way of such clear ones? Far be it from a sober reader and Catholic teacher to think so perversely about a pillar of the Church and a foundation of truth, about whom Pope Celestine in his decrees asserted that while Augustine lived no rumor of sinister suspicion ever touched him. Indeed, in every way, Pope Celestine said that St. Augustine faithfully professed and believed in that which every member of the Catholic Church now professes and believes, and what I also have professed in the brief confession of faith that I have set forth above, namely—to sum it up briefly—that it is, and is not, the same body. For we ourselves do not think, as they do, that it is in this way that we receive him; that is, we do not believe that it is the visible body of Christ that we eat, or the blood that had poured out in the sight of his per-

105. Ibid., PL 37: 1265.
106. Ibid.

secutors that we drink. But rather, we believe in that which we
do not see, so that the faith might grow strong, which it otherwise could not if these matters to be believed were placed before our bodily senses. That is why in explaining this fact, he
places this rather subtle distinction: "And even if it is necessary,"
he says [434 B], "for it to be celebrated visibly, it is to be invisibly understood nonetheless."[107] For they were thinking that the
Lord would command them in either a bestial or a human way
to eat that body which they saw, or to drink that blood which his
persecutors will have shed, that is, either raw, or boiled in water,
or like roasted meat drawn from the flaming coals of a brazier.
The Lord, disapproving of this carnal understanding of theirs,
said in the Gospel according to John: "It is the Spirit who gives
life; the flesh profits nothing."[108] About this, offering an explanation in tract twenty-seven in his treatise on this same Gospel,
St. Augustine says: "Why say this then? 'The flesh profits nothing.' It profits nothing, but how did they understand it? Indeed,
they understood the flesh in this way: just as a carcass is sectioned into pieces, or sold in a meat market; not as something
animated by the Spirit."[109] Thus far we have dealt with these
matters; let us now return to the proposition.

CHAPTER NINETEEN

Augustine, in Homily Eleven on John, writes: "For in the people of the Jews is a type of the Christian people. There was the
figure, here is the truth. There was the shadow, here is the
body."[110] Again, in Homily Thirty-One: "And those saw Christ dy-
ing by their crime and yet they believed in Christ's pardoning of
their crimes. Until they drank the blood they shed, they de-
spaired of their own salvation."[111] Again, in the Fortieth Homily:
"Those who in their rage killed him were changed[112] and be-

---

107. Ibid., PL 37: 1265. WSA 3/18: 475.
108. Jn 6.64.
109. Augustine, *In Ioannis Evangelium* 27.5, PL 35: 1618.
110. Ibid., 11.8, PL 35: 1479.
111. Ibid., 31.9, PL 35: 1640.
112. Reading *mutati* instead of *imitati*.

[Those who shed his blood drank it †]

lieved; and they who in their rage shed his blood, now in a spirit of faith drank it."[113] Again, in a sermon to the newly [434 D] baptized: "Receive in this bread what hung upon the cross, and receive in this cup what flowed from the side of Christ, for death, not life, will be for those who have thought that [he who is] life [itself] is a liar."[114] Again, in book four of *De Trinitate:* "Yet those who have remained with him are very few, since the nations acknowledge and with pious humility imbibe the price paid for themselves, and with trust in it abandon their enemy."[115] And in the subsequent chapter that follows a short time afterward: "And what is as clean for the cleansing of the faults of mortal men, as the flesh born in and from the womb of a virgin, without the infection of carnal concupiscence? And what could be so acceptably offered, and taken, as the flesh of our sacrifice made the body of our priest?"[116] And [435 A] Pope Leo in his sermon *De jejunio septimi mensis:*

[no concupiscence]

As you utter this confession with full heart, dearly beloved, cast off the wicked words of the heretics, so that your fasts and alms might not be polluted by any contagion of error. For then both the oblation of the sacrifice is clean and the generosity of mercy is holy when those who bestow it understand what they are doing. For since the Lord said, ["If you do not eat the flesh of the Son of Man and drink his blood, you will not have life in you" [Jn 6.53-54], you ought not, therefore, participate in the holy table in such a way that you call into question any further the truth of the body and blood of Christ.] For what is received in the mouth is believed by faith, and in vain do they respond "Amen" who argue against what they receive.[117]

[Pope Leo: what is received in the mouth in faith]

Again, in a letter sent to the bishop Anatolius:

If the true High Priest does not atone for us, using the nature proper to us, and the true blood of the spotless Lamb does not cleanse us, then a true priesthood and true sacrifices do not exist in any other way in God's Church, [435 B] which is the Body of Christ. Although he

113. Augustine, *Sermon* 352.2, "De utilitate agendae poenitentiae" 2, PL 39: 1550.

114. Sermon 228B, 2, *Ad infantes* (ed. G. Morin, *Miscellanea Agostiniana*, 18–20 = PL 46: 827). Augustine, *Sermons*, trans. E. Hill, WSA 3/6 (New Rochelle: New City Press, 1995), 263 n. 1.

115. Augustine, *De Trinitate* 4.13, PL 42: 900.

116. Ibid., 4.14, PL 42: 901.

117. Leo the Great, *De jejunio septimi mensis* 91.3, PL 54: 452B.

is seated at the right hand of the Father, he performs the sacrament of atonement in the same flesh which he assumed from the Virgin.[118]

Again, in a sermon on the Passion of the Lord: "As a result, his own malice deceived him. He inflicted punishment upon the Son of God, punishment that was to turn into healing for every child of human beings. He poured out that righteous blood which was the price and the cup for reconciling the world."[119] St. Gregory in an Easter homily: "And indeed you have learned what the blood of the lamb is, not now by instruction, but by drinking. For the blood that is placed on each of the door posts is now received not only by the mouth of the body, but also by the mouth of the heart."[120]

These are the testimonies of divine eloquence, a few texts which I have excerpted from many for the sake of conciseness, which, I have judged, clearly make the case that it is the true flesh of Christ and his true blood which is immolated, eaten, and drunk corporeally, spiritually, and incomprehensibly at the table of the Lord. And lest there be anyone who is so perverted or perverting as to understand these matters or explain them in a way other than the spiritual sons of the Universal Church explain and understand them, there are in many diverse churches, as much in ancient times as in modern ones, miracles that support this faith, when and where and to whom the eternal wisdom of God,[121] to which nothing is impossible, which extends from one end of creation to the other, which strongly and sweetly [435 D] orders all things, has willed to demonstrate such a great mystery. The existence of these miracles, no one who has given even a modicum of study to ecclesiastical history or the writings of the holy Fathers can ignore. These writings, although they do not enjoy the highest authority given to the prophets and the apostles, nevertheless have sufficient authority to prove this faith—a faith which we and all the faithful now have, and have had since

---

118. Leo, "Ad Anatolium," *Epistolae et Decretales* 44, PL 51: 713D. *St. Leo the Great: Letters*, trans. E. Hunt, FC 34 (Washington, DC: The Catholic University of America Press, 1957), 148–49.

119. Leo, *De Passione Domini* 62, PL 54: 351B. FC 93: 270.

120. Gregory the Great, *De evangeliis* 22.9, PL 76: 1178B.

121. MC: *Dei* added.

ancient times. On the other hand, when the decrees of the Roman pontiffs and sacred canons have condemned certain writings and identified them as apocryphal, it has been firmly established that these are specifically condemned and should not be read in the Catholic Church by Catholics.

CHAPTER TWENTY

Against such a great light of divine authorities, [436 A] you do not cease to counterpose a fog of questioning, saying: "What you assert to be the true body of Christ is what is called in the sacred writings *species, likeness, figure, sign, mystery,* and *sacrament.* These words, however, refer to a reality other than themselves, for no existing thing which is referred to another existing thing can be that to which it is referred. It is not, therefore, the body of Christ." This opinion, found in a certain writing of yours, although it is spoken of in different ways and with many drawn-out sentences, is, nonetheless, always the same. This is what your disciples and followers babble on about, subverting others while they themselves are subverted by your silver and gold and whatever other rewards that you offer. And so they themselves, erring from the truth, send others out in error, "not knowing," as the Apostle says, [436 B] "what they say, or what they affirm."[122] Their words, however, do not dictate anything that is true for the faith that we believe and the truth that we defend. For the words *species* and *likeness* are the vocabulary for those realities which describe what they were before, and from which the body and blood of Christ are confected. I say "bread" and "wine," whence at the end of a certain Mass it is prayed: "May your sacraments perfect in us, we beseech you, O Lord, what they contain, so that what we handle now in appearance [*species*], we might receive in the truth of reality."[123] Indeed, the priest prays that the body of

---

122. 1 Tm 1.7.

123. *Corpus orationum,* v. 6, "Orationes in ieiunio mensis septimi, die sabati in XII lectionibus, oratio ad complendum seu post communionem" (ed. B. Wallant, n. 4219, 233 = PL 78: 142D): "Perficiant in nobis, Domine, quaesumus, tua sacramenta quod continent, ut quae nunc specie gerimus rerum veritate capiamus."

Christ, which is brought forth in manifest vision under the appearances of bread and wine, may be received at some point as it truly is. For the Truth, to manifest himself, often does this in the sacred letters. About just this manifest vision, the Lord himself in the Gospel of John says to his disciples: "He who loves me, will be loved by my Father. And I will love him and manifest myself to him."[124] [436 C] And David in the person of God the Father said: "And I will give him length of days, and show him my salvation."[125] Although it is not improbable that what he is explaining here is the truth of the flesh and blood, nevertheless, what it brings about is the same thing: the remission of sins. For in every way the true flesh and blood of Christ exists in those who worthily receive, who, as a consequence of receiving, have the forgiveness of their sins. Whence in the canon of the Mass, the priest says: "So that it might become for us the body and blood of your most beloved Son, our Lord Jesus Christ," for us, I say, that is, for believers, and for those who receive it in a way that is worthy of your mercy. "For he who eats and drinks unworthily does so unto his own judgment."[126] [436 D] St. Gregory in book four of the *Dialogi:* "Then the true Host will be offered to God for us when we ourselves have confected the Host."[127] Indeed, it is even the true flesh of Christ and the true blood of Christ for sinners and those who receive him unworthily, but it is the essence, not the salvific effects. To this fact St. Augustine attests in the fifth book *De baptismo,* saying:

Just as Judas, to whom the Lord gave a morsel, prepared a place within himself for the devil, not by receiving anything evil, but by receiving it in an evil way; so it is that whoever receives the sacrament of the Lord unworthily, does not make the sacrament evil, since he himself is evil, nor will he have received nothing because he does not receive unto salvation. For it was no less the body and blood of the Lord for those of whom the Apostle said: "He who eats and drinks unworthily, eats and drinks judgment unto himself" [1 Cor 11.29].[128]

124. Jn 14.21.   125. Ps 90.16.
126. Cor 11.29.
127. Gregory the Great, *Dialogi* 4.59, PL 77: 428A.
128. Augustine, *De baptismo contra Donatistas* 5.8.9, PL 43: 181.

Ambrose in the sixth book of *De sacramentis:* "How is it true? I
see the likeness, but I do not see the truth of the blood."[129] And
a little later on: "Indeed, in the likeness you receive the sacrament, but as a consequence you receive the grace and virtue in
its true nature."[130] In no place is there any doubt that this likeness is understood as the appearance of the bread and the wine,
under which the nature of the body of Christ is hidden, and
without horror the blood is received by the worthy recipients
unto their salvation. Even *species, likeness,* and *figure* are found
to stand for the truth. Thus the Lord in the Gospel according
to John says: "You have neither [437 B] heard his voice, nor seen
his form [*species*]."[131] The Apostle, addressing the Corinthians,
says: "We walk by faith, not by sight [*species*]."[132] Ambrose in the
book *De mysteriis:* "And further we read of the likeness [*species*]
being accepted for the reality, both as it concerns Christ: 'found
in the likeness [*species*] of a man,' and God the Father: 'Nor have
you seen his likeness [*species*].'"[133] Again, in the fourth book[134] *De
fide* addressed to Gratian: "'My flesh is real food and my blood
is real drink.' You hear *flesh* and you hear *blood,* yet you recognize the sacraments of the Lord's death."[135] And a little while
later: "As often as we receive these sacraments, however, which
through the mystery of the sacred prayer are transfigured into
flesh and blood, we announce his death."[136] Augustine [437 C] in
the book *De catechizandis rudibus:* "For we are made equal to the
angels of God, and just like them; we hope and await to enjoy
equally with them the sight [*species*] of that Trinity in which we
now walk by faith."[137] The Apostle to the Philippians: "He was
made unto the likeness [*similitudo*] of a man, being found in
the appearance of a man."[138] And again to the Hebrews: "And
he is the radiance of his glory and the exact representation [*fig-*

129. Ambrose, *De sacramentis* 6.1, PL 16: 454C.
130. Ibid., 6.3.   131. Jn 5.37.
132. 2 Cor 5.7.
133. Ambrose, *De mysteriis* 1.4.25, PL 16: 396B; Phil 2.7; Jn 5.37.
134. MC: *libro* added.
135. Ambrose, *De fide ad Gratianum* 4.10.118, PL 16: 640A; Jn 6.56.
136. Ibid., 4.10.124, PL 16: 641A.
137. Augustine, *De catechizandis rudibus* 1.25.47, PL 40: 343; 2 Cor 5.7.
138. Phil 2.7, 8.

ura] of his nature [*substantia*]."[139] *Sign, mystery, sacrament,* and
whatever like terms are names used to designate the Passion of
the Lord, that is, however, if *sacrament* is understood as signifying those things which St. Augustine in *De civitate Dei* defines as
a sacred sign. Therefore, St. Gregory in the fourth book of the
Dialogi says: "For this unique victim saves the soul from eternal
loss, a sacrifice which, by way of mystery, renews that [437 D] death
for us of the Only-Begotten."[140] And a little later on: "Let us reflect, therefore, as to what type of sacrifice this is for us, which,
for our forgiveness, always imitates the Passion of the Only-
Begotten Son."[141] And some time later: "Because we celebrate
the mystery of the Lord's Passion, we ought to imitate that which
we worship."[142] Again, in an Easter homily: "And although on either door post the blood of the lamb was placed, when the sacrament of his Passion is received by the mouth, bringing about redemption, it is contemplated with an attentive mind as an object
of imitation."[143] Indeed, in the sacred codices, one does not find
only one definition of the word "sacrament." St. Ambrose, in his
book addressed to Gratian, says that the Only-Begotten [438 A] of
the Father has appeared to men through the "sacrament" of the
assumed man.[144] It means as much as if he were saying that he
appeared through the man he had assumed, and whom he had
consecrated as a worthy dwelling-place of his divinity.[145] He has
also other understandings of what the word "sacrament" means,
about which enough has been said above. It is called "bread" according to the custom of the sacred canons, which frequently
call some things by the names of the things from which they have
come, or which they are thought to be and are not, or which are
similar to them in some way. Thus St. Jerome says in the second
book *In Osee* (at the end of the preface): "After dust has returned
to dust, pale death will pull down us who write, as much as it does

---

139. Heb 1.2.
140. Gregory the Great, *Dialogi* 4.58, PL 77: 425C.
141. Ibid.
142. Ibid., 4.59.
143. Gregory the Great, *Homiliae in Evangelia* 22.7, PL 76: 1178A.
144. Ambrose, *De fide ad Gratianum Augustum*, PL 16: 527ff.
145. MC: *divinitatis* substituted for *divinitati*.

those who judge us."[146] And [438 B] to a proud man, it is said by a wise man: "How can you who are dust and ashes be proud?"[147] And it can be read that Abraham saw three men, although they were in fact angels; about this St. Augustine in the second book of *De Trinitate* says: "But under the oak at Mamre, Abraham saw three men, whom he invited and hospitably received, and ministered to them as they feasted."[148] And in the Book of Judges, the sterile woman said to her husband about the angel: "A man of God came to me."[149] And a little while later: "Behold, a man appeared to me whom I had seen before."[150] And sometime later: "And Manoah did not know that it was an angel of God."[151] And St. Jerome says about God in the same book of explanation on Hosea the prophet: "The worm and corruption have been made, as it were, not that God would be either the [438 C] worm or corruption, but because all these things appear to those who are undergoing punishments."[152] And in the Gospel according to John: "And they cursed him: 'You are his disciple,'"[153] when it is not a curse but a blessing to be a disciple of Christ. St. Augustine in his exposition on the same Gospel says further: "Such a curse be upon us and upon our children! For such a curse it is if you open your heart, not if you consider the words carefully."[154] And in the Gospel according to Matthew, and similarly according to Luke: "If you, evil as you are, know how to give your children good things."[155] St. Augustine treats this saying in the second book of *De sermone Domini*, in this fashion: "How is it that the evil give good gifts? For he not only called sinners evil, [438 D] but also those who love this age. They give good things, therefore, according to their senses, and they ought to be called good

---

146. Jerome, *Commentariorum in Osee Prophetam ad Pammachium* 2, PL 25: 861A.

147. Sir 10.9.

148. Augustine, *De Trinitate* 2.10, PL 42: 858.

149. Jgs 13.6.   150. Jgs 13.10.

151. Jgs 13.16.

152. Jerome, *Commentariorum in Osee Prophetam ad Pammachium* 2, PL 25: 864B.

153. Jn 9.28.

154. Augustine, *In Ioannis Evangelium* 44.12, PL 35: 1718.

155. Mt 7.2; Lk 2.13.

because they have these things for the sake of good."[156] And the Lord Jesus Christ, on account of certain likenesses, in the same writings is called a lion, lamb, worm, wood, rock, cornerstone, and many other things in a similar fashion. So also the body of Christ is called bread, either because it is confected from bread; or because to the eye's gaze the flesh seems like bread; or because by a certain likeness it is associated with corporeal and visible bread. With this distinction then, one could say that just as the consumption of material bread nourishes and sustains human flesh, so in a similar fashion does the invisible and spiritual body of Christ nourish and enliven the soul of the one who receives it worthily. And yet you object, and, by means of the authority of Ambrose, [439 A] you attempt to weaken Ambrose himself by saying: "Ambrose in the book *De sacramentis* says: 'For just as you have received the likeness of his death, so it is that you drink the likeness of the precious blood.'"[157] Explaining these words, you say: "What closer a comparison could there be, what could be a greater likeness? It cannot be denied that St. Ambrose has made a comparison between the sacrament of baptism and the sacrament of the altar. It is not, however, the true death of Christ in baptism, so it is not then his true blood in this sacrament." Let it be said, however, that although by [advancing] this understanding of these words you have deceived many, nevertheless, adverbs of comparison placed indiscriminately in a text signify neither an identity nor an equality. For the Savior says in the Gospel: "Be merciful, just as your Father is merciful."[158] It is not possible, however, for there to be an equality between the mercy found in men and the mercy of God. And in the Gospel according to John: "And I gave to them the glory that you gave to me, so that they may be one just as you and I are one."[159] And in another place: "You have loved them just as you have loved me."[160] Wherefore, St. Augustine in an exposition on the same Gospel says: "For one does not always intimate equality when he

156. Augustine, *De sermone Domini in monte secundum Matthaeum* 2.21, PL 34: 1303.

157. Ambrose, *De sacramentis* 4.19, PL 16: 443A.

158. Lk 6.36.   159. Jn 17.22.

160. Jn 17.23.

says, 'As this, so also that other'; but sometimes only, because this is, so also is the other; or, that the one is, in order that the other may be also."[161]

CHAPTER TWENTY-ONE

There is something else that you object to, because given the faculty of speaking, you cry out and say in many places: [439 C] "If bread is converted [*convertitur*] into the true flesh of Christ, then it would either be taken up into heaven, so that there it could be changed [*transferatur*] into the flesh of Christ, or the flesh of Christ would be carried down [from heaven] to earth, so that there the bread might be changed [*commutetur*] into the flesh of Christ. But neither is bread taken up, nor is flesh carried down; the bread, therefore, is not converted into the true flesh of Christ." You and your followers, however, have drawn this conclusion from human wisdom, not divine. For the Apostle, in his letter to the Romans, forbids inquiry into divine works by way of human wisdom, when he says: "One should not think highly of himself, but think soberly";[162] and to the Corinthians: "And my message and my proclamation were not with persuasive words of wisdom, but with a demonstration of spirit and power, so that your faith may not rest on human wisdom, but on the power of God";[163] and to the Colossians: "See to it that no one captivate you with an empty seductive philosophy according to human tradition, according to the elemental powers of the world."[164] And St. Gregory in an Easter homily: "It must be known to us that the divine work, if it is understood by reason, is not admirable. Faith has no merit where human reason offers a proof."[165] When dealing with such inscrutable matters, therefore, it is necessary for you to pray to God, so that you might understand these matters, insofar as human capacity is capable of understanding them; or that you might bear up humbly and patiently while you continue to believe those things that are so obscure

161. Augustine, *In Ioannis Evangelium* 110.5, PL 35: 1923.
162. Rom 12.3.   163. 1 Cor 2.4.
164. Col 2.8.
165. Gregory the Great, *Homiliae in Evangelia* 2.26.1, PL 76: 1197C.

and far removed from the human intellect, and in so doing, you will at least arrive at a minimal understanding of them in this life. This is something which is altogether different from generating a dispute, dissenting from the Universal Church, and bringing about a new schism by speaking and writing against the precepts of the holy fathers. Having profited in this way, you would act in the way that the Legislator has prescribed that one should, when he says: "Do not transgress the ancient boundaries which your [440 A] fathers have set."[166] And St. Augustine says in the first book of *De sermone Domini in monte* that: "Because something either seems obscure, or sounds absurd to someone does not mean that, because of it, he should raise an objection against it; rather, he should pray so that he might come to understand it."[167] And in the third book of *De Trinitate:* "But it is certainly a useful caution to myself, that I should remember what my own powers are, and admonish my brethren that they also remember what theirs are, lest human infirmity pass on beyond that which is safe."[168] And in the book against Felix the heretic: "It is enough that I strive to obey the authority of the Scriptures in simplicity rather than in pride."[169] And a little later: "What reason can be given if you preach the Virgin birth, if you do not deny that he returned sight to the blind, if you should show that the buried return from the dead? If, therefore, of all of these, the reason is most incomprehensible [440 B] yet the truth is obvious, the public testimonies of the faith are believed more easily than a reason is sought."[170]

CHAPTER TWENTY-TWO

Having proved those things which needed to be proved, and excluded those things which reason forces one to exclude—just

---

166. Prv 22.28.

167. Augustine, *De sermone Domini in monte secundum Matthaeum* 1.21, PL 34: 1245.

168. Augustine, *De Trinitate* 3.10.21, PL 42: 881.

169. *Contra Felicianum Arianum de unitate Trinitatis* 2, PL 42: 1158: This work is listed as dubious by the *Clavis Patrum Latinorum* under Vigilius (n. 808), and attributed to Ps. Augustine.

170. Ibid.; MC: *investigatur* omitted.

what it is that you believe, and the corollary to that belief, let us see. You believe that the bread and wine of the Lord's table, during the consecration, as far as it applies to its substance, remain unchanged, that is, bread and wine existed before the consecration, and bread and wine exist after the consecration. Therefore, [what is consecrated] is only to be called the flesh and blood of Christ in memory of the flesh that was crucified and the blood that poured forth from his side. You say that these are celebrated by the Church, so that we, chastened by them, might always call to mind [440 C] the Lord's Passion, and in remembering it, we constantly crucify our flesh with its vices and sinful desires. But if these things are true, then the sacraments of the Jews are more excellent and divine than the sacraments of the Christians. For who does not know that the manna the Lord rained down from heaven, or that the living and sensate creatures which that people were accustomed to sacrifice, were more excellent than a small mouthful of bread and a little bit of wine? Again, who does not know that it is more divine to announce future events than it is to narrate past ones; that to foretell the future is impossible unless someone is filled with the Spirit of God? Yet the sacraments of the Christian will often be performed by someone who is not even an expert, or maybe even a simpleton. But far be this from the hearts of the faithful and far from Christian understanding! For Ambrose, a soldier of Christ, in the book *De mysteriis,* confirms these sacraments of the Christians to be more powerful and worthy, and those of the Jews inferior, saying: "We will take great pains to prove that the sacraments of the Church are both more ancient than those of the synagogue, [440 D] and more excellent than the manna."[171] And a little while later: "We have proved the sacraments of the Church to be more ancient; now recognize that they are more powerful."[172] And a little while later, "you recognize now which are the more excellent, for light is more powerful than shadow, truth than a figure."[173] Moreover, in the fourth book of *De sacramentis:* "Accept what I say: the sacraments of the Christians are more divine than those of the

171. Ambrose, *De mysteriis* 1.8.44, PL 16: 404A.
172. Ibid. 1.8.47, PL 16: 404B.
173. Ibid. 1.8.49, PL 16: 405B.

Jews."[174] False, therefore, are the things which you propose. Furthermore, if what you believe and assert about the body of the Lord is true, then that which is asserted and believed about this reality everywhere by the Church is false.

All those who [441 A] rejoice to be and be called Christian, glory in the fact that they receive in this sacrament the true flesh of Christ and the true blood of Christ, each taken from the Virgin. Ask all those who are of the Latin tongue and have seen the publication of our works. Ask the Greeks, the Armenians, or whatever nation of Christian men; with one mouth they will testify that they themselves have this same faith. If, then, the faith of the Universal Church appears false, it either never was the Church, or the Church itself has disappeared. There is, however, nothing more effective for the destruction of souls than this pernicious error. For no Catholic would ever concede that the Church did not exist or could perish. Otherwise, it is not true what the Truth promised to Abraham: "In your offspring, all nations will be blessed."[175] Again, the Psalm: "Ask me, [441B] and I will give to you the nations as your inheritance, and the ends of the earth as your possession."[176] Again: "All the ends of the earth shall call to mind and be converted and return to the Lord."[177] And further on: "He redeems them from the hand of their enemy, and has gathered them from their regions, from the rising of the sun to its setting, from the north and from the sea."[178] Again, St. Augustine in the first part of the exposition on the Psalms: "Brothers, what is the great Church? The great Church is not a tiny part of the orb of the earth, is it? No, the great Church is [extended over] the whole orb of the earth."[179] Again, in the same work: "I have announced your justice in the great Church."[180] How great? In the whole orb of the earth. How great? Amongst all the peoples. Why is it amongst all the peoples? Because "in all [441 C] the earth their sound has gone out."[181] Again, in the third part of the same work: "The body of Christ is made from the

---

174. Ambrose, *De sacramentis* 4.3.10, PL 16: 438A.
175. Gn 22.18.   176. Ps 2.8.
177. Ps 21.28.   178. Ps 106.2, 3.
179. Augustine, *Enarrationes in psalmos* 21.2.26, PL 36: 177.
180. Ibid.   181. Ibid. See Ps 18.4.

multitude of believers throughout the whole orb of the earth."[182] Again, in the same work: "The tabernacle of the Lord is this holy Church, spread out through the entire world."[183] And elsewhere: "The choir of Christ is now the whole world. The choir of Christ resounds from the east to the west."[184] Again, in the book *De agone Christiano:* "We should not listen to those who reject the holy Church, which is one and universal and spread throughout the entire globe."[185] And further on in the same work: "His own people, however," Augustine says, "when they did not listen to the prophets and the Gospel, in which it is most openly written that the Church of Christ is to be spread out far and wide amongst all the nations, and instead listened to the schismatics, those who were not seeking the glory of God but their own, they sufficiently showed themselves to be slaves, [441 D] not freemen."[186] And the Lord in the Gospel: "The field is this world."[187] And a little later on: "The kingdom of heaven is like a net cast into the sea, into which every type of fish is gathered."[188] Again, to the disciples: "Go into all the world and preach the Gospel to every creature."[189]

CHAPTER TWENTY-THREE

You, and those who have been deceived by you, have not only set yourselves up in opposition to the clear testimonies given by the Lord himself and his Holy Spirit about the Church and its establishment, but strive to deceive [442 A] others about it as well. So you say: "The Gospel has been preached to all peoples, the world has believed, and the Church has come into being, it has grown and borne fruit, but afterwards it blundered by the ignorance of those who misunderstood, and it perished. In us alone, and those who follow us, the holy Church remains upon the earth." Gospel truth and the inviolate authority of the prophets and the holy fathers, however, overturn this false sacrilege. From

---

182. Ibid. 130.1, PL 37: 1704.   183. Ibid. 146.19, PL 37: 1912.
184. Ibid. 149.7, PL 37: 1953.
185. Augustine, *De agone Christiano* 1.29.31, PL 40: 306.
186. Ibid.   187. Mt 13.38.
188. Mt 13.47.   189. Mk 16.15.

his own Gospel, the Lord promises his holy Church, saying: "Behold, I am with you all days until the end of the world."[190] That he could not have said, if he knew his Church would perish before the end of the world. For elsewhere it says: "Then, if someone will have said to you: 'Behold, here is the Christ, or behold, there he is, do not believe him.'"[191] [442 B] Augustine, in the second part of the exposition on the Psalms, says: "The body, however, is the Church, not this one or that one, but the one that is diffused throughout the whole world."[192] Again, in the same work: "This hope is for all the ends[193] of the earth. Not the hope of only one corner of the earth, not the hope of Judea alone, not the hope of Africa alone, not the hope of Pannonia alone, not the hope of the east and the west alone, but the hope of all the ends of the earth and the broad expanse of the sea."[194] And in the same work: "This prophecy has been sent forth for those who think the religion named Christian will prevail for a specific time in this age and afterward will no longer exist. It will remain, however, with the sun, as long as the sun rises and sets. As long as this age lasts, therefore, the Church, which is the body of Christ, will not cease to exist upon the earth."[195] [442 C] Again, in the same work: "'Holiness befits your house, O Lord'; your house, your entire house. That is, not this one or that one, not here or there; but your whole house throughout the entire orb of the earth. Why throughout the entire orb of the earth? 'Because he has made straight the orb of the earth, which will not be moved.' The house of the Lord will be strong throughout the whole orb of the earth."[196] Again, in the last part of this same work: "What is that which you say, O heretic: that the Church already has perished from all the peoples when the Gospel is still preached so that it might still exist amongst all the peoples? The Church, therefore, shall exist amongst all the peoples up until

190. Mt 28.20.
191. Mt 24.23.
192. Augustine, *Enarrationes in psalmos* 56.1, PL 36: 662.
193. MC: *finium* substituted for *filiorum*.
194. Ibid., 64.9, PL 36: 780.
195. Ibid., 71.8, PL 36: 906.
196. Ibid., 92.8, PL 37: 1189; Ps 92.5; 95.10.

the end of the age."[197] In the same work: "Where are those who say that the Church has perished from the world when it cannot be turned aside?"[198] [442 D] Again, in the same work: "Whoever shall have thought the Church to be in one part [of the earth], and shall have not known it to be diffused throughout the whole orb of the earth, and shall have believed in those who say: 'Behold, here is the Christ, and behold, there is the Christ' (the same way you heard it when the Gospel was read), although [Christ] bought the whole earth because he paid so great a price for it, he is offended, so to speak, in his neighbor, and is burnt by the moon."[199]

Therefore, that which is asserted and believed by you about the body of Christ is false. It is his true flesh which we eat, and his true blood which we drink.

197. Ibid., 101.9, PL 37: 1310.
198. Ibid., 103.5, PL 37: 1353.
199. Ibid., 120.12, PL 37: 1615; Mt 24.23.

GUITMUND OF AVERSA

ON THE TRUTH OF
THE BODY AND BLOOD
OF CHRIST IN THE EUCHARIST
IN THREE BOOKS:

A DIALOGUE BETWEEN
GUITMUND AND ROGER,
MEMBERS OF THE BENEDICTINE
CONFRATERNITY

FIRST BOOK

SALUTATIONS OF GUITMUND AND ROGER[1]

Guitmund

 EAR BROTHER Roger, [1427 A] you call upon me to address a matter truly necessary in these times—but one that should be enjoined upon someone better than I. For you ask me to treat of the truth of the Lord's body in the face of current questions, and especially to refute in writing, to the best of my ability, the foolishness of Berengarius of Tours. Although my will—even necessity—leads me to deal with other matters useful to the soul, nevertheless I cannot lay aside your desires and entreaties, which I look upon quite favorably, since I know how your devout request serves the common good. You, however, I ask to do me this one service—and in this matter you should certainly act in obedience: pray unceasingly that the Lord will most readily come to my assistance. [1427 B] "For we are in his hand, both we and our words."[2]

Roger

2. What you ask of me is surely most reasonable; indeed it is not fitting to discuss such great mysteries without constantly accompanying prayers. Therefore, with the help of the Lord, let it be so. Moreover, I beg you to deal with me in this manner: listen to my questions, and, what is more, do not hold back from introducing anything on your own, either from the books of Berengarius, or the questions of many others who have many times asked you about this matter, or what in your own right may occur to you to present as significant.

---

1. Subtitles have been added by the translator.
2. Wis 7.16.

PROPOSED PLAN OF THE WORK

Guitmund

3. With the help of the Lord, I will set forth such things concerning these mysteries as seem to be sufficient, and in the manner in which my conscience speaks to me before God, but first let us speak a little about the way of life of the man and his doctrine so that you may know fully the cause and [1427 C] source of all his error.

Roger

4. Indeed, what you say is appropriate because some, paying attention to his bearing and to his scorn for ancient doctrine, want to [1428 A] imitate him as if he were an authority.

ADOLESCENCE AND EDUCATION
OF BERENGARIUS

Guitmund

5. When he was young and still in school—so they say who knew him then—he, carried away by the levity of his temperament,[3] paid no attention to his teacher, considered his fellow students as of no account, and even condemned the books of liberal arts. Since, by himself, he was not able to reach the secrets of a higher philosophy—both because the man was not smart enough and because at the time the liberal arts had declined among the French—he sought, to the extent that he was able, to obtain for himself the praise [of creating] a unique knowledge, with the interpretation of words (in which he rejoices a great deal). He hunted for the glory that the excellence of such a knowledge would provide for him: and thus it came to pass that a man of almost no education professed himself to be a doctor of letters, [1428 B] with his pompous stride, a loftiness above others, simulating the dignity of a teacher rather than demonstrating it by deeds, shutting himself deeply within his cowl, and fooling the unwary with the pretense of long medita-

---

3. Faber edition uses *novitate* instead of *levitate*.

tion, speaking most slowly, as it were with pain, in a voice long-
awaited but barely audible.

After, however, he was refuted—to his shame—by my Lord
Lanfranc over an insignificant matter of philosophy, and when,
through the same Lord Lanfranc, that most learned man, God
made the liberal arts come to life and flourish in a most excellent way, Berengarius, grieving that he was being abandoned by
his disciples, impudently turned to spewing forth opinions on
the mysteries [*sacramenta*] of the divine Scriptures, to which Lanfranc, still a young man tied up by other studies, had not yet
turned his attention. [1428 C] But even there he lacked wisdom,
because "into a soul that plots evil, wisdom enters not,"[4] and he
studiously sought out those things by whose novelty he might
move the hearts and eyes of all to himself, preferring to be a
heretic with the approval of men, rather than to live without
public notice as a Catholic before the eyes of God. At that time,
to curry the favor of worldly men and those who wished to sin, if
they could do so with impunity, he made these things known,[5]
destroying lawful marriages, in so far as he was able, and overturning the practice of infant baptism; the devil in the former
case, through his mouth, said it was licit for evil men to abuse all
women; in the second case, having abolished infant baptism altogether, he urged people to rush with impunity into the depths
of every form of evil and be baptized afterwards. [1429 A] Read
the letter that the Bishop of Liège wrote to King Henry of
France against Berengarius,[6] and there you will find what I have

4. Wis 1.4.

5. According to Hurter, the text should read: "Tunc aperuit illa quibus placeret hominibus mundanis et cupientibus peccare, si inulte licet . . ." instead of,
"Tunc illa, quibus mundanis hominibus, et, si inulte licet, semper peccare cupientibus placeret, aperuit . . ."; for contextual reasons, I have chosen to follow
Hurter's version.

6. *Deoduini Leodiensis ad Henricum regem contra Brunonem et Berengarium epistola* (PL 146: 1439B–1442C). In this letter, Durandus accuses Berengarius and a
certain Bishop of Angevin named Bruno of introducing old heresies into modern times [*antiquas haereses modernis temporibus introducendo*]. These heresies are
three in number: (1) the body of Christ in the Eucharist is present only in shadow and figure [*umbram et figuram*], (2) the destruction of legitimate marriages
[*legitima conjugia destruant*], and (3) the overturning of the practice of baptiz-
ing infants [*baptisma parvulorum evertant*]. He goes on to say that these heretical

written in almost exactly the same words. Indeed, in those same days he also dared, mindlessly, to propound this blasphemy (against which, with the help of God, we are taking action): namely that, having blotted out the truth [*veritas*] of the Lord's body, he, fighting for the devil, counseled those who wished to sin not to pay any reverence to Holy Communion, nor let the fear of having committed any wrong keep them back from receiving it.[7] [1429 B] I do not wish to detain you at this time with the many other impieties that he vomited forth in those days. So we have taken, then, what has been said about the beginning of this pestilence. Shall I now tell you how and by whom such a pestilence has been held, and also how and by whom it has been fought and condemned, so that having learned of the beginning, the progress, and the outcome, you may know better what to think of it—unless you think it will take too long?

Roger

By all means continue; I shall listen thirstily to these things. For I think that it will be of great benefit to understanding the matter in question.

SOURCE OF BERENGARIUS'S HERESY

Guitmund

6. Since, therefore, not even the ears of the very evil could put up with these above-mentioned blasphemies, first of all because of injuries and other effects done to the mothers, and secondly, [1429 C] because of the damnation of their children, and

---

notions have spread to the very borders of Gaul and throughout the whole of Germany.

7. This eucharistic heresy of Berengarius, as Guitmund describes it, is similar to that of Messalians in the sixth century, chronicled by Theodoret in his *Ecclesiastical History* 4.10, NPNF, 2nd ser., v. 3, trans. B. Jackson (repr., Peabody, MA: Hendrickson Publishers, 1994), 114: "who did not hold aloof from the communion of the Church, alleging that neither good nor harm came from the divine food of which Christ our Master said, 'Whosoever eateth my flesh and drinketh my blood shall live forever.'" Thus Berengarius, according to Guitmund, like the Messalians, believed that the Eucharist neither harmed nor benefited the recipient, so that there was no consequent obligation to abstain in the case of serious personal sin.

like Lanfranc's text [handwritten]

because Berengarius himself could find no place for defending
his opinions in the Sacred Scriptures, especially since an abundance of works of St. Augustine argued against them,[8] he then
tried to defend himself in a way that depended on the testimony
of the senses, and he was not aware that this was abundantly dis-
puted by some of the holiest of the Fathers (indeed the Church
was not lacking these problems in those days when many of the
wisest of them wrote clearly and lucidly what they held about
these opinions). Looking, therefore, for some rationalizations
(for not even heresy can ever grow strong without some verisi-
militude of reason), [1429 D] and sticking to a few passages of Sacred Scripture badly understood—a snare of death to many who
err—in whatever way he could, he secretly poured forth the poison of this great evil by way of his needy students, whom he
nourished at that time with food, along with his sweet-sounding,
malevolent words. *feeding students - but with poison* [handwritten]

Moreover, if there were some who accepted him in any way,
they were those who were terrified by the apostolic teaching
which says: "He who eats and drinks unworthily, eats and drinks
unto his own judgment,"[9] and, forced to receive Holy Communion because of ecclesiastical custom, would rather consider it
as either nothing or no great matter, rather than refrain from
sinning in any way because of fear of it. [1430 A] In this way, then,
and by such means, this damnable plague grew little by little. As
a result, Catholics, soon beginning to hear these things openly
and being gravely disturbed by them, and finding them intolerable, held the Council of Vercelli,[10] presided over by Pope Leo
of blessed memory. About this council you desire that we say
something; now then, put forward those things which seem to
you to be in need of a discussion.

8. E.g., *Pro nuptiis; De baptismo parvulorum.*

9. 1 Cor 11.29.

10. Council presided over by Pope Leo IX (1049–1054) in the year 1050, in
which the eucharistic doctrine of John Scotus Eriugena, the ninth-century philosopher and theologian, was condemned, and Berengarius himself was excom-
municated *in absentia.*

OBJECTIONS TO THE REAL PRESENCE AND
TRANSUBSTANTIATION FROM BERENGARIUS

Roger

7. Berengarius and those who follow him assert that the Lord's Eucharist is not truly [*vere*] and substantially [*substantialiter*] the body and blood of the Lord, but is called such [1430 B] because it is a signifying image or figure of the body and blood of the Lord. None of this would trouble me, save for the fact that some, as you mentioned above, thinking in only a materialistic way, are deceived according to the senses, and offer rationalizations, and seem to fortify them with various lines from St. Augustine. They even put forth words of our Lord and Savior by which those weak [in faith] might be scandalized. First I will set forth the rationalizations, and then the authorities [they claim].

Nature, they assert, does not undergo this kind of change. When the Scripture text is offered them which says: "The Lord has done all things whatsoever he has willed,"[11] this change they say he has not willed. For it cannot be right for Christ to be chewed with our teeth [*atteri*], or to be broken into pieces [*dissipari*], just like those things that teeth chew and break up into pieces. If you are willing, respond now to these things; later I will propose others, so that by distributing the task in a diligent manner and comparing your answers to each item [1430 C] proposed by me, I may understand everything to my complete satisfaction.

NUMBER AND TYPE OF EUCHARISTIC HERESIES
ADVANCED AGAINST TRANSUBSTANTIATION

Guitmund

8. Since you have asked me earlier to add to your questions anything that I think should be added, you should know first of

---

11. The origin of the association of this verse with the ability of nature to allow this change is Paschasius. In his work *De corpore et sanguine Domini* (ed. B. Paulus, CCM 16, 14, lines 46–47 = PL 121: 1269), Paschasius, in dealing with the objection that the change of bread and wine into the body and blood of Christ is somehow "extra vel contra Dei velle," cites Ps 134.6: "Omnia enim quaecunque voluit fecit in coelo et in terra."

all that not all who err about these sacraments walk the same
path of error.

For all the Berengarians agree on this: the bread and wine are
not changed essentially [*essentialiter*],[12] but what I could wring
from certain people was that they differ greatly on this point.
Some say that absolutely nothing at all of the body and blood of
the Lord is present in these sacraments, claiming that they are
only shadows or figures. Others, however, ceding to the correct
reasoning of the Church but not receding from foolishness—so
that in some way they seem to be with us—say that the Lord's
body and blood are truly [1430 D] contained there, but in a hidden way, and they are impanated—if I may say it in that way—so
that they may be consumed. And they claim that this is the more
subtle opinion of Berengarius himself. Others, however, although
they are not now followers of Berengarius, and who even fiercely
repudiate him, are wounded nonetheless by his arguments and
some of the Lord's words (which we will speak about more fully
at the proper time), and are accustomed at times to think that
part of the bread and wine change and part remain. Others, however, shying far away from the irrational understanding of people
such as these, are troubled by the same words of the Lord, which
they do not sufficiently understand, and to them it seems that the
bread and wine are completely changed [*mutari*], but when someone unworthy goes to receive the flesh and the blood of the Lord,
they are again changed into bread and wine. Inasmuch as all of
these are errors, [1431 A] according to the help the Lord gives, we
will undertake to refute them.[13]

---

12. As is the case with *substantialiter,* here Guitmund uses *essentialiter* three
times in a synonymous fashion, joining it to the verb *mutare* (twice) and *trans-
mutare* (once), in order to describe the nature of the change in the elements of
bread and wine in the eucharistic sacrifice.

13. To sum up Guitmund's position, according to him there are four different types of eucharistic heresies, two of which are of the Berengarian type, and
two of which involve the unworthy reception of Communion. Both types of Berengarian heresies deny a substantial change in the elements, and the first group
believes that bread and wine remain after the consecration, but Christ is now
present in shadow or figure. The second type, which Guitmund says is the more
subtle opinion of Berengarius himself, is the one where the body and blood of
Christ are somehow hidden in the bread and the wine. The first group he will

THE PROPOSITION ADDRESSED AS TO WHETHER
OR NOT NATURE ALLOWS THIS CHANGE

9. First of all, let us respond to the followers of Berengarius, of whatever type. For all of them, although they differ among themselves, nevertheless hold almost the same opinion against us and rely on the same arguments. For all of them assert that nothing of the bread and wine is essentially changed [*essentialiter mutari*].

Now let us look at their reasoning, and first of all, let us talk about what they assert about nature. Since they say: "Nature cannot undergo this type of change," either they must say it absolutely and without any exception, that is, so that it is not possible even if God wills it, or they say that it allows of some exception. And if they say it absolutely and without any exception, then they declare themselves to be manifest adversaries of the will of God because they say something is impossible for him. Furthermore, they refute themselves every time they sing the verse of the Psalm you cited, viz.: "The Lord has done whatsoever he has willed."[14] For if they do not accept this verse, then they sing it in vain; [1431 B] nor do they now believe in an omnipotent Lord when they contend that some nature can oppose his will. Now if they do not believe in an Omnipotent One, then they do not believe in God. For he is not a true God who cannot do what he wills. But I think that they do not deny that they believe in God. Therefore, let them accept that "the Lord has done whatsoever he has willed," and along with it, let them also accept that if he has willed it, the Lord has made this change in such a way that nature can undergo it. For if the very nature of all things has come to exist by the will of God, since it would be nothing at all [had God not made it], and if that nature has been formed into

---

call the *Umbratici,* and the second, the *Impanatores.* The non-Berengarian heresies, however, hold for a change in the elements, but when some unworthy person approaches to receive communion, the first group believes that part of the consecrated Hosts changes for the worthy to receive, and the rest remain unchanged for those who are unworthy. The second group, however, believes that there is a total change in the elements of bread and wine, but when the unworthy communicant approaches, they revert back into what they once were.

14. Ps 134.6.

such a variety of different species of created things, [1431 C] how is it, then, that the nature of bread and wine now existing is able to resist the will of God so that one reality cannot be transferred into another? O very foolish men, who, while they think they are defending nature, instead show their ignorance of the power of nature! For just as you yourself know the natures of food and men through the art of medicine, surely you must know that every day the natures of the bread that we eat and the wine that we drink are naturally transformed into our flesh and blood. If, therefore, the stomach of a man or any animal whatsoever can change bread and wine, or whatever other food that is enclosed within it, into living flesh and living blood daily, [1431 D] is not God just as great, such that he can, by the power of the majesty of his presence and by the strength of his word, if he wishes, transform [*transformet*] bread and wine into his flesh and blood? But if Christians are willing to concede to God at least as much as Plato, the great philosopher of the pagans, was willing to concede, when he said the nature of things is that which God wills,[15] then what could be more absurd than the proposition that God would wish something contrary to his own will? Therefore, these people, unless they lack all heart, will never speak so absolutely that they say nature admits no change unless God wills it; and so they assert this in vain as a significant point against us. Through this they are achieving nothing at all against us. For no Christian believes that this change happens except by the will of God. Therefore, let them stop saying inanely: "Nature does not undergo this change," and instead [1432 A] let us investigate only whether or not God wills it.

OBJECTIONS TO THE PHYSICAL ASPECT OF THE REAL PRESENCE ADDRESSED: ABILITY TO TOUCH CHRIST

10. But far be it, they say, that God should will any of this, for it is not right that Christ be chewed [*atteri*] by teeth! In the first place, I want to investigate just what they mean by the word

---

15. Plato says that God has made all things "by and in nature." *Republic* 10, trans. P. Shorey (Cambridge: Harvard University Press, 1969), 597.

"chew" [*atteri*]. For if they understand "chew" as either to touch more closely or to press more forcefully, then I ask, how is it not right for Christ to be chewed [*atteri*] with teeth? For if it is not right because it cannot happen, then they are using the same reasoning stated above about nature, namely, that nature cannot undergo such a change. And this is very empty reasoning. Certainly there is no so-called "impossibility" in created reality that can impede the will of God. Why cannot he be pressed by the teeth, who, after the Resurrection, could be touched by the hands of Thomas? And it is written of the holy women, whom he met after the Resurrection, [1432 B] "they held on to his feet."[16] So there is no reason that a tooth cannot touch that which a hand touches; because the sense of touch applies to the whole body just as much as it does to the hand. Therefore, whatever the hand touches can be touched by the whole body, and therefore it can also be touched by the teeth. Moreover, why cannot what can be touched gently, although it is a solid body, be touched a little more forcefully, which is what "chew" means? If, therefore, after the Resurrection the body of the Lord could be touched by the hands of the Apostle Thomas and the holy women, why can it not be touched either lightly or more forcefully by the teeth of the faithful today, that is, be chewed? There seems to be no reason to prevent it.

OBJECTIONS TO THE INAPPROPRIATENESS OF THIS CHANGE ADDRESSED

11. If, however, they say that it is not right that Christ be chewed [*atteri*] by the teeth, not because it is impossible, but because it seems to be unworthy [of him], again I ask, why should this seem unworthy? Is it because Christ [1432 C] seems to be humbled too much by it? But shall he who did not deem it unworthy to be irreligiously crushed [*atteri*] by the unfaithful for the salvation of the faithful, by their rods, the crown of thorns, the cross, the nails, the lance, as it is written: "He was crushed [*attritus*] on account of our offenses,"[17] deem it unworthy, for

16. Mt 28.9.
17. Is 53.5.

the salvation of the same faithful, to be chewed [*atteri*] by their teeth as religiously as they are able? For if for our sake he was willing to suffer what was more unworthy of him, how will he not deign to suffer that which is less unworthy? Just as it was most necessary that the Lord Jesus Christ hang upon a tree, so that death, which had come through a tree, might be conquered by the tree of the cross, so it is also necessary that Christ be truly eaten, since the old man¹⁸ did not merely eat a shadow of the fruit of the forbidden tree, but by truly eating the real fruit of the forbidden tree, truly incurred death by eating it; so the new man does not eat the shadow of him who hung upon the tree of obedience, that is the cross, but truly eats him, so that he may [1432 D] escape death and receive life.

EUCHARISTIC BANQUET FORETOLD BY ISAIAH

12. This is the mystery about which Isaiah prophesied when he said: "On this mountain the Lord of hosts will provide for all peoples a feast of rich food and choice wines, juicy, rich food and pure, choice wines. On this mountain he will destroy the web that is woven over all peoples, he will destroy death forever."¹⁹ The prophet was in Jerusalem. What does he mean when he says, "on this mountain," except the one on which Christ was crucified? And what is meant by saying: "He will provide a feast for all peoples," save only that all people will eat what hangs there? And what is meant by: "those juicy, rich foods," except that flesh made most rich [1433 A] by the grace of the Holy Spirit, "in which the fullness of the divinity dwells bodily"?²⁰ And what is signified by "refined wine," if not the holy blood which is drunk in the species [*species*] of wine? And what will happen for us in this banquet? "He will destroy death," he says, "forever."

18. Guitmund uses *veteres homines* in literary opposition to *novi homines*; I have changed it to the singular to retain the parallel between Adam and Christ, a rendition that I believe is more faithful to his theology.

19. Is 25.6–8.

20. Col 2.9.

NATURE OF THE GLORIFIED BODY EXPLAINED

13. And perhaps it is the teeth that are unclean? But the Apostle says: "Everything is clean to the clean."[21] Therefore, there is no tooth, or anything else that is unclean to Christ. Certainly hands seem to be dirtier than teeth. Certainly with hands we touch many filthy things which we shudder to approach with the teeth. Therefore, he who after the Resurrection offered himself to be touched by hands will not shun the teeth because of their uncleanliness. But perhaps these people who do not fear to wound him by insolent lies fear to wound the Savior by chewing him with teeth? [1433 B] O, for the sake of their salvation, may God destroy these unfriendly defenders if they do not know that the flesh of the risen Lord has retained what belongs to it by nature, and lost what belonged to it through weakness. To be touched is natural to the flesh; to be wounded, however, belongs to weakness. And so Christ is able to be touched by the teeth in such a way that no kind of pressure from them can wound him any further.[22]

FURTHER OBJECTIONS AGAINST THE PHYSICAL ASPECT OF THE REAL PRESENCE ADDRESSED: BODILY DIVISION

14. Therefore, since there exists no impossibility, nor does the humility of Christ shun it (if it is necessary for our life), and since there is no possibility of bringing uncleanness to the Savior in this, or wounding him bodily, then there is no reason why it would be unlawful for Christ to be chewed [atteri] with the teeth. Therefore, if atteri means "to be touched more forcefully," then what they arrogantly say, that is, "It is not right for Christ to be chewed [atteri] by teeth,"[23] has no value as an argument

21. Ti 1.15.

22. Here Guitmund states his governing principle delineating Christ's presence in the Eucharist: he is chewed yet unharmed. It is not impossible to touch or rather *chew* Christ in the Eucharist, for the Eucharist is the body of Christ, but resurrected and foreign to any hurt or harm, so that although he can be touched, he cannot be wounded.

23. One can summarize Guitmund's position as follows: The Berengarians say that nature cannot allow this change, to which Guitmund counters with the

against us. But if, by "to be chewed" [*atteri*] they understand "to be broken" [*frangi*], or "to be ground up" [*comminui*], then there are not now two objections, [1433 C] but only one. For what is it to say "chewed by the teeth and ground up into pieces," except that to say "ground up into pieces" is to assert something further than "to be chewed by the teeth"? Thus the whole argument should rather be: "It is not right that Christ be ground up into pieces, either by chewing with teeth, that is, by grinding, or in any other way."

15. This then is what we confess: That it is certainly not right for Christ to be ground up into pieces by any form of violence, either by the teeth or in any other way. If [1433 D] indeed it has pleased him to whom "all things are possible"[24] in the reasoning of his deep and inscrutable counsel, that his body be capable of division into particles in such a way that he may no longer die, or be wounded, nor suffer any corruption (so that he endures no further misery), who would dare to think that this is impossible? What about their claim when they assert that these sacraments are chewed by the teeth and ground up into pieces so that a certain reduction takes place? Let us respond this way: If he for whom "nothing is impossible,"[25] and who can "do whatsoever he wills in all things" (just as it has been said), should be pleased to allow his body to be divided up in these sacraments, and be disbursed through particles—not through our violence, but through his will in our ministry, without death or injury, or any inconvenience to himself—if we believe in this way, then no one should be able to find anything inconsistent in this. For [1434 A] here (as St. Gregory says), "his flesh is divided up for the salvation of the people."[26]

omnipotent will of God. They then say that even if nature allowed it, it is unworthy for Christ to suffer it, to which Guitmund responds with the humility of Christ. The first is an argument from possibility; the second, suitability.

24. Mt 19.26.
25. Lk 1.37.
26. *Dialogi* 4.60 (ed. A. De Vogüé, SCh 265, 202, lines 16–17 = PL 77: 425D).

PROPOSITION THAT CHRIST IS WHOLE AND ENTIRE
IN EVERY PARTICLE OF THE HOST ADVANCED

16. If, however, it does not please him to have his flesh divided up and disbursed through particles without any inconvenience to himself; if this is in fact the case, then we believe that his body is not crushed by teeth, or ground up into pieces in any way. Then, that which has been said: "His flesh is divided up for the salvation of the people," should not be understood by us as meaning that in being divided up it is ground up, but rather, this happens because of a likeness to the *fractio*, where Christ is said to be immolated daily in a likeness to the Passion.[27] For although the priest seems to divide these [sacraments] because of the great mystery, nevertheless, we should believe that when the venerable body of our Lord and Savior is distributed to the faithful, he has not divided himself up among the individual recipients, but rather, we ought to believe that it is by way of participation that he comes into the diverse members of his faithful. We are also able to say that he is as much in one little portion of the Host as he is in the whole Host. It is as when one reads about the manna, that neither he who gathered more had more, nor he who gathered less [1434 B] had less.[28] Thus the whole Host is

27. According to Jungman: "Among the preparatory acts regarding the Sacrament, the oldest and most important one, the one that therefore reappears in all the liturgies, is the fraction or the breaking of the consecrated bread." As something that comes about in the Mass as part of the constant tradition going back to the Last Supper, Jungman says that its symbolism, however, has had varying forms. In some rites it is meant "to show how the Lord distributes His presence among the many, just as after the Resurrection He made Himself known and 'distributed His appearance among many': the women, the disciple at Emmaus, the apostles." Jungman goes on to comment that the association of the breaking of the bread with the fraction, as indicative of Christian fellowship at the table, has not survived in any of the liturgies, but other understandings have, such as that of the Greeks, who saw it as a "violent separation, a splitting, a sundering, and consequently as a figure of Christ's death on the cross." Idem, *The Mass of the Roman Rite: Its Origins and Development,* trans. F. Brunner (New York: Benziger Bros., 1949), 2, 299–301. It would seem that Guitmund's understanding admits of a symbolism that reflects both the distribution and Passion of the body of Christ.

28. Ex 16.18.

the body of Christ in such a way that each and every separate
particle is the whole body of Christ. Three separate particles are
not three bodies, but only one body. Nor do the particles themselves differ among each other as if they were a plurality, since
the one particle is of the whole body as the rest of them are that
same body. Therefore, they must not now be called many particles, but rather, one Host, intact and undivided, even though it
seems to be divided by the priestly ministry, because of the great
mystery, as I have said, which must be celebrated in this way. In a
like manner, if the Host seems to be broken by the teeth or in
some other way, we understand it to be unbroken, [1434 C] because we believe that the whole body is contained in each single
part.

17. No one, however, should consider this idea as a commentary from my own understanding, for in fact, it can be found in
the preface used by almost the entire Latin world on a certain
Sunday between Epiphany and Septuagesima Sunday:

Eternal God, [it is right and just] to offer you this victim of sacrifice,
which is the salvific and ineffable sacrament of divine grace: which is
offered by the many, and becomes the one body of Christ by the infu-
sion of the Holy Spirit. Each receives Christ the Lord, and the whole
Christ is in each portion; he is not diminished by each one of them,
but instead offers the whole of himself in each one. Because of it, we
who receive the communion of this holy bread and cup are made into
the one body of Christ.[29]

Furthermore, Eusebius of Emesa says:

The Old Testament narrative says: "he who had gathered a large
amount did not have too much, and he who gathered a small amount
did not have too little."[30] This means that the holy reception of the Eucharist consists not in quantity but in power. That body which is distributed by the priest is as much in the tiniest particle as it is in the whole
Host; wherefore, when the Church of the faithful receives it, it is whole
in all of the members together, as much as it is whole in each recipient. For this is the sense from which that apostolic teaching is derived,
which says: "He who had much had nothing left over, and he who had

29. Gregory the Great, *Liber Sacramentorum,* "Dominica V post Theophaniam,"
(ed. E. Moeler, CSL 161/C, 477, n.1578, lines 1–10 & 161/D, 783 = PL 78:
48D).

30. Ex 16.18.

a little was not wanting."[31] If perhaps we were to set before the hungry bread to be eaten, one would not arrive at the whole loaf from the singular portions, for each one would take individually and gradually his own individual portion. From this bread, however, when it is received, each individual person has no less than all of them together. [1435 A] For one receives the whole, two receive the whole, many receive of the whole; without diminution they receive it, because the blessing of this sacrament knows how to be distributed, but knows not how to be destroyed in the distribution.[32]

ANALOGY OF THE THOUSAND MASSES TO EXPLAIN THE PHYSICAL PRESENCE PROPOSED

18. We also say the same thing if a thousand Masses are celebrated at the same time. For we believe the whole Christ to be present in each Mass in such a way that the diverse number of priests or places does not bring about many Christs or a divided Christ. Those who believe that the body of the Lord is invisibly present at every Mass are not able to oppose us in this. For, when a thousand Masses are celebrated at one time, and, just as they themselves agree, in every Mass it is the whole body of Christ (for they also deny the possibility of dividing the body of the Lord), then either there will be a thousand bodies of Christ, or they will confess with us that at one and the same time in a thousand places, the one and the same body of Christ can be whole and undivided. But they [1435 B] do not say that there are a thousand bodies of Christ. And so it remains, that in the thousand Masses offered at the same time, they should believe that the one and the same body of Christ is undivided. And so it is in one Host as well; even if it seems as if it is divided into many parts, we know that none of the flesh is divided up in these portions, because it is the whole Christ who is present when they are all joined together or individually separated.

31. 2 Cor 8.15.
32. *Homilia de corpore et sanguine Christi* 17.4 (ed. F. Glorie, CSL 101, 200, line 88–201, line 102).

ANALOGY OF THE VOICE AND THE SOUL PROPOSED
TO EXPLAIN THE PHYSICAL ASPECT OF
THE REAL PRESENCE

19. This should not seem to be incredible to anyone. For we know by daily experience that our intellect, that is, the word of our heart, when we clothe it, as it were, by the voice, while, hidden in our heart, it was known to us alone, now by means of the voice can be made known to others at one and the same time, while it still remains whole and entire within our heart. So also when the voice is heard equally by a thousand men so that, clothed as it is with the voice, our thought not only illuminates at the same time the hearts of all, but whole and entire touches the ears of all.[33] If, therefore, God so greatly dignifies the human word, so that not only the word itself, but even the voice in which it is clothed in a certain way, is able to touch a thousand men

33. Clearly Guitmund is developing a theme from St. Augustine and his understanding of the Incarnation of the Father's Eternal Word. Guitmund's Augustinian parallel of the Incarnation with his doctrine of Christ as whole and entire in each portion of the Host is quite evident in Augustine's *Sermon* 28.4: "Ears too have a kind of food, which is sound. And what is that like? What we are trying to do, you see, is put together an idea of the mind's understanding from these sense experiences of the body. Here am I, speaking to your honors; there are your ears, there are your minds. I have mentioned two things, ears and minds. And in what I speak there are two things, sound and meaning. They travel together, together they reach your ears. Sound remains in the ears, meaning goes down into the heart. . . . Even so, something as transitory as this has a positively miraculous quality about it. Look, if you were all hungry and I set a lot of bread before you, it wouldn't reach each of you. You would divide among you what I had put out, and the more of you there were, the less you would each have. But now what I am offering you is a sermon. You do not divide the words and syllables among you; you don't cut up my sermon, one taking this piece, another one that, and thus what I say comes to you in bits and pieces. No, each one hears it all, two hear it all, as many as have come hear it all. It is enough for all, it is complete for each one." *Sermons,* trans. E. Hill, WSA 3/2 (New Rochelle: New City Press, 1995), 112–13. See also *Sermon* 196, *In natali Joannis Baptistae* (PL 39: 2112). The point of the analogy of the voice, then, is that just as it carries the thoughts of the human heart undivided to a thousand men at one time, and the voice itself also touches their ears whole and undivided at one and the same time, so in each and every particle of the sacred Host is the flesh of Christ, in which the eternal Word of God is enclosed, and delivered to each and every recipient whole, entire, and undivided, to all at one and the same time.

whole and entire at the same time, then no one ought to say it is
incredible that this same thing can be true regarding the unique,
omnipotent, and co-eternal Word of the almighty God, and regarding his flesh with which he likewise clothed himself in order
to appear to us, even if we cannot understand it, and this because it happens to the very fragile and transitory word of men
and to their momentary and barely existing voices, which we can
never catch hold of and yet almost always have experience of.
For certainly our soul itself, which is weighed down by a body
that is corrupted, is not divided up piece by piece into individual
members of the body, but is whole and integrally contained in
each individual portion of the body, as St. Augustine most pow-
erfully proves.[34] Why would he who has bestowed such power
upon our soul, so that it is simultaneously one and the same, and
indivisible in each and every portion of its own body, not also be
able to give that same dignity to his own flesh if he wished to? Is
not his flesh just as powerful, so that it also could be whole and
entire in the diverse portions of his body, which is the Church,
since, just as the soul is the life of our body, [1436 A] so also is the
flesh of the Savior (by all means many times better than our soul
through the grace of God) in a similar way the life of the Church?
Indeed, it is through the soul that the body lives temporally, but
through the flesh of the Savior, the Church lives happily not just
for a time, but forever.

20. Since in truth the most wise Solomon has said that all
things [that exist] are so difficult to understand[35] that man cannot even begin to explain them, is it not insane, then, to attempt to discuss these divine secrets in a violent way before the
eyes [of all]? For all the creatures of God are inexplicable miracles to us; Christ, however, is a unique miracle among the others—or, better, he is beyond them all. If Christ is able to bring it
about that (just as we have said) each and every separate particle is the whole body of Christ, and nevertheless all of them sep-
arately are not many bodies but one body: just as the voice
strikes the ears of a thousand men, and is whole with each and

---

34. See *De quantitate animae,* CSEL 84, 131–231. Also *De Trinitate* 6.6.8, CSL
50, 237.

35. Eccl 1.8.

every one, [1436 B] so that it is not said that there are many voices, but only one: just as the whole soul fills a thousand particles
of the human body, and when it offers itself whole to each part,
it is not many souls, but only one soul: if he has indeed done
this, then there now seems no reason hindering the breaking of
the Host in this way, and it cannot be said that Christ cannot or
should not wish to transform the bread and wine into his body
and blood, just as he has taught and the Church has believed.[36]

UNTRUSTWORTHINESS OF THE SENSES EXPLAINED

Roger

21. About the matter of a thousand Masses which can be celebrated at the same time; [1436 C] you certainly seem to have
made more than sufficiently clear a very difficult matter for me.
Nevertheless, in the act of breaking up one Host, I still have a
slight hesitation, because at first I only see the one, and then by
my dividing it, it appears to be broken up into many, so that
each portion seems less than the whole. And even if the Host
were divided, not by my strength, but by itself, after the division
its size would still appear wholly changed. I would now like to
believe, to my complete satisfaction, that both every individual
piece and all of them together are one intact body without any
division.

Guitmund

22. If you think enough has been said about a thousand Masses celebrated at one time, it is a marvel that you could be dis-

---

36. In his discussion of *dissipari*, Guitmund has established four principles
that have become axiomatic in eucharistic doctrine ever since:

(1) Not a part of the body of Christ (as the flesh), but the whole body, the
whole Christ is present in the Eucharist in virtue of the change.

(2) The whole body, the whole Christ, is present not only in the entire Host,
but no less entirely in each particle.

(3) Christ is present whole and entire in every Mass, even when a thousand
Masses are celebrated simultaneously.

(4) By the breaking of the Host and its being chewed by teeth, the one and
indivisible body of Christ is not divided.

turbed over one Host. For just as before you break up the Host, you see only one, so also, before a thousand Masses are celebrated there is only one body of Christ, who is in heaven; for although you do not discern it with your eyes, [1436 D] you nevertheless perceive it by the mind or by faith. And just as you think that the Host is divided by your work, so also can it be concluded that it is by the work of the priests that the body of Christ, which is one in heaven, is present in a thousand places at once. But far be it that one should think that, either by their act or yours, the one Christ may be divided in those many places or pieces! For it is he himself who effects in your act, not what your eyes perceive, but what he wills. For although he seemed to die by the violence of the Jews, yet it was he himself who said: "No one takes my life from me, but I lay it down of myself."[37] Therefore, although the Host is thought to be broken by violence, nevertheless Christ must be believed to effect what he himself wills, and not what the carnal senses judge. Therefore, just as after the fraction of the Host, single particles seem to be less than the whole Host, so also [1437 A] in all those Masses the body of the Lord appears to be less than it is believed to be in heaven. But this is only and wholly due to the senses, and just the senses are often fooled in other things so in this case they are always fooled. But if the eye of flesh can never perceive this, is this any reason, then, for the eye of the mind to be extinguished?

23. For when Mary Magdalene, weeping at the tomb of the Lord, saw the Lord himself, was it not most certainly Jesus, although, deceived by the eyes, she thought instead that she was looking at a gardener?[38] Or, when the Lord himself, on the day of his own Resurrection, as if he were a pilgrim, explained the Scriptures to two of his disciples while they were walking along the way, was it anyone other than Jesus? For it is written: "Their eyes were held lest they recognize him."[39] Or, when the disciples, laboring upon the sea, saw him walking upon the waters, who would dare to say that it was not truly he, but because their eyes were deceived, [1437 B] did they not, instead, think him to be a ghost?[40] But, now seeing him with them aboard the boat, and

37. Jn 10.18.   38. Jn 20.11–17.
39. Lk 24.16.   40. Mt 14.26.

marveling at his miracle of calming the sea, one might assume
from the Gospel that they did not recognize him until they came
to the shore. For it is written: "and when they had gotten out of
the boat, immediately they recognized him."[41] From these words
(as we have said) one might assume that in the boat, perhaps
still stupefied by the recent miracle, some of them did not recognize him. What happened then? Certainly it must not be
thought that he deluded them as a joke? Far be it! For he was
everywhere the same; he was everywhere the truth; he was everywhere wisdom. But it was necessary for us to be shown through
these things that, as long as we stand [1437 C] with Mary weeping
at the tomb of the Lord,[42] mortifying ourselves[43] and announc-
ing the death of the Lord until he comes;[44] as long as we are on
the road, traveling apart from the Lord;[45] as long as we are laboring upon the sea of this age and the wind of temptation is
against us; as long as we walk by faith and not by sight:[46] although the Lord would always console those weeping at his
tomb, although he would always explain the Scriptures to those
who travel along the way, although he calms those troubled
upon the sea, although he would always be present with us in the
ship of Holy Church "until the consummation of the age,"[47]
nonetheless, we do not have the means to discern him except in
the guise of a pilgrim, that is, with the eyes of flesh, [1437 D] although it is none other than he himself whom we have in these
sacraments.

24. And rightly so. For since the fruit of the death-bearing
tree had closed the spiritual and trustworthy eyes of the old
man, and opened the carnal and deceitful ones, it is just, therefore, that the fruit of the life-giving tree of the cross should close
the carnal eyes of the new man, and open the trustworthy eyes
of the mind by which truth is seen. For just as the diseased pal-
ate considers bitter those things which are sweet to the healthy
one, so that no one who is healthy believes it, so in the same way,
no one, unless he were irrational, would trust the judgment of

41. Mk 6.54.

42. Jn 20.11.

43. Col 3.5.

44. 1 Cor 11.26.

45. 2 Cor 5.6.

46. 2 Cor 5.7.

47. Mt 28.20.

the infirm carnal eyes against that of the healthy eyes of the mind when it concerns the very Medicine itself for the interior light.[48] For this matter is so great that one is not strong enough to comprehend it by the weak vision [of the carnal eyes], so that our faith, which is most useful in this matter, must be exercised in the interim; thus by acting in a way contrary to the sight of flesh in this so necessary a sacrament, we might learn to transcend the visible and hurry to the invisible, [1438 A] hold as more certain what is hidden and what the truth, which never lies, teaches, rather than what the false eye presents to us.

25. Therefore, since it has been shown to you that it is the same [body] in the particles of one Host that is present in many Masses celebrated at the same time, Masses about which you said that enough has been explained, and that from Gospel examples and clear reasoning you should not judge according to the vision of the carnal eyes, please respond whether or not you judge that enough has been said up to this point.

Roger

Indeed, for me, I confess that you seem to have explained the truth of the genuine faith with cogent reasoning: nevertheless, I will not be silent about the fact that there is still something that gnaws at me. For you said above that it only seems as if the priest divides the Host because of the mystery which must be celebrated in this way. Therefore, if I should see it, that is, the Host after

---

48. The *interior light,* as Guitmund refers to it, is an allusion to Augustine's concept of knowledge, known as his theory of "illumination." Although Augustine makes direct reference to the interior *lumen* in the *De beata vita* 4; *De musica* 6.8; and the *De moribus ecclesiae Catholicae et de moribus Manichaeorum* 2.8 (see PL 32), the theory is actually developed in the *Soliloquies* 1.6.12, and *On the Teacher* 11.38 (also PL 32). Augustine formulates the theory in these terms: The eye sees the sun; the mind sees God. The sun's rays make the earth and earthly things visible to the eye. God makes certain truths of the sciences visible to the mind. Thus, just as the bodily eye must be healthy to have proper vision, so the mind must be healthy to have proper understanding. For the mind to be healthy it must (1) be purged from desire for mortal things (faith); (2) never despair of healing (hope); and (3) desire the promised light (love). Used in this context, the *medicine* of the interior light refers to the Eucharist, which inspires faith in the mind of the believer, so that it might perceive the inner reality of the truth of Christ, beyond the visible testimony of the senses.

it has been consecrated, I now no longer see it as capable of being divided, save for the grace of the mystery, which as you have said must be celebrated in this way—and I must confess that the entire sequence of your disputation has been confirmed with unshakable truth. But because it might seem to be capable of division to someone who elects to disregard the mystery, my thoughts suffer from a darkness—where this darkness comes from I do not know—yet my mind would like to get rid of it, but it is not strong enough to free itself from it completely.

EXPOSITION ON THE WAYS IN WHICH
THE SENSES DECEIVE

Guitmund

26. If you go over again thoroughly in your mind those things said above, [1438 C] in my opinion nothing of this darkness will remain in your thoughts. For the senses often fail, as the many arguments of the ancient philosophers once taught, and the experience of daily life now thoroughly teaches. "For," Boethius says, "the senses are equally confused in matters both great and small."[49] And so it is, about these matters in which the senses are confused, they cannot have a true and accurate judgment. About commonplace realities as well, the senses do not judge according to the truth of the matter, but instead, they judge by the impressions made by the sensation. For to anyone with a healthy appetite, if he is very hungry, even bitter foods seem sweet; to one who is sick, or to the fully satisfied, however, even sweet things are bitter. Likewise, if someone is languishing in love with the hideous shape of a prostitute, is not her form extremely pleasing to his eyes, yet offensive to almost everyone else, [1438 D] that is, all those whose minds are not captivated by the same misery? Take, for example, the oar in the water:[50] if you ask the eyes, they assert that it was bent, which, as soon as it is removed, reason proves by the tes-

---

49. See Boethius, *De musica* 1.9, PL 63: 1176C.

50. See Augustine, *Contra litteras Petiliani Donatistae Cirtensis episcopi* 3.21: "Remum in aqua fractum cum sit integer." Also *De vera religione* 1.29: "Cur in aqua remum infractum oporteat apparere cum rectus sit," and ibid., 1.32: "Si quis remum frangi in aqua opinatur, et cum inde auferetur integrari."

timony of the eyes that it remains straight. And what about the judgment of the ears? When a sultry tune sounds in the ears of a sober person, it seems most foolish to him, while at the same time it delights a vulgar buffoon.

NECESSITY OF FAITH TO DISCERN CHRIST IN THE SACRAMENTS OF THE ALTAR

27. But why do I dwell on this matter so long? For who ought to marvel if the external sense is often deceived, when the soul, the inner judge of all the senses, would be in such frequent and great danger unless the grace of God were to rule over it? Therefore, none of what the sick and nearly blind eye thinks that it sees [through the external sense] should be any impediment against the reasonable faith of Holy Church; for [1439 A] I now believe that you accept that those eyes which the food of disobedience has opened,[51] must consequently be closed by this food of obedience, so that through this spiritual and life-giving food, the spiritual eyes, which that deadly and carnal eye has closed, may be reopened, so that we may no longer be wise according to the flesh unto death,[52] but rather, with face unveiled, we may now contemplate those spiritual things which lead to eternal life. And so it is, that as long as we struggle in the contest of faith, as long as we are on a pilgrimage apart from the Lord, it is appropriate that our faith be diligently tested, so that by testing it might be instructed, and by instruction it might be fed, and by being fed it might grow, and by growing be perfected, and, once perfected, be crowned.

28. But what test of faith would that be, or what merit would the faithful have for the test of that faith, as far as it concerns so great a sacrament, if the sacred Host could not be divided, except by the priest and only at Mass before the eyes of anyone? Who would not give consent, even if they were one of the unbelievers, simply because of such an evident miracle, rather than [1439 B] because of the discernment of faith? In fact, the Apostle says that miracles are revealed, not for believers, but for the un-

51. Gn 3.7.
52. 2 Cor 5.16.

believers; these sacraments,[53] however, are not for unbelievers, but for believers.[54] Therefore, it is wrong not only to dispense them to unbelievers, but even to disclose them to them.[55] They are not, then, revealed to unbelievers by way of open miracles; instead, only the faithful discern them, not with a fleshy vision, but with the mind. For our Lord Jesus Christ himself called these sacraments *mysterium fidei*.[56] In what way is it a mystery, then, save for the fact that it is hidden? And what is there of faith, save for the fact that it allows itself to be contemplated, not by the eye of flesh, but by faith's inner vision? For, just as the most holy Gregory says, [1439 C] "faith has no merit where human reason offers a proof."[57]

29. If, then, you have clearly understood about the deceptiveness of the carnal senses, which should not be believed contrary to reason in small things or about those things which the senses are accustomed to experience, let alone about great and hidden matters; and if you have learned that the spiritual senses are to be opened to the spiritual sacraments, and that the carnal ones must be closed; and if, furthermore, for you the mystery of faith is that these things should be hidden from unbelievers in this

53. The term *sacramenta altaris,* or simply *sacramenta* as Guitmund uses it here, refers to the Eucharist proper. Its earliest usage seems to be with Augustine, who speaks of the *sacramenta altaris,* in *Sermon* 351.1.4, "De utilitate agendae poenitentiae," PL 39: 1546.

54. 1 Cor 14.22.

55. It seems that in this context, Guitmund is making a veiled reference to the *disciplina arcani,* which called for a certain level of secrecy about the practice of the sacred mysteries.

56. *Mysterium fidei:* words that were originally part of the institution narrative of the Roman Canon, but were removed by Pope Paul VI in the liturgical reform after Vatican Council II. In this context, Guitmund obviously thinks that they came from our Lord, but the origin of the phrase is uncertain. According to Jungman: "In the middle of the sacred text [institution narrative], stand the enigmatic words so frequently discussed: *mysterium fidei.* Unfortunately the popular explanation (that the words were originally spoken by the deacon to reveal to the congregation what had been performed at the altar, which was screened from view by curtains) is poetry, not history. The phrase is found inserted in the earliest texts of the sacramentaries, and mentioned in the seventh century, it is missing only in some later sources." Joseph Jungman, *The Mass of the Roman Rite,* v. 2, 199–200.

57. *Homiliae in Evangelia* 2.26.1, PL 76: 1197C.

way, but for believers, it is for the exercise and growth of faith unto their merit and great profit: then enough has been said. In fact, as far as I am concerned, it is inappropriate for you to be involved any further in the darkness of shameless subterfuge. Finally, who can explain or grasp with the mind, how much future glory and power even our flesh will have after the resurrection? For we will be changed, "for that which is corruptible will clothe itself with incorruptibility," and "this natural body will rise as a spiritual body,"[58] and then, "what eye has not seen, nor ear has heard, or what has not yet arisen in the heart of man,"[59] will be given to us. When, therefore, reason cannot now even comprehend how much power the flesh of the least significant man will have, how can you, then, dispute impudently and carnally according to the senses about the body of the Savior, which all the angels ineffably venerate? For certainly, whatever occurs to the human intellect about what could be given to us, it is either far less or nothing compared to that which is promised us. Since, therefore, we believe in those things which we are going to receive, which will come about in a way that now we do not have the strength to know, save for the fact that for God all things are possible, will you not cease chattering on like an infant about the body of the all-powerful God [1440 A] because you do not now have before your bestial eyes whatever is being accomplished?

ABSOLUTE INTEGRITY OF THE BODY
OF CHRIST ASSERTED

30. Accordingly, give greater consideration to retracing what has been said above, and faithfully hold that either the Lord our God is ineffably capable of distributing his flesh in particles [*per partes*] without any detriment to himself, or, if that is not pleasing to him to do so, then the sacraments of his table remain undivided—either for the reasons that we have said, or for others, if perhaps God has deemed to give you better ones—even though it may seem otherwise because of the infirmity of the

58. 1 Cor 15.53 and 44.
59. Is 64.4; 1 Cor 2.9.

carnal eyes. And if that which I said before is in fact pleasing to the Lord, then it is right that, not by our violence, but rather by Christ's condescension, his flesh be chewed [*atteri*] by teeth, and his body be served to the faithful by way of particles [*per partes*]. If, however, it does not please him, there is still nothing disagreeable to us that ought to be objected to about the division or fragmentation of the sacraments, which, as we have said, can be reasonably proven [1440 B] to be indivisible and inseparable.

Roger

I confess that reason has competently met all the objections that I raised, so that I rejoice, and I see that nothing remains that would justify my troubling you further.

DIFFICULTY OF TRANSUBSTANTIATION ADDRESSED

Guitmund

31. To be sure, there is a difficulty which troubles some who believe that this change cannot occur, and it is this: in the physical world there is hardly any change in the whole of nature which is even remotely similar to it. For when one thing is substantially changed into another [*substantialiter transmutatur*], it is usually changed into that which did not exist before: for example, [1440 C] the staff of Moses changed into a serpent,[60] which was at first not a serpent, but then began to be a serpent; when, however, we say that the bread is changed, it is not changed into that which had not been flesh, but we confess that it is changed into the flesh which was already the flesh of Christ, without any increase in the flesh of the Lord himself. And although we do not deny that this change is difficult for us to understand in this age, it is, however, not difficult to believe.

32. But why is that? Ought we not to believe in this [change] which is great and most salvific, even if we cannot understand in this life how it comes about, [1440 D] since by necessity we take many other things on faith, things which are far more—or certainly no less—offensive to our blindness? Consider providence

---

60. Ex 7.9.

and free will, since we faithfully hold them both—and it is necessary that they both be held: it seems to human reason that they
are so much opposed to one another that they would destroy one
another, rather than the one concede that the other exists. No
human mind can grasp how a thing which is whole in one place
can at the same time be whole in another, while all hold it about
the human voice. That the whole soul dwells in each member of
the body at the same time is something which St. Augustine demonstrated with unassailable reason. And behold, the creation of
all things is believed, even though man cannot comprehend it.
For who, [1441 A] if I may speak plainly, can grasp when that which
was made first had its coming to be [*fieri*]? For up until that moment, what was altogether non-existent did not exist; for coming
to be [*fieri*] pertains to that which already exists.[61] After it exists,
however, it does not come into being, for it indeed already exists.
But neither was that which was first made between being and
non-being, because it was capable of being something [else]. For
that something which was between [*interesset*] would first have to
be made: then, after it was made, it could be another thing.
When, therefore, did that which was first made have its *fieri*?
Nonetheless, it had it. For that which does not lack a beginning
would not be at all, unless it first came to be. Indeed, "He spoke,
and they were made."[62] O admirable *fieri*, which is necessarily believed, but no thought can comprehend! And if someone thinks
my reasoning is absurd, and all these ideas displease him, let him
say what he will, and he will most certainly find that in all his
words, and in all his thoughts—should he subtly consider them—
they would be found wanting in expression of the primal origin

61. Here Guitmund embarks in a most original way upon a lengthy metaphysical discussion of the term *fieri*, designating it as an attribute of being, or
esse. The point that he will ultimately try to make is that in any philosophical
speculation about creation and coming into being, something must first exist
before it could ever be another, and in this sense it seems that Guitmund is
speaking about that property of being which the later Scholastics would term
obediential potency. In this case it refers to the Eucharist, where the body of the
Lord Jesus is already existing in heaven, before it ever comes to be under the
forms of bread and wine in the sacrament of the Lord's table, and the bread and
wine themselves have the ability to become the body and blood of the Lord.
62. Ps 32.9.

of things.[63] Therefore, when these matters necessarily demand faith, and in no way admit of discussion, [1441 B] when it concerns the body of their Creator himself—do not these matters reasonably call out for a simple believer and argue against a shameless disputant?

33. It is appropriate at this time, then, to call to mind the beginning of this disputation. We have proposed this: that when they say "nature cannot allow this change," they should be willing to add, "except if God does or does not will it." For if they are unwilling to allow this addition, and instead assert that nature without exception is not able to undergo this change, even if God wills it, then they do not believe that "everything the Lord has willed, he has done."[64] And if they do not believe that everything the Lord wills, he does; then they despise not only the canonical Scriptures that they very frequently recite, but even him, that is to say, God, whose Scriptures they are. Furthermore, neither do they believe in God himself, nor that God is all-powerful; for neither is he truly all-powerful, nor is he truly God, who cannot do all that he wills. [1441 C] But because these assertions are too evil, even for them, they also find it necessary to assert that whatever the Lord has willed, he has done. And this change, therefore, no matter how difficult it may be for us to understand, if God has willed it, without a doubt, he has done it.

34. It should only be inquired, then, as to whether or not God has willed this change. That God has willed it, we shall demonstrate, with his help, in an opportune place,[65] for whether or not it is possible to understand how it comes about, we will, nonetheless, prove with necessary reason that he has indeed done it. For it is not enough to argue that, since the blindness of our infirmity can never grasp it in this life, you should not be-

---

63. Guitmund's point, then, is that speculation on existence and the act of creation, which is so evident to the senses, is nonetheless beyond the mind's ability to understand, and therefore demands faith. Arguing from the standpoint of the *rationality* of this article of faith, he then asks why it should take more faith to accept this change, which is far more familiar to our common experience, than something which is so much further removed from it, such as creation *ex nihilo*.

64. Ps 134.6.

65. See 3.47.

lieve it, especially if the matter is one which, as I have said, will be proven by the necessity of clear reasoning. For Christ did not command you to "understand," [1441 D] but to "believe."[66] It is his to care how he does that which he wishes to bring about; yours, however, is not to discuss, but humbly to believe that whatever he thoroughly wills to happen, happens. For it should not be understood first, so that you might believe afterwards: but it should be believed first, so that afterwards you may understand.[67] Nor did the prophet Isaiah say, "Unless you shall have understood, you will not believe," but: "Unless you will have believed, you will not understand."[68] Therefore, let us use the words of St. Augustine against Felicianus, when he says: "Let faith believe this, let not understanding search for it, lest it deem unbelievable that which it does not find, or lest it not believe to be unique that which it finds."[69] He says the same thing in his second letter to Volusianus: "If a reason is sought, this would not be miraculous: if an example is demanded, it will not be unique. Let us grant to God the ability to do what we [freely] admit we cannot understand. In such matters, [1442 A] the whole reason for the deed is the power of the One who does it."[70] St. Hilary says that one should not speak in a human or temporal sense of divine matters.[71] In dealing with this issue, St. Ambrose in his

66. Lk 8.50: "Crede tantum et salva erit." Mk 5.36: "Crede tantummodo."

67. See Augustine, *De Scripturis, Sermon* 43, PL 38: 256.

68. Is 7.11, Vulgate: "Si non credideritis, non permanebitis," Guitmund's text says: "Nisi credideritis, non intelligetis." It appears that in this translation, Guitmund is following Augustine, who, following the LXX, quotes Is 7.9 as "Nisi credideritis, non intelligetis," a text that Augustine cites in numerous works, most notably: *De libero arbitrio* 1.2, *De magistro* 11, and *De doctrina christiana* 2.12.17 (ed. J. Martin, CCSL 32, 43, lines 19–20), in which Augustine recognizes both translations: "Nisi credideritis, non intelligetis; alius interpretatus est, Nisi credideritis, non permanebitis."

69. *Contra Felicianum Arianum de unitate Trinitatis* 8, PL 42: 1163: "Hoc fides credat . . . credat singulare." This work is listed as *dubius* by the *Clavis Patrum Latinorum* under Vigilius (n. 808), and attributed to Ps. Augustine. According to Hurter, *De veritate* 1.42, n.1, the work is by Vigilius of Thapsis, although the Maurists included it among the works of Augustine.

70. *Secunda epistula ad Volusianum* 137.2.8 (ed. A. Goldbacher, CSEL 44, 107, lines 10–14 = PL 33: 519).

71. *De Trinitate* 8.14 (ed. P. Smulders, CSL 62A, 329, lines 1–2 = PL 10: 247).

book *De sacramentis* says: "Why do we use arguments? Let us use his examples, and to the example of the Incarnation, we will add the truth of the mystery. Why do you seek the order of nature in the body of Christ, when Christ himself was born of the Virgin apart from the order of nature?"[72]

35. Therefore, because the Incarnation or virginal birth speaks to us as a fitting example, of all the important works on the subject, I consider this one an apt starting point to illustrate an analogy, which will allow us to ascend to a higher understanding. For truly we receive from the Sacred Scriptures a fourfold generation of man.[73] The first is of a singular man, neither from a man nor a woman, but from the clay of earth, which is Adam. The second is in a way its contrary, [1442 B] which of all of them is the most customary, and that is from a woman and a man, whereby men and women are born. The other is again without any precedence, where a virgin man produces a virgin woman, that is to say, the generation of Eve from Adam. The fourth is no less singular and unique, accomplished for the sake of all the others, and is better and more useful than all of them; it is in a way contrary to the third, since a Virgin man is born from a Virgin woman; that is, Christ, born from Mary, the Savior of all, has enlightened our age.

36. From these generations then, the one which involves a man and a woman, whereby men and women are born, no one marvels at because it is part of our daily experience, and no one

72. The text cited by Guitmund is not from the *De sacramentis*, but rather from the *De mysteriis* 9.53 (ed. Faller, CSEL 73, 112, lines 45–46 and 51–52 = PL 16: 407A).

73. Cf. Anselm's *Cur Deus Homo* 2.8 (PL 158: 406C): "Quattuor modis potest Deus facere hominem; videlicet aut de viro et de femina, sicut assiduus usus monstrat; aut nec de viro nec de femina, sicut creavit Adam; aut de viro sine femina, sicut fecit Evam; aut de femina sine viro, quod nondum fecit. Ut igitur hunc quoque modum probet suae subjacere potestati, et ad hoc ipsum opus dilatum esse; nihil convenientius quam ut de femina sine viro assumat illum hominem quem quaerimus. Utrum autem de virgine, aut de non virgine, aut de non virgine dignius hoc fiat, non est disputare; sed sine omni dubitatione asserendum est quia de virgine Deum hominem nasci oportet." Since Anselm's work was published at a later date, the use of this example by Anselm means either that Anselm used Guitmund, or that both drew from a common source, which is likely, since both studied at the same monastery in Bec. See n. 80.

judges it to be unbelievable. Nevertheless, there is a certain sense in which it is more remarkable than the others: for from two non-virgins a virgin is born, and a virgin is never born except from two non-virgins [1442 C] so that from two opposites, as it were, an opposite comes about. Truly Solomon testifies to its mysteriousness when he says: "How are the bones joined together in the womb of a pregnant woman?"[74] That generation, however, whereby a man comes about from what was not of man, namely, the generation of Adam, formed from the clay, is the one that is seen to be far more miraculous in this respect than all the others, even more so than that generation whereby virgin Eve was produced from virgin Adam. Hardly, however, does any one ever dispute it, nor hardly ever does anyone find fault with it. But when Christ's birth from the Virgin Mary is preached, the whole world groans against it with innumerable objections. [1442 D] For by force, deceit, and every kind of evil, the world has tried to remove this generation from its midst. Certainly this is most unjust, since this generation is far more useful and excellent than all the rest, not only because it has an honor and nobility beyond them all, but also because it is medicinal. For this generation, distinct from the other ones, draws unto itself only the nature of our race, and nothing of its dignity; moreover, it receives most of the infirmities and trials of our race, yet it is in every way, by the divine power within it, sufficient for our perfect happiness. Truly, all the other generations because of this one have been raised up from being under the feet of the devil—the most unhappy of all conditions—to being a companion [1443 A] of the all-powerful and sublime God. For as St. Peter says, we have been made "sharers of the divine nature,"[75] and unless the other generations made use of the work and medicine of this one, they would all go into incurable perdition.

37. Furthermore, when a diligent inspection of the three unique generations[76] is made, this one is found to be far more similar and closer to the most familiar generation, and there-

---

74. Eccl 11.5.

75. 2 Pt 1.4.

76. That is, Adam from the clay of the earth, Eve from the rib of Adam, and the Savior Christ from the Virgin Mary.

fore more credible than the others. For to whom is it not sufficiently clear that, in regard to the common generation, which is
from a man and a woman, this one is more similar because it is
from one of these,[77] rather than that generation that is from neither? In fact, if we were to contemplate that generation whereby
a woman issues forth from a man alone, we can see that it is far
more remote from the one of our common experience. Indeed,
it is far more customary and suited to our common nature that
a woman give birth to a man (for that happens daily) than that
a man should give birth to a woman. But perhaps the generation
of Eve should not be called in any way a birth, and such would
make it further still from the common form of generation. Furthermore, what is this whereby a woman suddenly bursts forth
from the side of a sleeping man, out of the rib from which she
was made, [1443 B] against the usual course of nature?[78] In this
one, however [that is, the one in which Christ has come forth
from Mary], just as with the rest of men, the child gradually grew
in the mother's womb for nine months, and came out by the
common law of birth, with this exception: that the Mother did
not suffer *in partu;* and so that this birth might befit so great a
Son, he adorned the Mother with the singular prerogative of
preserving her virginal integrity. For it was not right—because
he came to restore those who were corrupted and to make honorable those who were made dishonorable—that he should violate her who was intact, and make dishonorable her who was
honorable. It was far more suitable, then, that if Eve came forth
from a virgin man to violate the world, Christ should come forth
from the Virgin woman to restore it. I add further that all the
other generations are of servants; this one, however, is of the
Lord. From the others came men; from this one came God. All
the other ones, just as I have said, God made from one command; this one God makes, as it were, through a great effort, by
words and deeds, and he did not cease from the beginning to
prefigure and promise it by new miracles. Therefore, it has been
written about this special work: "Wisdom has built herself a

77. That is, from a woman (the Virgin Mary).
78. See Gn 2.22.

124 GUITMUND

house."[79] Having given worthy consideration to all these and many other matters, one ought to judge this generation as more credible and evident than the first two.

38. But how these things pertain to the matter about which we have been speaking is now worth considering. For there are in fact no less than four changes of created things, whether substantial or efficacious, that the divine Scriptures commend to us.[80] One is the change from completely nothing into that whereby all things exist; the other is contrary to it, in that, although we do not know it by experience, we nonetheless can gather it from reason, namely, the one whereby those things that exist, as much as existence is within them, [1443 D] can return to non-existence. For if all things exist by this fact alone, that is, because God wills it, then if his will, by which he is present to them so that they might exist, were withdrawn even a little, then immediately they would return to their own nothingness. This is what St. Augustine says against Felicianus: "Creation has come forth from nothing; therefore, inasmuch as existence is within it, by the quality of its own nature, it can be turned from existence into non-existence, that is to say, into nothing, unless a constant grace were to keep it in existence."[81] In another case, that is, the one about the singular accidents that depart when other accidents supervene, it would appear that someone cannot say that they become completely nothing.[82] Indeed, if they were something, they would be

79. Prv 9.1.

80. Guitmund's rather elaborate section on the four births, derived from Ambrose's example in the *De sacramentis*, is an attempt to establish an analogy showing the *reasonableness* of a substantial change in the Eucharist. His main point is based on the principle that something that is more familiar to our experience is more credible and easier to believe. Guitmund's argument, then, is that the substantial change in the Eucharist approaches our everyday experience more than many other objects of faith and therefore should be all the more believable.

81. See n. 69; *Contra Felicianum Arianum de unitate Trinitatis, liber unus* 7 (PL 42: 1162).

82. It is at this juncture that Guitmund begins a philosophical speculation into the nature of substance and accidents that is decidedly Aristotelian in tone. His source could very well be Boethius, and the commentaries that he published on Aristotle's works; in this case it seems to be the *Categorias Aristotelis libri quattuor*, especially book one entitled *De denominativis* (PL 64: 168–77). In it,

in a subject. But with contrary ones supervening, they cannot remain in their subject, nor pass over [*transmeare*] into another one. Therefore, they become completely nothing, unless perchance someone could say that they are changed [*transmutari*] into those accidents which supervene. But if this is so, then innumerable examples occur to us of those things which are essentially changed [*essentialiter transmutantur*] into those things which exist in like manner. Take, for example, very white paper touched by very black ink: white is turned into black, so that it has now turned into that which it was not. For it cannot be said that, at that moment, the place where the black increases is one where the white has been removed, seeing that the ink is not blacker than it once was, or that some of the paper is filled with black from something other than the ink.[83] The same thing can also be found in numerous other examples. Therefore, it is just as we have said: the accidents having receded, either they become absolutely nothing, or, if they are changed [*permutantur*], then they are changed into the supervening accidents, which in no small way approaches the matter we are investigating.[84] This leads us to conclude that things are often changed [1444 B] into

---

Boethius makes a number of significant points on the relationship of substance and accidents, which seem to parallel Guitmund's philosophical development of the nature of the substantial change in the Eucharist. The first is the metaphysical distinction between the two, in that substance and accidents differ *essentially*, so that one can never become the other: "Neque substantia in accidentia, neque accidens in substantiae naturam transit." In fact, Boethius says, the relationship between the two is such that the accidents come into the substance (*accidens quidem venit in substantiam*), and the substance in return receives (*suscipit*) the accidents. The second major point is that a substance exists (*subsistit*) by itself per se (*ipsa vero substantia per se constant*), while accidents do not (*accidentia vero per se ipsa non constat*), but instead exist in a subject (*accidens in subjecto est*), and, once separated from the subject, return to nothing (*ad nihilum redigatur*). From what has been said above, it is clear that Guitmund's thought has been drawn from Aristotle's categories, as it was commented on and handed down by Boethius, and it is within this context that his treatise should be understood.

83. Here, in both of these examples, Guitmund denies independent existence to the accidents, for if white turned into black, the paper would be darker, and if the black inhered in the white, it would not be in contact with the paper.

84. Clearly in this illustration of the receding accidents, Guitmund finds a parallel in the substantial change of the Eucharist, where the preexisting substance of the bread becomes the preexisting, supervening substance of the body of Christ.

those things which already existed. The third type of change that
we ordinarily discern is the one readily seen to be where substances change [*transeunt*] into those substances which they were
not, either by an operation of nature, or by a miracle; just as a
nut changes into a tree, a seed into a plant, food and drink into
flesh and blood; or just as a staff into a serpent, a serpent into a
staff, and various other similar examples.

39. The fourth change, however, is the one where that which
exists passes [*transit*] into that which is no less existing, in the
way that we believe by divine power bread and wine are changed
[*commutari*] by a certain unique power into Christ's own body
[and blood]. And indeed this change is readily judged by believers to be far better, far more useful than the other three. [1444 C]
Better indeed because that into which it is changed is divine
flesh, which of all things is the best. More useful, moreover, because this change, which has been made for the sake of the other ones, Christ has established as a unique medicine for us. Indeed, the primal elements have been made from nothing, and
we have not been made happy by them. In fact, the other two
changes would offer us nothing except to hand us over to the
greatest misery, if the fourth, medicinally supervening, had not
come about.

40. Since this change is both more honorable and useful than
all the rest, as well as closer to, and more like, the one of our
common experience, it is, then, even more believable than the
other two. For to whom does this not shine more clearly than
light: that, as far as concerns this change, it is the one where one
thing comes to be in another, it is the one that is most familiar?
And although the change of one thing into another is to some
degree more miraculous, is it not far closer and more similar
than that change whereby something comes into being from
non-being, [1444 D] or goes from being into non-being? For the
former changes can be considered in two ways; the latter change,
in only one: and therefore they are remote from the capacity of
our intelligence, so that perhaps it is not possible for someone to
call them changes: and if it might be very difficult just to find a
word to describe them, it would be of the greatest difficulty to try
to do so from one's own experience. And indeed, the other

changes are of things which pertain to the subjects; this one, however, is of the Lord; those others are of the other creatures; this one the Creator himself has retained for his own body. Indeed, in regard to the others, God ordered once in the beginning that they should be, and they were made; this one, however, he has not ceased from the beginning to promise and to prefigure by prophetic oracles, public events, and especially by sacrifices and new miracles: indeed God himself, our Lord Jesus Christ, so as to bring this change about, has ordered his very own words to be repeated and offered daily, with devotion and great solemnity of prayers. [1445 A] Once these things and very many others have been worthily examined, this change can, and ought to be, judged more believable and precious than the other two. For if God has done that which is more difficult and further removed from our intellect, because he has willed it, how is it that he has not done, if he willed it, that which seems in some way to be easier and more understandable? And that God has done that which is more difficult, no one doubts. Therefore, no one should doubt that God, if he wills it, does that which is easier. Or why should God, who has added the fourth generation (as we have shown) for man's salvation and reparation, not add this fourth change for man's medicine? It is appropriate, therefore, that, just as God, the highest good, willed without envy all the good things in his creatures, which were fitting to be in them, so, considering the wondrous beauty of variety, God has so willed it that, just as there should be no lack of a fitting generation among [1446 A] men, so also there should be no lack of a suitable change among created things.

41. Therefore, because the proposition, as I judge it, has been sufficiently established (that is to say, if God willed this change, he did it), the only thing that is left to be proved is the assertion that he has in fact willed it. But because many poisons are left to be drawn out, we will keep that discussion for a more opportune place. Now, therefore, with the prior calumnies of our adversaries having been discussed, if it is agreeable, let us rest a little bit so that you may recall more diligently what has been said, and we may rise up by a new beginning into the things that follow, with your mind restored by a new intention.

SECOND BOOK

Guitmund

ET ME JUST say that, while I respond to your objections, if someone should read them, he would wisely observe that my effort at this time is not to counter the enemy entirely by our disputations, but rather to strengthen the Catholic faith against hostile arguments [1445 B]. For the former goal will come about at a later time with the help of God. For now, we wish so to distinguish the matter, as to show both the weakness of the enemy's position and the impossibility of bringing anything against our faith. For when the enemy fails in his attacks in every possible way, he will, with God's favor, find himself completely overwhelmed by our exhaustive arguments. And I judge that, through this approach, heretical deception will be more readily silenced, and Catholic truth shine forth more clearly. But these things have been said because of those who, wishing to be satisfied more quickly than the matter allows, might disparage us for placing before them a defective work, since up until now, we have not completely covered the entire subject. [1445 C] Therefore, let us now proceed to the rest of our discussion.

OBJECTION OF BERENGARIUS TO THE CORRUPTION OF THE EUCHARIST

Roger

2. Berengarius says: "The flesh of Christ is incorruptible; the sacraments of the altar, however, if they should be reserved too long, can be corrupted, for they are seen to putrefy."

INCORRUPTIBLE NATURE OF
CHRIST'S FLESH ASSERTED

Guitmund

O most lying tongue! O tongue accustomed to blasphemy! He is quicker to wrench from the Scriptures of God through pride his own damnation than to receive salvific refreshment from them with the faithful. For he has believed the Holy Scriptures which say that Christ is incorruptible, and yet he has not believed in Christ's statement: "The bread that I will give [1445 D] is my flesh for the life of the world."[1] Instead, he contradicts that testimony by positing corruption [in Christ]. Therefore, let it seem to sick and corrupt men in their lack of faith that the divine bread can be seen as corruptible and perishable, and, just as it has been written, let the impious man be carried off, lest he should ever see the glory of God.[2] Let Berengarius forever dream shameful things about God, and forever meditate upon scandal, for then Christ will forever be for him "a stumbling block and rock of scandal."[3] But to us, however, that Eucharist, that divine manna, is the heavenly bread from God. [1446 B] For truly we receive from the sacred altars the flesh of the immaculate Lamb rendered incapable of suffering, through which we both live and are healed from corruption; this flesh can never be corrupted, nor perish, because, although from day to day it renews us, it itself never grows old.

3. St. Ambrose, in his book *De sacramentis,* is in full agreement with this thought, when he says:

Consider now whether the bread of angels is more excellent or the flesh of Christ, which indeed is the body of life. That manna was from heaven, this is above the heavens; that was of heaven, this of the Lord of the heavens; that was subject to corruption if it were kept for a second day, this is foreign to every corruption, because whosoever shall taste in a holy manner shall not be able to feel corruption.[4]

1. Jn 6.51.   2. Is 26.10.
3. 1 Pt 2.8.

4. The text cited by Guitmund is not from the *De sacramentis,* but rather from the *De mysteriis* 8.48 (ed. Faller, CSEL 73, 109, lines 52–58 = PL 16: 404C). *St. Ambrose: Theological and Dogmatic Works,* trans. R. Deferrari, FC 44 (Washington, DC: The Catholic University of America Press, 1963), 23.

If, therefore, it may seem to someone to be corrupted by age or putrefied at times, [1446 C] and if the one [who sees it] does not believe that what he sees is in fact the body of the Lord, then we believe it happens just as he sees it in his heart (as St. Gregory says about Christ the pilgrim and the two disciples speaking with him along the way).[5] Consequently, although Christ might appear outwardly in such a form, he is still believed to be as he is seen within one's own heart. On the other hand, if he believes that what he sees is the body of the Lord, we believe that this has happened to him either to correct or to punish some negligence, since either he has treated the body of his Lord unworthily to the extent of his ability, or he has acted disobediently and violated ecclesiastical rule by retaining the sacrament too long. In any case, the solidity of faith will be more abundantly [1446 D] rewarded for the man, who, contrary to what his eye discerns about these things, does not doubt the power of his Lord and the common faith of the Church.

VARIOUS APPEARANCES OF CHRIST FOR TESTING AND APPROVING FAITH

4. There are ready examples from the divine books that pertain to these matters that we have mentioned. For truly Mary Magdalen, not yet believing the Lord had risen, on account of her lack of faith thought that she was seeing a gardener.[6] Also, on the day of the Resurrection itself, Christ appeared in the likeness of a pilgrim to the doubting disciples.[7] And it is here that one can see how the negligence of believers would be either punished or corrected. [1447 A] Because they had attended to the prophecies about Christ in a half-hearted way, for their negligence, they deserved to be punished, then called foolish, and finally corrected when the Scriptures were opened to them. Moreover, St. Gregory attests to the fact that the incorruptible Christ would condescend to be seen as corruptible for the purpose of testing and rewarding the faithful, telling the story about a cer-

5. *Homiliae in evangelia* 23, PL 76: 1182D.
6. Jn 20.15.
7. Lk 24.15.

tain monk Martyrius, who merited to carry the Lord Jesus on his own shoulders when he appeared to him in the form [*species*] of a leper.[8] "And when," he says, "he who appeared as a leper had vanished from his shoulders, the monk immediately received from him the pronouncement of his reward: 'Because,' he said, 'you have not been ashamed of me on earth, O Martyrius, neither will I be ashamed of you in heaven.'" Therefore, just as our Lord Jesus Christ had appeared in a deformed and horrible form [*species*] on earth, for [1447 B] the purpose of testing and rewarding the humility or the love of Martyrius, so it is, for the purpose of testing and rewarding the faith of his servants—if there is no lack of faith or negligence to be punished or corrected—that he appears in the form [*species*] of corrupt bread; and if this is ever encountered, one should believe it is [Christ] whom they see. And just as that very deformed leper, vanishing from the shoulders of Martyrius, was none other than Christ who revealed himself, so it is none other than the flesh and blood of Christ in the divine sacraments, even if they are sometimes seen under the appearances of putrefied bread and wine—as anyone of orthodox prudence knows enough to believe.[9] But if you should object (as is usually said) that Berengarius does not accept the *Lives of the Saints* for an authority, you should know that, although he does not accept certain lives of the saints, I have learned that he has never rejected the books of St. Gregory, [1447 C] as far as I can recall. For this reason then, we also accept this dialogue of St. Gregory as an authority, in which, as we have said, these things about Martyrius have been commemorated. For so great an author would not have written them unless he also believed them to be true, and judged them as worthy of belief by posterity.

8. *Homiliae in evangelia* 2.34, PL 76: 1300C.

9. In this statement, it is clear that Guitmund holds the Real Presence of Christ in the sacrament, even though the species of bread and wine may be corrupt.

HUMANITY OF CHRIST A SCANDAL FOR UNBELIEVERS
AND SALVATION FOR BELIEVERS

5. Next, let us review the entire saving history [*dispensationem*] of the Lord's humanity. Indeed, the whole dispensation existed in such a way that, on the one hand, the disbelief of the enemies is scandalized, which is to be censured and afterwards damned, while, on the other hand, the faith of believers is made to grow, and afterwards crowned. For what of this fact: that he willed to be born of the Virgin espoused to Joseph? Was it not both to [1447 D] increase the deadly impiety of the enemy, for the sake of scandal, so that they might call him the son of a carpenter; and at the same time to make a profitable opportunity for believing Peter? For did not Peter merit an increase of faith, when, in no way impeded by this fact, he said: "You are the Christ, the Son of the living God"?[10] Why then all the infirmity of Christ's flesh? Did he not by it blind the devil himself, so that when the devil— paying no heed to previously unheard-of miracles—rose up to kill him, he did not foresee in that action his own irrevocable damnation, which was to come? Yet from that same weakness, the faithful are today continuously illuminated by faith, so that they are not only made strong by the help of this same faith not to fail in their own infirmities, [1448 A] but moreover, trusting in the help of their same Lord, they dare to invoke, more trustingly on every occasion, the charity by which he was made weak for them. And what should I say about his death? Is it not the Apostle who says that, because of it, "Christ is a scandal to the Jews and foolishness to the Gentiles"? For the Christians, however, "Christ is the power of God and wisdom of God."[11]

6. Therefore, just as when Christ was still living as a mortal among men, this scandalous talk was spread all around about his flesh, so it will continue to be as long as his Church shall be mortal unto the consummation of the age. And so it is today, that, for the sake of the Church, for whom those things were done in regard to this same flesh, with its incorruptibility preserved, something can appear in an outward aspect whereby unbelievers are scandalized and brought into darkness, but the

10. Mt 16.16.   11. 1 Cor 1.23.

elect are strengthened and receive greater illumination. [1448 B] Therefore, let men of corrupt and putrid minds cease positing corruption and putridity in the sacraments of God; because just as when the appearance [*species*] of a pilgrim, a gardener, or leper was assumed, it either chastised or corrected the negligence of the faithful, or tested their love and faith, but did not void the truth of the essence of Christ: so it is the same [today], that if putridity or some other similar unfitting thing should appear in the sacraments of the Church, so as to punish or correct the negligence of ministers, or certainly to test love and faith (as we have said), the truth still holds, that putridity in no way vacates the truth of the essence [*essentia*] of the flesh and blood of the Lord. Consequently, let not the Church of God fear the trickery of the heretics. For the Church herself does not ignore the fact that the whole fleshly dispensation [1448 C] of her Lord, while he was here upon this earth, was salvation for her but was a constant cause of scandal for the reprobate.

OBJECTION OF BERENGARIUS ABOUT RODENTS

Roger

7. They also object that these sacraments can be gnawed or consumed by mice or similar types of animals.

Guitmund

As far as I am concerned, these sacraments can never be seen as capable of being gnawed by mice or other brute animals. But if at times they appear to have been gnawed, as it were, then one can respond as we have said about the gardener, about the pilgrim, or about the leper, that is, that they have not been gnawed but rather they can be seen in such an appearance [*in tali specie*], either to punish or correct [1448 D] the negligence of the ministers, or to test the faith of those who see these things. Consequently, as far as it concerns this matter, that is, that these sacraments are said to be capable of consumption by brute animals, we can respond with the aforementioned reasons: namely, it should either test faith, or condemn or correct the custodian's negligence, that human sight is capable of seeing brute animals approach that closely to the body of Christ. Immediately, however, it is taken up and invisibly reposited in heaven, either [1449 A] by the ministry of angels always in attendance upon it, or by Christ's own power. The glorious martyr Tarsisius's own witness comes to our mind in support of this opinion.[12] He, when carrying the venerable sacraments of the body of the Lord, was forcibly seized by pagans, who attacked him and searched for what he was carrying. And the [celebrated Tarsisius] chose to die rather than "to give that which is holy to dogs,"[13] and thereby earned the palm of a precious death. In fact, those who most curiously searched everything found nothing further, save only the cloth wrapping, the body of the Lord having been taken up into heaven. *taken up to heaven*

8. Furthermore, if anyone should say that he has truly seen these sacraments devoured by brute animals, and found them within their bodies (even though those against whom we are fighting do not care what ideas they advance, for they are always offering objections, lest they should come to proper faith), still, although such testimony is not easily accepted, and seems unworthy of a response, [1449 B] nevertheless, lest we be thought evasive or negligent, this answer can be given. If it should be the case that Christ deigns (either because of those reasons which we have just stated, or because of whatever other reasons that he himself knows) that these sacraments can be eaten by either beasts or birds without any corruption to him, how does this obstruct the truth that we believe about the body of the Lord? Certainly he is not wounded more by beasts or birds than by our eating. Furthermore, he who had lain on the stone of the sepulcher, and who after the glory of the Resurrection trod the earth, does not flee the mouths of beasts or the beaks of birds because of their lowliness.[14] To be sure, it is most manifest, by reason of the order established by God, that animate bodies are better than the inanimate, the sensate are better than the non-sensate. Nor do I believe that any half-educated man is going to refute

12. See Pope Damasus, *Opuscula, Carmen* 18, PL 13: 392A.

13. Mt 7.6.

14. Hurter amends that text here from *pro utilitate* to *pro vilitate;* based on what follows, one may conjecture from context that this is in fact the correct reading.

this conviction even tentatively. Moreover, sensate beings are better, dearer, to the good Lord, [1449 C] and therefore more honorable, so that no body of any living animal would be lower in the sight of God than earth and stone. But if the very body of Christ, as we have already said, lay on the stone and trod the earth, would he then abhor the body of any animal because of its lowliness? For this reason then, even if by some divine judgment some brute animals are able not only to touch but even to devour the most holy mysteries, from this fact there is still no argument that stands in our way or forces us to deny the truth of the body and blood of the Lord that we hold in the sacred mysteries. Therefore, having sufficiently driven out this blasphemy as well, we shall now see to the rest.

OBJECTION OF BERENGARIUS ABOUT FIRE

9. Also, the important question about fire arises because they say that [1449 D] in certain canons, the sacred mysteries are ordered consigned to the flames to be consumed. But this is prescribed, not so that they may be consumed by combustion, but rather, they are ordered to be honorably committed to the most pure, the most worthy, the most cleansing of all the elements. It purifies all the remaining elements; it, however, cannot be rendered impure by the others, nor does it have any need of purification. Nevertheless, it would be sufficiently pleasing to me that whenever negligence, or certainly when a new miracle might occur about such great mysteries, what should be done is that which my teacher, the Lord Lanfranc—a most noble man, to be believed without doubt—told me was done when he was a boy in Italy. For when a certain priest celebrating Mass found true flesh upon the altar, and true blood in the chalice, according to the proper species of flesh and blood, [1450 A] he was afraid to consume it, and, seeking counsel, immediately made the matter known to his bishop. The bishop called together many of his fellow bishops on the matter, and enclosed that chalice with the same flesh and blood of the Lord, lovingly covering and sealing it in the middle of the altar, so that it might be reserved perpetually as the greatest of relics.

THE SENSE IN WHICH THE EUCHARIST IS
SAID TO BE BURNED

10. If the sacred mysteries are therefore placed in the flames, they are certainly not handed over to the fire to be burned, but rather, are faithfully committed to the most pure element to be hidden from us, as I said, and reposited in heaven. But if perchance to some attentive person they seem to be burned, certainly he will know that the substance of the Lord's sacrament is never burned; but as we have already said, it is taken away from us and seeks a heavenly place; the sensory qualities, however, which God wills in his most sublime counsel to remain after the change in substance, [1450 B] manifest their own properties. Whence it happens that color, taste, and odor, and any accidents of this sort of the prior essence, that is, of the bread, have been preserved,[15] and what occurs is the same as what normally happens to bread that has been burned or kept too long. Here also, in a similar way, the substance of the Lord's body[16] is completely preserved, although the accidents themselves seem to some degree vulnerable to external corruption. In this way, then, the spiritual depth of mystery, veiled in the preserved accidents, on the one hand is not heedlessly revealed to the non-believer, but on the other, is more fully and gracefully entrusted to the just, because of the merit of tested faith.

OBJECTION OF BERENGARIUS THAT THE BODY
OF CHRIST SHOULD BE TOTALLY CONSUMED

Roger

11. If bread and wine were to be converted into the flesh and blood of Christ, they say, [1450 C] so much of it would have been consumed so often that, even if the body of Christ were as big as

15. In this case, Guitmund clearly makes a distinction between species and accidents, where the former refers to the appearance of Christ as bread after the change in substance, and the latter refers to the sensory qualities of the prior bread itself.

16. In this context, the interchangeable use of "substance of the Lord's sacrament" and "substance of the Lord's body" gives one an insight into how Guitmund views "body" and "sacrament" as equal realities.

an enormous mountain, he still would have been entirely devoured and consumed by now.

Guitmund

Indeed, even if we were to concede that the body of the Lord is dispersed into individual portions to be eaten by the faithful, in such a way that it cannot remain whole within itself without any harm to itself, it should follow nevertheless that, because of the analogy of the voice (as it has been described above), where among a thousand men, the whole voice proceeds from one man and arrives at each individual man in a such way that what has been said remains whole and entire with the speaker, we believe that it is the same for the Lord's body when it is eaten by individuals. Thus we confess, that [when the body of the Lord is individually dispersed in portions to be eaten by the faithful,] that body remains whole and entire within itself. Thus this false objection should be silent, since it is in no way a hindrance to us, [1450 D] for, just as St. Augustine and Eusebius of Emesa have said: "This gift of God knows how to be distributed, but does not know how to be destroyed in the distribution."[17]

Augustine + Eusebius — gift can be distributed but will not be destroyed in the distribution

OBJECTIONS OF BERENGARIUS ABOUT THE SEWER ADDRESSED

Roger

12. It is unbefitting for the body of the Lord to be expelled into the sewer; but "everything that enters through the mouth," as the Savior says, "goes into the stomach and is then expelled into the sewer."[18] Furthermore, as far as this pertains to these sacraments, they say that if a great deal of bread and wine are consecrated, someone can live a long time eating or drinking nothing else; and since he will have need of the latrine during that time, what other than these sacraments would go into the sewer? These are the matters that derive from the rationalizations of Berengarius, which at present need to be answered for

17. Eusebius of Emesa, *Homilia de corpore et sanguine Christi* 17.4 (ed. F. Glorie, CSL 101, 201, lines 101–2 = PL 30: 273D).

18. Mt 15.17.

me. After you answer them, I will put forward the supporting arguments.

Guitmund

13. We believe without a doubt [1451 A] that the body of the Lord in no way goes into the sewer.[19] Furthermore, we do not concede that everything that enters into the mouth is expelled into the latrine. For that statement of the Lord cannot be competently understood, except as it pertains to foods that are ingested to sustain the life of this mortal body. For no one would even dare to speculate about what the Savior ate after his own Resurrection, or about the angels who ate in the presence of Abraham.[20] Therefore, just as when corruptible food is consumed by immortals, that food is not fittingly believed to be bound by the law of the sewer; so it is a sacrilege to think that incorruptible food, which is the body of the Lord, when it is eaten by mortals, must endure the necessity of the latrine. Indeed, far be it that the food which prepares body and soul for eternal glory should undergo the [1451 B] inglorious evacuation of the body.

14. But if what we have said seems insufficient to anyone, then he should hear what physicians and doctors themselves especially say about our incorruptible food. For they teach with most sound reasoning that the part of the food and the drink which is more corpulent and corrupt leaves the body by way of the latrine; at the same time the part of the food that is more subtle and useful by nature is distributed through various parts of the body and is turned into the nature of flesh and blood; another part that is indeed subtle, but less useful, is in a similar way transfused through parts of the body and evaporated through pores; the remaining part, which is not quite as subtle nor as corpulent as the first, however, is dispelled either through the nasal passages or sputum or some other similar fashion. Since this is so, not all of the food [1451 C] that goes into the stomach is expelled into the sewer.

19. Guitmund is asked by Roger to proffer an opinion on the heresy of *Stercorianism,* a term coined by Cardinal Humbert, which held that the eucharistic bread was subject to the same process of digestion as any other food.

20. Gn 18.6–9.

15. But the Lord did not say this in the Gospel. In fact, we understand from the Lord's statement that all food and drink which enters the mouth for the sustenance of the body naturally passes into the stomach; but he did not say, "and everything is expelled into the sewer," but rather, said only, "and is expelled into the sewer," speaking, that is, about the most obvious part of food. And indeed, insofar as it concerns this part of the body, enough has been said about this Gospel statement. For all the rest, if there are any who wish this statement of the Lord to be expounded more clearly for them, let them first studiously read the expositions on the Gospels. For the present, what we have said up until now is enough, lest any should think that we are contradicting the Lord's statement. [1451 D] In any case, whether or not this question asked about the saying of the Lord is resolved in this way or in some other that is more agreeable, for now this argument should stand for a sufficient defense, that is to say that not all that enters the mouth is expelled into the latrine. This objection is also offered to us in vain, because we are in no way impeded in the belief that we receive the body and blood of the Lord from the table of the Lord, when we know that so many other things which enter into the mouth do not go into the sewer.

THE POSSIBILITY OF THE EUCHARIST SUSTAINING THE LIFE OF THE BODY

16. Now let us see what they add further on that topic. "From these sacraments," they say, "if a great deal of bread and wine is consecrated, someone is able to live a long time by eating and drinking nothing else; therefore, what will go into the sewer during that time, if it is not these sacraments?" Certainly, I confess, because of the virtue of the most holy body, [1452 A] that if it should so please God (because of some reason that he himself knows), someone can be sustained for a long time better than by all the foods of this world—I do not say from a great quantity of bread, but from the smallest portion. For if Elijah, by virtue of that refreshment which came from two baked loaves and a little water that he would receive from the ministering angel, lived

a total of forty days and nights,[21] how much more so, by virtue of
this celestial and divine banquet, which is not now baked loaves
and water from the hand of an angel, but rather the very flesh
and blood of the Word of God himself, which we receive from
Christ's own hand, someone can—taking no other food—be
sustained in the best way, if ever God so wills! Furthermore, we
have also read the same thing about some holy fathers, who fed
on no other food than the Lord's Communion on Sundays,
[1452 B] and lived many years.

BLASPHEMOUS EXPERIMENTS WITH
THE EUCHARIST DISCUSSED

17. We can concede that it is possible, by virtue of the Lord's
body, that someone could live a long time by way of a divine miracle; however, we completely deny that it goes into the sewer. Indeed, if at any time someone should have need of the latrine, it
is due either to the remains of previous foods, or to a defect of
someone's body. But this, Berengarius says, has now been manifestly proved (as in fact some have responded to us on his behalf), that not from the remains of previously digested food nor
from the defect of one's own flesh, but rather, because of a long-
time consumption [of eucharistic nourishment], [1452 C] there is
in fact the customary fattening of the body and those so fed
have need of the latrine. O heretical malice, have you dared to
prove this by an experiment? Have you also dared to say that
you have proved this? Do you openly dare to make this public?
With such enormous audacity, have you not either feared the
tremendous majesty of the presence of God in the experiment,
or dreaded the righteous indignation that you were going to
rouse in the Christian people for so great a crime?

18. Nevertheless, what I want to know is, when or by whom has
this been proved? For if he should say that it has been proved in
ancient times, since none of the approved authors report this,
then it should not be believed at all. And if it has been proved
recently, then who proved it? Certainly no one of the Catho-

21. 1 Kgs 19.6–8.

lic party. For who, believing this consecrated bread to be truly
the body of Christ, would think of carrying out such a nefarious
crime? [1452 D] But if Berengarius himself or one of his followers
has consecrated a great deal of bread, or one very large loaf, so
as to prove such a thing, we ourselves are not at all concerned
about a Mass conducted by such unfaithful men, and especially
by those wishing to prove so great an evil, or whatever pertains
to them. For we do not believe that the bread and wine necessarily change into the body and blood of Christ except among
those who believe that the words of Christ work so great a thing
by the divine power.[22] For among those who hold the faith in this
matter, however, we believe and confirm that through the words
of Christ, this change does necessarily come about [*fieri*]. And
if perchance at some time he has deceived some simple Catholic priest to do this unwittingly, so that he should consecrate either several loaves or one great one for the purpose of this same
experiment, or if perchance one of his followers in a like manner did it [1453 A] while celebrating Mass with Catholics, indeed
we believe that the body of Christ has been consecrated, but we
respond either that it never went into the sewer, or that at the
time the body of the Lord was invisibly taken away, so as rightly
to confute and deceive heretics who would make it for the sewer,
and was replaced with bread by angels, or perchance by malig-
nant spirits.

19. For it is read in the *Lives of the Fathers*[23] (which, even if Berengarius does not wish to accept, I shall nevertheless offer for
the instruction of others), that a certain most holy Father, whose
eyes God had opened for the purpose of beholding [the sight],
saw an angel invisibly withdrawing the body of the Lord from
some who were going to communicate unworthily, and offering

22. Guitmund propounds the opinion that the confection of the Eucharist
is an ecclesial act, which must be performed in union with the Church for va-
lidity. Although Hurter thinks that Guitmund is denying the doctrine of *ex opere
operato* in this context, it is more like the case of the priest who stands outside
the bakery: no valid consecration takes place. So in the same way, those who
perform the sacred rites for the sake of a sacrilegious experiment cannot bring
about the Body of Christ, when the intention is to make bread for the sewer.

23. Cf. Rufinus of Aquileia, *Historia monachorum seu liber de vitis patrum* 23,
"De Macario Alexandrino," PL 21: 455.

them coal [in its place]. And it just might be that this [was shown to him] to fortify future generations against this question about the sewer—not that he would always do this with one who is going to receive unworthily, however, which, God willing, we will demonstrate in a later discussion. [1453 B] St. Augustine, whom Berengarius has never rejected, also says in the book *De civitate Dei*[24] that a similar withdrawal by apostate spirits occurred with the virgin Iphigenia, the daughter of King Agamemnon, when she was going to be sacrificed to the gods by her father. Here the devil had removed her, so that by a novel miracle he might deceive those miserable people more profoundly, and obtaining a deer from someplace, replaced her with it. In regard to a certain man, Augustine reports that great wonders happened in his own times. The man was seen in the form of a horse carrying grain among other pack horses, because he, snoring heavily as if in a deep sleep, had his outward appearance taken away by the devil, who transformed it into a packhorse carrying grain among a group of men.[25] For these reasons then—either because in the Mass of unbelievers there is no power in the Lord's words [1453 C] to confect the body of the Lord, or by divine power or angelic ministry the body of the Lord is invisibly borne away—one can safely conclude that the bread suitable for heretics is subjected to the sewer either by angels or by demons. Therefore, let Berengarius and his followers cease railing against the Church of God about such an experiment, since each and every time the truth of the body of the Lord in these most holy mysteries is pre-

---

24. *De civitate Dei* 18.18 (ed. Dumbart and Kalb, CSL 48/2, 609, lines 75–79 = PL 41: 576).

25. Guitmund is again referring to Augustine's *De civitate Dei* 18.18 (op. cit. 609, lines 49–56), where Augustine tells the story of a man that he knew by the name of "Praestantius," who "narrated his experience as being a dream, [where] he had become a horse with other pack animals which carried Rhaetic corn (so called because sent to Rhaetia) to the soldiers. It was discovered that this had happened just as he told the story; and yet it seemed to him to be simply a dream." Trans. H. Bettenson (London: Penguin Books, 1985), 783. Guitmund, paraphrasing Augustine's text, is making the point here that, on the authority of Augustine, demons have been known in the past to create illusions and transport bodies, and so it is reasonable to conclude that this same thing can happen with the bread that has been consecrated for the sewer.

served, and they themselves in their stupid curiosity are shown
to err more profoundly.

Roger

20. Indeed, armed with the sword of God, you have slain the
many-headed serpent of this question with marvelous vivacity.
And I give thanks to God that the matter over which I was greatly anguishing, as I see it, has been quite satisfactorily answered
for me.

DERISION OF BERENGARIUS CONCERNING
THE REAL PRESENCE

Guitmund

[1453 D] Have you not also heard what [Berengarius] glories in,
or rather, greatly derides Catholics about?

Roger

What, pray tell, is that?

Guitmund

"Christ," he says, "has never been sown nor harvested in the
field; but these sacraments have been sown and harvested in the
field: How therefore can they be the body of Christ?"

Roger

I had never heard of this argument, or else it has slipped out
of my mind; by all means it deserves a suitable response, so I desire a reasoned explanation from you.

Guitmund

21. The insane mockery of the heretic is obviously worthy of
ridicule. For who among men [1454 A] has not had what he has
eaten, which was sown and harvested in the fields, changed into
his own flesh? For so it is that all men who feed on these foods
that have been sown and harvested in the fields can themselves
be said in a certain sense to have been sown and harvested in
the fields. And so that which Berengarius says is false: "Christ

has never been sown or harvested in the fields." But even if, for this reason, no man is believed to be sown or harvested in the fields, why on the other hand is it not possible [to say] that those things that have been sown and harvested in the fields are converted into the body of Christ, which has been neither sown nor harvested in the fields? For we do not say that those things that have been sown and harvested in the fields are changed, but say instead that bread is converted into flesh. But it is not the bread that has been sown or harvested in the fields, but rather the grains from which [1454 B] the bread has been confected. Since this is so, then what Berengarius says is false: "These have been sown and harvested in the fields." Therefore, even in this he is to be laughed at, nor is the false mocker to be feared, since all the adornments of his opposition have been broken by an easy effort as if they were spider webs.

Roger

I think that everything you say should be most worthily received and embraced wholeheartedly.

Guitmund

22. So these are all the points, insofar as we have heard up to now, in which—as if they were rational arguments—Berengarius and his followers have mocked the Church of God. I judge such objections, however, sufficiently refuted, and now let us come to those arguments [1454 C] that they seem to use from the writings of the holy Fathers as a defense.

THE OBJECTIONS OF BERENGARIUS TO AUGUSTINE'S USE OF SYMBOLISM ADDRESSED

Roger

23. They assert that Augustine, in the book *De doctrina christiana,* calls the food of the Lord's altar a sign and figure, saying:

In this time, though, after the clearest indication of our freedom has shone upon us in the resurrection of our Lord, we are no longer burdened with the heavy duty of carrying out even those signs whose meaning we now understand. But the Lord himself and the discipline of the apostles has handed down to us just a few signs instead of many, and

these so easy to perform, and so awesome to understand, and so pure
and chaste to celebrate, such as the [1454 D] sacrament of baptism, and
the celebration of the Lord's body and blood. When people receive
these, they have been so instructed that they can recognize to what
sublime realities they are to be referred, and so they venerate them in
a spirit not of carnal slavery, but rather of spiritual freedom. But just as
following the letter and taking signs for the things signified by them is
a matter of slavish weakness, so too interpreting signs in a useless way is
a matter of error going badly astray.[26]

Have you not heard, then, that they say he calls the sacraments of the altar signs? Then he infers: "When people receive
these, they have been so instructed that they can recognize to
what sublime realities they are to be referred, and so they venerate them in a spirit not of carnal slavery, but rather of spiritual
freedom."[27] Have you not heard that he says these things are to
be venerated, not in carnal slavery, but rather in spiritual freedom? And if you were to ask: what does it mean to venerate a
sign by carnal slavery? "To follow the letter," he says, "and to take
signs for the things that are signified by these signs, is slavish
weakness."[28]

24. Likewise in the [1455 A] following:

But if the expression seems to command infamy or crime, or to forbid
usefulness or kindness, then it is figurative. "Unless you eat," he says,
"the flesh of the Son of man and drink his blood, you shall not have
life in you" [Jn 6.53]. He seems to be commanding a crime or an act of
infamy; so it is said figuratively, instructing us that we must share in the
Lord's Passion, and store away in our minds the sweet and useful memory that his flesh was crucified and wounded for our sakes.[29]

Have you not heard that they assert it is a figure? Why would
you inquire further? Add further, however, that not only with all
the ecclesiastical authors, but also in the collects of the Masses
which the Church celebrates everywhere, the bread of the altar
is said to be a sacrament, that is, a sacred sign.

26. *De doctrina christiana* 3.9.13 (ed. J. Martin, CSL 32, 85–86, lines 11–23 = PL
34: 71). Quoted from *St. Augustine: Teaching Christianity*, trans. E. Hill, WSA 1/11
(Hyde Park, New York: New City Press, 1996), 175.

27. Ibid.

28. Ibid.

29. *De doctrina christiana* 3.16.24 (ed. J. Martin, CSL 32, 92, lines 3–9 = PL
34: 75). Augustine, *Teaching Christianity*, WSA 1/11: 180.

Guitmund

25. O foolish wise men who do not understand [1455 B] either
Augustine, or the other holy authors, or the Church's customary
words; more accurately, they wickedly pervert them with remarkable diligence! And, truly, Augustine in the book *De doctrina christiana* never called the food of the altar of the Lord a sign or figure, but he said that the celebration of the Lord's body was a
sign, and this we also believe [to be true]. For as often as the celebration of the body and blood of the Lord occurs, truly we do
not kill Christ again, but instead we commemorate his death in
and through that celebration; and the celebration itself is a certain commemoration of the Passion of Christ. The commemoration of the Passion of Christ, however, signifies the Passion itself.
Therefore, the celebration of the body and blood of the Lord is
a sign of the Passion of Christ. And this [1455 C] is what blessed
Augustine says:

> In this time, though, after the clearest indication of our freedom has
> shone upon us in the resurrection of our Lord, we are no longer bur-
> dened with the heavy duty of carrying out even those signs whose
> meaning we now understand. But the Lord himself and the discipline
> of the apostles has handed down to us just a few signs instead of many,
> and these so easy to perform, and so awesome to understand, and so
> pure and chaste to celebrate, such as the sacrament of baptism, and
> the celebration of the Lord's body and blood.[30]

But he has added that to follow the letter and to take signs for
the things which are signified by these signs are slavish weakness;
he says this about the signs of the Old Testament, about which
he was speaking at that time. For certainly, merely to be circum-
cised according to the letter was slavish and weak, as well as to
immolate cattle, to celebrate new moons and Sabbaths, [1455 D]
and to take for Christ the lamb, the rock, and other similar
things that signified Christ. But if Augustine said this even about
the celebration of the Lord's body, which he called a sign, we
also follow him further. For, when we say in the celebration of
the body of the Lord, "Christ is immolated," no one should take
this carnally according to the letter. For "Christ" has died once,

---

30. *De doctrina christiana* 3.9.13 (ed. J. Martin, CSL 32, 85–86, lines 11–18 =
PL 34: 71). Augustine, *Teaching Christianity*, trans. E. Hill, WSA 1/11: 175.

"now he does not die, death no longer has power over him."[31] But while we remember his Passion when we celebrate Masses, it is indicated [by the words] that he died at one time for us. Therefore, if anyone says: "The celebration of the body of the Lord is the Lord's Passion, that is to say, carnally," the thought is rejected by us. For the celebration is not the Lord's Passion itself, but rather a commemoration of the Lord's Passion, [1456 A] now symbolically carried out.

26. Augustine, however, continues and says:

But if the expression seems to command infamy or crime, or to forbid usefulness or kindness, then it is figurative. "Unless you eat," he says, "the flesh of the Son of man and drink his blood, you shall not have life in you" [Jn 6:53]. He seems to be commanding a crime or an act of infamy; so it is said figuratively, instructing us that we must share in the Lord's Passion, and store away in our minds the sweet and useful memory that his flesh was crucified and wounded for our sakes.[32]

In the matter where it seems to prescribe infamy or crime, Augustine himself diligently sets forth a satisfactory explanation in another place. Let us not follow our own opinion about the words of Augustine, but let us hear him carefully explaining himself. For in [1456 B] expounding Psalm 98, he says thus:

What he said seemed hard to them: "Unless anyone eats my flesh, he will not have eternal life" [Jn 6.54]. They received it foolishly, and understood it carnally, and they thought that the Lord meant to hack off small pieces of his body to give them, so they said, "This is a hard saying."[33]

27. Also, in the exposition on the Gospel of John, he more copiously treated these same words about the infamy or crime that they thought he commanded, by setting forth a most detailed exposition, saying:

"This scandalizes you," because I said, "I give you my flesh to eat and my blood to drink." Of course this scandalizes you. "What then if you

31. Rom 6.9, Vulgate: "iam non moritur, mors illi ultra non dominabitur." Guitmund: "mors ei ultra."

32. *De doctrina christiana* 3.16.24 (ed. J. Martin, CSL 32, 92, lines 3–9 = PL 34: 75). Augustine, *Teaching Christianity,* trans. Hill, WSA 1/11: 180.

33. *Enarrationes in psalmos* 98.9 (ed. E. Dekkers–I. Fraipont, CSL 39, 1385–86, lines 41–48 = PL 37: 1265): "Durus est hic sermo."

should see the Son of man ascending where he was before?" What does this mean? By this did he resolve what had disturbed them? By this did he make clear why they had been scandalized? Clearly he did this, [1456 C] if only they understood. For they thought that he was going to disburse his body; but he said that he was going to ascend into heaven whole of course. "When you see the Son of man ascending where he was before," surely then, at least, you will see that he does not disburse his body in the way in which you think; surely then, at least, you will understand that his grace is not consumed in bite-sized pieces.[34]

And again:

But these men quickly defected, when the Lord Jesus spoke such words; they did not believe him although he was saying something great and veiling some grace with these words. But just as they wanted in a human way, so they understood that Jesus could, or that he was proposing, because the Word had been clothed in flesh, to cut himself up, as it were, and distribute himself [1456 D] to those believing in him.[35]

And a little later: "Why say this then? 'The flesh profits nothing' [Jn 6.63]. It profits nothing, but only in the way in which they understood it. For they understood the flesh in this way: just as a carcass is sectioned into pieces, or sold in a meat market; not as something animated by the Spirit."[36] And again: "'It is the Spirit that gives life; the flesh profits nothing,' as they understood the flesh, but not so do I give my flesh to be eaten."[37]

28. Certainly then, St. Augustine has sufficiently declared in these words that the Lord seemed to order a crime or a vice: and one can see that for those who were hearing it, it seemed a hard saying. And they were also scandalized, he says, because they took those words in a foolish and carnal way. But why foolishly and carnally? Because they had thought, he says, that the Lord would be cut up into pieces, and that he was going to give certain portions of his body to them, and that his grace would be consumed in bite-sized pieces [1457 A], and that the flesh in

34. *In Ioannis Evangelium* 27.3 (R. Willems, ed., CSL 36, 271, lines 5–15 = PL 35: 1616). *Tractates on the Gospel of John: 11–27*, trans. J. Rettig, FC 79 (Washington, DC: The Catholic University of America Press, 1988), 278–79.

35. Ibid., 27.2 (ed. R. Willems, op. cit., 270, lines 6–12). Augustine, *Tractates on the Gospel of John: 11–27*, trans. J. Rettig, FC 79 (Washington, DC: The Catholic University of America Press, 1988), 278.

36. Ibid., 27.5 (ed. R. Willems, op. cit., 272, lines 9–13).

37. Ibid., 27.7 (ed. R. Willems, op. cit., 272, lines 30–32).

which the Word had been clothed would be cut up, as it were, in the way that a carcass is divided up or sold in a meat market, as it were, and in that way, not animated by the Spirit, it would be distributed to the faithful. This, therefore, is the crime or vice that, as St. Augustine says, the Lord seemed to order. Not, however, that he would order a crime or a vice by ordering his flesh to be eaten, but rather, that he seems to order it (he says)—at least so those [who heard it] thought—that, by ordering his flesh to be eaten, he would necessarily order that he be killed, and cut into pieces, and that his flesh thus be eaten either cooked or raw. Therefore, as it applies to this expression, he says, it is a figure.

29. At one time the Shadow-Lover [*Umbraticus*][38] cries out; at another time he rejoices. Do not be preposterous, O Shadow-Lover, do not glory precipitously: patiently and diligently turn your attention to whose reality is said to be a figure. [1457 B] For it is a figure, Augustine teaches. Teaching what? Figurative of what? He says it is figurative of what it teaches: communicating with the Passion of the Lord and holding in our memory both sweetly and usefully that his flesh was crucified and wounded for us. Thanks be to God. For whatever it is that Augustine calls a figure here (for what he calls a figure in these words of his is not so easy to know), he most manifestly demonstrates that the figure is not of the body of the Lord, but of his crucifixion and wounding, that is, of his death and our communication with it, so that we may imitate Christ and communicate with his Passion by suffering with him. Paul the Apostle is also in agreement with this, who says: [1457 C] "As often as you will eat this bread and drink the cup of the Lord, you will announce the death of the Lord until he comes."[39] And if we inquire as to why Augustine has called this a figure, certainly there seems to be nothing so agreeable that comes to mind, as what the same doctor had already said a little above, that is, the celebration itself of the body

38. *Umbraticus* or "Shadow-Lover": a term which Hurter says "most aptly describes" those who denied the Real Presence of Christ in the Eucharist and said that he was present only in a "shadowy" fashion (*umbratilem*), i.e., by way of sign and figure. Hurter, *De veritate*, 83, n.1.

39. 1 Cor 11.26.

and blood of the Lord. For these reasons, the Berengarians un-
wisely and foolishly put forward against us the book *De doctrina
christiana,* since the food of the altar of the Lord is never called
a figure there, never called a sign there. And whatever it may be
that is called sign and figure there, it has been most certainly
demonstrated that it is certainly not a sign and figure of the
body and blood of the Lord, but rather, a sign or figure of the
Passion of the Lord and our communication with it.

THE SYMBOLIC NATURE OF THE EUCHARIST
AS A SACRAMENT DEFENDED

30. But furthermore, if they contentiously assert that the Eucharist itself is called a sign or a figure [1457 D] by the Church
(for indeed it is called a sacrament [*sacramentum*],[40] that is, a sacred sign), what, I ask, would they gain for themselves in this
matter, how will they hinder us? For we are most certainly not
afraid to call the Eucharist "figure" and "sacrament." Perhaps
the Shadow-Lover will respond here with what he is accustomed
to say: if it is a figure, how is it a reality [*veritas*]? If it is a sacrament, how is it a reality? O most foolish reasoning of a malicious
sage! Have you not read in the Gospel that Christ himself is
called a sign? Simeon says: "Behold, he has been destined for
the fall and rise of many in Israel, and for a sign that will be
contradicted."[41] And in the Song of Songs, the bridegroom says
to his spouse: "Place me as a sign upon your heart."[42] Also in Isaiah: "There will be Jesse's root, which stands as a sign for the

40. Herein, and what is to follow, is Guitmund's rich understanding of the
word *sacramentum,* for one finds throughout the entire work his Augustinian
freedom in its application. For Guitmund, it is at times the whole mystery of
sign and inner reality. It is at other times used interchangeably with, and in the
sense of, *mysterium,* from the *Vetus Latina* found in Eph 5.23 and 1 Tm 3.15,
and still other times it is simply the sign, or *signum.* But probably the usage
that seems to be unique to Guitmund is the equivalence *sacramenta altaris* enjoys
with *corporis et sanguinis Domini,* for, as it is clear in the text, these two are used
interchangeably in Guitmund without distinction or clarification, which reveals
to the reader that for him, the "sacraments of the altar" *are* "the body and blood
of the Lord."

41. Lk 2.34.   42. Song 8.6.

peoples."[43] Because of these things, [1458 A] if it is Christ, it is
both the true Christ [*verus Christus*], and sign [*signum*]; there is
no obstacle for us if that which we receive from the altar of the
Lord, although it is the true body of Christ, is also called a sign.
But of what thing, you may perhaps inquire, is it a sign, if not of
the body of the Lord? On the other hand, I ask you in turn, of
what reality is Christ a sign? If you respond to me, you yourself
will answer your own question. If you do not respond to me on
that point, then neither do you force me to respond to you in
this.

Christ is a sign

CHRIST HIMSELF AS A SIGN EXPLAINED

31. For the instruction of the faithful, however, I will say something about this matter as the Lord may allow: for Christ, because
he offered himself for us, has been made for us a sign of redemption. For every price of a passage is a sign, the price of the reality
to which it belongs. Christ, because he is our Redeemer, passed
over from death to life for us, and because he himself is [1458 B]
our price, he, for us, is the sign of this passage, namely, the sign
of our redemption. We are not foolish to believe, then, if also
from a similar reasoning, that the food of the Lord's altar effects
our salvation because of the power of the Divinity fully dwelling
within it, and because it is our price, we believe that it signifies
our very salvation.

32. Christ, indeed, is the Mediator between God and men,[44]
since he is for us always the rainbow in the clouds, as it were,
composed of divine and human substances. He shines forth in
his preachers, and when the Father beholds him constantly in-
terceding for us, he is the sign of an eternal covenant between
God and man, as it is written: "I will place my bow in the clouds,
[1458 C] and it will be a sign of my covenant between me and the
earth."[45] Of this divine covenant and of this most salvific peace,
the most holy offering on the altar is believed by us also to be a
sign.

33. But the Christ who was born of the Virgin is a sign for us

---

43. Is 11.10.   44. 1 Tm 2.5.
45. Gn 9.13.

as well—a sign that we are also reborn, in Christ, from the virgin mother who is the Church, whom the Apostle has "promised to present in marriage as a chaste virgin to the one man, Christ."[46] For in Christ, as he grows, we see our own progress pre-signified "until we all grow into the perfect man."[47] He drives out the devils, perfects health, and completes his work on the third day. First we drive out our vices, then we nourish our virtues, and in the third place we are perfected. Why should I propose more, when the whole of his earthly life in this world, and his every human discourse, is set forth as a sign [1458 D] of our Christian life? "For if indeed we say that we remain in Christ, then we ought to walk as he walked."[48]

34. Nevertheless, as I also call to mind something about his end, the same flesh was crucified, died, was buried, rose, and ascended finally to the right hand of the Father. Does this not signify to us—according to the Apostle—that, just as he has commanded, daily we should carry our cross,[49] and daily we should die to this world, and, "buried with him," should attend not to present things, but as sons of the resurrection, "we should walk in a new life," so that after the labors of this age we also might ascend unto a celestial reign? "For if," the Apostle says, "we have grown into union with him through a likeness to his death, we shall also be united with him in the resurrection; for we know that our old self was crucified with him, so that this sinful body of ours might be done away with. We who were baptized in [1459 A] Christ Jesus were baptized into his death, and buried with him through baptism unto death, so that, just as Christ rose from the dead by the glory of the Father, we too might walk in newness of life."[50] For the approved faith of every orthodox Christian is that after living this life well, we shall seek after a heavenly one. "For we know," according to the blessed Apostle, "that if this earthly habitation of ours is destroyed, we have a dwelling from God, a home not made by hands, in heaven."[51] In all these ways, therefore, Christ shows himself to us as a sign of his Holy Church, [a sign] that, hanging upon the cross, he him-

---

46. 2 Cor 11.2.
48. 1 Jn 2.6.
50. Rom 6.3–6.

47. Eph 4.13.
49. Lk 9.23.
51. 2 Cor 5.1.

self has confirmed this by his own most holy authority, saying: "O God, my God, why have you abandoned me?"[52] For where or when did the Father abandon [1459 B] him, since he himself had said: "I am not alone because the Father is with me,"[53] and again: "Father, I know that you always hear me"?[54] Beyond any doubt, then, he was symbolizing in himself his Church, which was once abandoned in Adam. And since, just as St. Paul the Apostle has taught us: "He is the head of the Church," and "the Church is his body,"[55] then his own proper body, which is the body he assumed from the blessed Virgin, is a sign, figure, and sacrament of his body which is the Church. It is easy to see that the body of the Church, in a likeness to its head, is born of the Holy Spirit and the Church, whose heart is virginal, so that from every race, just as from diverse members, it is gathered together into one new man.

APPROPRIATENESS FOR THE EUCHARIST TO BE CALLED A SACRED SIGN

35. Therefore, we believe that it is not contradictory, that all these things are signified through that which is received from the altar of the Lord. Let me summarize with ready brevity, then, and without carelessly advancing the deep reasons of the divine mysteries, [1459 C] the certain testimony that the universal Church offers about this matter: namely, that as often as we receive the sacrament of the altar, we show ourselves to be Christians, that is, spiritually born. Consequently, we declare that we were crucified, and died, and were buried together with our Lord through baptism into his death, but also that we rose with him. Through this death we also expel vice; through this death we trust that we are confirmed in a new life; through this death we hope that we will be perfected and ascend to the eternal kingdom. Now I need not labor to prove further that the sacred oblation is a sign of the unity of the body of the Church. For Paul the Apostle has sufficiently proved it when he says: "The bread that we break [1459 D] and the cup that we bless, is it not a participation in the

52. Mt 27.46.   53. Jn 16.32.
54. Jn 11.42.   55. Eph 1.22–23.

body and blood of the Lord? Because we who are many are one in Christ."[56]

36. This is what St. Cyprian understands and pursues in a letter to a certain Magnus:

Finally, the very Sacrifices of the Lord declare that Christian unanimity is bound to itself with a firm and inseparable charity. For when the Lord calls Bread made from the union of many grains his Body, he indicates our people whom he bore united; and when he calls Wine pressed from the clusters of grapes and many small berries and gathered in one his Blood, he, likewise, signifies our flock joined by the mixture of a united multitude.[57]

Whence St. Augustine [1460 A] also in *Super Joannem* says: "And so he wants this food and drink to be understood as the society of his body and his members, namely, the holy Church."[58] And a little later:

For this reason, indeed, even as men of God knew this before us, our Lord, Jesus Christ, manifested his body and blood in those things which are reduced from many to some one thing. For the one is made into one thing from many grains, the other flows together into one thing from many grapes.[59]

37. The sacred oblation, therefore, is most aptly and reasonably called a sign, both of many other goods, and also of the body of the Lord, that is, the Church from many men and peoples, as if from grains, ground, that is, humbled, between the two Testaments, as it were between upper and lower millstones, [1460 B] and through the water of baptism and the fire of the Holy

56. 1 Cor 10.16–17.

57. *Ad Magnum de baptizandis Novatianis et de iis qui in lecto gratiam consequuntur*, Epistle 69.5 (ed. G. F. Diercks, CSL 3C, 476, lines 105–7 = PL 3: 1142B): "Unanimitatem christianam . . . conexam," Guitmund: "Unanimitate christianos . . . conexos," which is Augustine's rendering of the text in the *De baptismo contra Donatistas* 7.50, *Sententiae Concilii Carthaginensis* (ed. Petschenig, CSEL 51, 369 = PL 43: 240), which is most likely Guitmund's source for the citation. *St. Cyprian: Letters (1–81)*, trans. R. Donna, FC 51 (Washington, DC: The Catholic University of America Press, 1964), 248.

58. *In Ioannis Evangelium* 26.15 (ed. R. Willem, CSL 36, 267, lines 27–29). Augustine, *Tractates on the Gospel of John, 11–27*, trans. J. Rettig, FC 79 (Washington, DC: The Catholic University of America Press, 1988), 273.

59. Ibid., 26.17 (ed. R. Willems, op. cit., 268, lines 6–11). Augustine, *Tractates on the Gospel of John, 11–27*, trans. J. Rettig, FC 79, 274.

Spirit, they are collected and compacted into one.[60] But of the body itself, in which the divinity of the Savior was properly clothed, in some of the authors, you will never or rarely find it openly called a sign. And indeed, where the Eucharist is found to be called a sacrament of the body of the Lord, we have interpreted this usage of words as follows: The Eucharist is a sacrament, which is the body of the Lord, so that the Eucharist itself would truly be the body of the Lord, but it would be a sacrament of other things, that is, of good things foretold, just as we are accustomed to say: God is the font of goodness, that is, the font who is goodness, and the fullness of divinity, that is, the fullness that is divinity, and many other expressions of this sort. Or rather, we certainly understand that the Eucharist itself is truly the body of the Lord, that is to say, [1460 C] the proper body of the Word of God himself and a sacrament of the body of the Lord, that is, the Church, as the blessed Apostle has taught.

THE PROPOSITION IS ADVANCED THAT ONE REALITY CAN BE A SIGN OF ITSELF

38. But if it were to be found anywhere that the Eucharist is called a sacrament of the body itself, in which the Word of God has been clothed (which clearly never, or hardly ever, occurs), how would that thwart our position? In what way would it shake our faith? Can a sacrament never be the reality of which it is a sacrament? Or rather, cannot a figure be the reality of which it

60. Guitmund is obviously building on a theme from *Sermon* 227 of Augustine: "In this loaf of bread you are given clearly to understand how much you should love unity. I mean, was that loaf made from one grain? Weren't there many grains of wheat? But before they came into the loaf they were all separate; they joined together by means of water after a certain amount of pounding and crushing. Unless wheat is ground, after all, and moistened with water, it can't possibly get into this shape which is called bread. In the same way you too were being ground and pounded, as it were, by the humiliation of fasting and the sacrament of exorcism. Then came baptism, and you were, in a manner of speaking, moistened with water in order to be shaped into bread. But it is not bread without fire to bake it. So what does fire represent? That's the chrism, the anointing. Oil, the fire-feeder, you see, is the sacrament of the Holy Spirit." *Sermons,* trans. E. Hill, WSA 3/6 (New Rochelle: New City Press, 1995), 254.

is a figure?[61] Why does Paul say about the Son of God in the Epistle to the Hebrews: "Since he is the splendor of his glory and figure of his substance,"[62] that is, of the Father? Is the Son not that which the Father is? Far be it to think otherwise. The Son is completely that which the Father is, and nothing other than that which the Father is. It is false to say, then, that no figure is that reality of which it is a figure. Therefore, when Christ was at one time teaching, [1460 D] working miracles, living most justly among men, eating, drinking, sleeping, and showing in himself the other qualities of our humanity, was he symbolizing himself to us as anything other than God and man? But even now he intercedes for us, and today, when he shows his body with wounds to the face of the Father, he symbolizes himself as born for us, as having suffered and risen again and ascended to the heavens. Therefore, the same Christ is a sacred sign of himself, that is, a sacrament. And this same divine oblation is able to be a sign to us, without being a danger to our faith. Since this is the case, that our Eucharist is found to signify to us all the same things which are Christ, and those things of which Christ is a sign, so it is that the Eucharist is a sign as Christ is a sign. [1461 A] For this reason, then, no one says that Christ is a shadow of Christ, and not the true Christ; nor does anyone say that his body is only a shadow and not a true body, because, as we have shown, it is also a sign of his body, which is the Church, and of Christ himself. Let no one say, then, that our Eucharist, because of the meanings already mentioned, is a shadow of that body of the Lord, with which the divinity of the Savior clothed himself as his own, and does not exist as the true and proper body of the Savior. For if, on account of the aforementioned significations, the Eucharist itself is not the true and proper body of Christ, then on account of the same significations, neither will Christ be the

61. Hurter (*De sacramentis*, 92 n.1) comments on Guitmund's point, that just because something is a sign or figure of one reality, that does not mean that the reality must be absent from the sign, as was the case with the tongues of fire over the heads of the apostles at Pentecost, for with the fire was also the presence of the Holy Spirit. So it is the case in the Eucharist that there is a certain fullness of the reality with the body of Christ being truly present.

62. Heb 1.3.

true Christ. But far be this from all minds: that, since Christ is wholly a sacrament [1461 B] of so many and such great goods, therefore the truth of his own reality is vacated in any way because of it. Far be it equally from all hearts, as well, that our Eucharist, since it signifies for us the same goods, for that reason is denied to be the true and proper body of Christ. In my judgment, then, it has been satisfactorily and abundantly shown that nothing from the aforementioned writings of St. Augustine, whether from the words "sacrament," "figure," and "sign," which the Church continues to use and which the adversary objects to, is any real obstacle to our faith, and it is evident in these things, as in the other matters, that his childishness should cease.

Roger

39. By all means, you have certainly proved that Christ is a sign of himself as well; nevertheless, I desire a fuller explanation [1461 C] on just how such a thing can be.

PROPOSITION DEFENDED THAT CHRIST IS A SIGN OF HIMSELF

Guitmund

Why do you wonder about this? For the matter is such an established fact that no one should doubt it. For who is the man (for example) who by doing something, or even acting on his own power alone, would not signify that he is alive? So it is, then, that one man, in substance always the same, can signify himself through different acts. It follows, therefore, that Christ, always substantially [*substantialiter*] the same, by doing visible acts, signifies himself invisibly at work. For by word, demeanor, or appearance of his body, Christ signified that he was kind or angry to those to whom he appeared at different times. So it is that, in the same way, the oblation of the sacred altar, where the substance [*substantia*] of the body of Christ is truly [*veraciter*] present, according [1461 D] to visible species [*species*] and visible mysteries [*mysteria*], can signify something either with respect to the Lord himself or to his Church, without any danger to our faith.

Roger

40. Proceed with what you intend; for concerning these matters it is utterly insane to doubt further.

DIFFICULTIES WITH AUGUSTINE'S EXPOSITION
OF PSALM 98 RESOLVED

Guitmund

Truly, that which Berengarius was especially accustomed to
bring forward as an argument, was what Augustine says about
the words of the Lord to the disciples, in the aforementioned
exposition on Psalm Ninety-Eight, where he says:

When the twelve disciples remained behind with him, he instructed
them, and said to them: "The Spirit is he who gives life; the flesh, however, profits nothing. The words which I have spoken to you are spirit
and life" [Jn 6.64]. It is not this body that you see that you are going to
eat, and that blood [1462 A] which will be poured out by those who will
crucify me that you are going to drink.[63]

If, therefore, Berengarius says, it is not "this body," nor "that
blood," then it stands to reason that what is received from the
altar would be only a shadow and figure of the body and the
blood.

41. But if he had diligently turned his attention to the above
words of Augustine, in his exposition of the same Psalm, or certainly in the exposition on the Gospel, where these same words
of the Lord are treated, perhaps he would never have constructed the calumny of this error from them. But the unhappy man,
long grown old in heretical pestilence, with the devil's urging,
utterly and almost inexplicably caught in his snares, would more
willingly adjust all his forces to pursue one word, which he had
understood badly, which seemed to defend the foolishness he
propagated, rather than pay the slightest attention to the provi-
dential watchfulness of the divine Scriptures crying out mightily
against him. [1462 B] Indeed on the same Psalm, St. Augustine
preached: "[Christ] took earth from the earth, because flesh

---

63. *Enarrationes in psalmos* 98.9, "Sermo ad plebem" (ed. E. Dekkers–I. Fraipont, CSL 39, 1386, lines 52, 55–59 = PL 37: 1264).

comes from the earth, and he received his flesh from the flesh of Mary. He walked here below in that flesh, and even gave us that same flesh to eat for our salvation."[64] If the same flesh that he received from the flesh of Mary, in which he walked here below, he gave us to eat for our salvation—how is it not "this body," since he gives us flesh to eat in the same substance? But not "this body" in the same form as if he were to say: "My body, just as you have heard, I will give to you, but not according to what you see, that is, not such as you see it, that is, not in this form [*forma*] and appearance [*species*] which you see."[65] Otherwise, [1462 C] why did [Jesus] add: "which you see," when it would have been sufficient to say "not this [body]," unless, of course, it was because it was according to essence [*secundum essentiam*],[66] and not according to what you see?

42. Therefore, so that you may know that Augustine meant what we say he meant, note well why he blames those who were scandalized by those words in the exposition of this Psalm or the Gospel. For there is no doubt that they thought that the substance they discerned with their eyes was to be given to them to eat, and not bread or anything else. Augustine says, however, that they received these words foolishly and carnally. "They thought," he says, "that the Lord was going to cut off some parts of his body and give them to them."[67] They thought that his grace would be consumed in bites,[68] and the flesh in which the

Aug: they received the words foolishly + carnally

64. Ibid. (op. cit. 1385, 21–23). *Enarrationes in psalmos: 73–98*, "Exposition of Psalm 98," trans. J. Rotelle, WSA 3/18 (Hyde Park, NY: New City Press, 2002), 474.

65. Central to Guitmund's eucharistic theology is the fact that Christ is "substantially" present in the bread and the wine, and it is here that one finds an insight into what exactly he means by that term. For Guitmund, the "substantial" presence of Christ means that it is the same body born of Mary, now at the right hand of the Father in heaven, also with the faithful in the sacraments of the altar. The only difference between the glorified presence and the real presence of our Lord is the appearance, or species.

66. Cf. St. Thomas, ST III, q. 76, a. 1, and his understanding of *per modum substantiae*.

67. *Enarrationes in psalmos* 98.9, "Sermo ad plebem" (ed. E. Dekkers–I. Fraipont, CSL 39, 1385).

68. *In Ioannis Evangelium* 27.3 (ed. R. Willem, CSL 36, 271).

Word had been clothed would be distributed to the faithful,[69] not whole, [1462 D] as it ascended into heaven, but rather cut up as it were, in the same manner that a carcass is cut up and sold in the market,[70] not as the spirit animates, that is, not alive. For if the spirit animates,[71] it is alive. But what if they had thought that they themselves were going to receive the whole flesh, not cut up into portions, not dead but alive; not as it is sold in a market, but alive, just as the spirit animates it? Would they have erred? Certainly they would not have erred. For at that time they were blamed, not because they were thinking that they were going to eat that flesh, that is, flesh of the same substance, but rather, only because they thought that it would be neither whole nor alive. They would have been without fault then, if they instead thought that they were going to eat the same flesh (that is, flesh of the same substance), whole and alive. If this follows, [1463 A] nay rather because it follows, see how effectively it demolishes the thought of Berengarius, and the whole error of the Shadow-Lovers.

Idolators — because they don't believe in real presence

FORCE OF THE ARGUMENT CALLS FOR THE ACCEPTANCE OF AUGUSTINIAN REALISM

43. Why then, if, after all we have said, the previously mentioned words of Augustine can be understood most fittingly without contradicting any part of the Scripture, but instead a whole series of texts, carefully inspected, and the exposition of the Gospel urge it, or rather force it, then what charge can Berengarius bring against us? If I may speak in a more indulgent manner, even if these words were ambiguous, they still do not support the position [of Berengarius] over our own. Now, however, since the testimony of the text itself and the most lucid reasoning of the Gospel treatise, as well as the authority of the universal Church, agree with our understanding, let this infection of heretical corruption fall silent, having no further grounds for

69. Ibid. 27.2 (op. cit., CSL 36, 270).
70. Ibid. 27.5 (op. cit., CSL 36, 272).
71. Ibid. 27.7 (op. cit., CSL 36, 272).

argument.[72] [1463 B] But if he is confident in his ability to disprove our conclusion in some way, or demonstrate a better one, we are prepared to hear him with an open mind. For we do not wish to dodge anything we have not diligently discussed, with the help of Christ.

AUGUSTINE'S USE OF 'HOC' IN HIS EXPOSITION OF PSALM 98

44. Furthermore, I say the following, because I think I heard that Berengarius rationalizes about the pronoun *hoc* as follows. *Hoc*, he says, is a pronoun; pronouns, however, signify a substance without qualities. When he [Augustine] says,[73] therefore, "not this body," he is talking about the substance of the body, not about the qualities. I am compelled to cry out here along with the prophet and the Apostle: "Where is the scribe? Where is the arbiter of words? Where is the one pondering over the words of the Law?"[74] [1463 C] "Did not God make foolish the wisdom of this world?"[75] Truly I have called this wisdom foolish. For these same grammarians, who defined the property of the parts of this sort of speech, have handed down and praised exceedingly "figures of speech," which lack even the most essential parts of perfect grammar. For who, either speaking or talking in a common parlance of speech, is criticized if he should say: "I am not the one [*ille*] I once was," or "You are not 'this one' [*is*] or 'that one'

72. Here, Guitmund lays out three independent doctrinal fonts: (1) Sacred Scripture, (2) sound theological reasoning, and (3) the authority of the Church.

73. Guitmund is offering at this point a critique of Berengarius's interpretation of Augustine's eucharistic commentary from the exposition of Psalm 98.9 (cf. paragraph 41). For Guitmund, Augustine understood our Lord's words "not this body," to mean not this body as you see it, i.e., the quality of appearance, although the substance would remain the same. What follows is a debate as to whether Augustine really meant *hoc* to apply to the quality of Christ's body, or its substance. If it is in fact the latter, then Guitmund will make the case that Augustine uses that pronoun in many other texts that only further reinforce his conviction that Augustine was a eucharistic realist, and not a symbolist.

74. Cf. Is 33.18.

75. 1 Cor 1.20.

[*ille*] you used to be," when the substance would be the same, but the qualities different. The dialecticians also, who place altogether too much emphasis on words, daily both say and teach that things differ and are the same, not only according to substance, but also according to quality. But if *ille, is,* and *idem* are pronouns, and according to the most learned doctors [1463 D] very often signify not always substance, but also the qualities, why then is the pronoun *hoc* not allowed to do the same? Is it because it does not please Berengarius, who has nothing else with which to defend his heresy? It was pleasing, nevertheless, to certain authors of the grammatical art, of the highest authority, who not only acknowledge that qualities can be designated by pronouns, but even number among pronouns *talis* and *qualis,* which are significative of particular quality.

45. But he should have looked at what the famous Donatus has said, the most expert grammarian, who wished *qualis* and *talis* to be considered as pronouns.[76] I do not now have the task of passing judgment about the authors of the grammatical art, since I can use the argument of the adversary for myself more readily, namely, that *ipsa* is a pronoun. Pronouns, however, signify a substance [1464 A] without qualities. Therefore, when Augustine says: "In the same [*ipsa*] flesh he walked, and the same flesh [*ipsa*] he gave us to eat for our salvation," he says that we eat the substance of Christ's flesh, not the figure. Again, *hoc* is a pronoun. Therefore, when the same Augustine says in a sermon to the neophytes: "Receive in this [*hoc*] bread what hung upon the cross, and receive in this [*hoc*] cup what flowed from the side of Christ,"[77] he declared that what we eat and drink is the substance of the body and blood of Christ, not a figure.

76. Donatus Aelius, a celebrated grammarian born around 333 A.D., who was a teacher of Jerome, and composed commentaries on Virgil and Terence, as well as a treatise on grammar entitled *Ars Donati grammatici urbis Romae,* which was a popular textbook used for teaching the *trivium* in the Middle Ages.

77. *Sermon* 228B.2, "Ad infantes" (ed. G. Morin, *Miscellanea Agostiniana,* 18–20 = PL 46: 827), listed as "dubious authorship," by Morin and the Maurists. The text in Migne reads: "Hoc agnoscite in pane quod pependit in cruce; hoc in calice, quod manavit ex latere." Guitmund's version exchanges "accipite," for "agnoscite." Hill's notation on the question of authenticity is this: "Some scholars question the sermon's authenticity. There is nothing obviously

46. This argument of yours, O whoever you are who will advance it, if it is in fact weak, then it would be of no concern to us. If it is strong, however, it profits us more than you, since you would have it in only one place, but we in many. And should Augustine be in disagreement with himself, either he should not now be accepted, [1464 B] or he should be believed in many testimonies rather than one. To be sure, it is easier even for him to err in one place than in many, or for his codices to be susceptible to corruption by some falsifier. Choose, therefore, that which pleases you: either your reasoning is weak, and accomplishes nothing; or it is strong, and it profits us a great deal. For if it is weak, it proves that, where [the text] says, "not this body," this is not said about substance. If, however, it is strong, it confirms that, where [the text] says, "He gave us his very flesh to eat," and, "Receive this," and other similar sayings, this must be understood about substance.

47. Or if perhaps you might say: "I explain those pronouns in this way: 'He gave his very flesh for us to eat for our salvation,' that is, 'the figure of the very flesh'; and, 'Receive this in bread,' means, 'Receive the figure of this body in bread'; [1464 C] and the same way in all the other cases." If this, I say, is what you would say, then we explain your pronoun in the same way, saying: "'I will give to you, not this body which you see,' that is, not a figure of this body, not a shadow, but the truth I will give to you." For such a conclusion follows those resolutions of your own. If, then, drawing figures from among pronouns, you bring a case against us, how could you have the audacity to object if the same is brought against you? And so either employ these figures, so that they draw out your shadows for you; or reject them, and [the pronouns] overwhelmingly agree with us. For if you place the

un-Augustinian about the content; if the preacher was someone else, then he was clearly a devoted disciple. There is, perhaps, a certain lack of the spontaneity, of that sparkle and occasional flash of brilliance which one has come to associate with Augustine; but not even he could be at the very top of his form all the time. I think it must be regarded as genuine until the contrary is much more convincingly proved." *Sermons*, trans. E. Hill, WSA 3/6 (New Rochelle: New City Press, 1995), 263, n. 1. Inasmuch as I accept Fr. Hill's assessment of the sermon's authenticity, it reinforces Guitmund's arguments in favor of Augustinian eucharistic realism.

aforementioned conclusions regarding pronouns against us, then that [Scriptural] passage which you had brought against us, you manifestly turn against yourself and against your shadows. If, on the other hand, you reject them, so that you always obstinately [1464 D] search for a substantial signification among pronouns, then, as I have said, either we do not accept that Augustine opposes this one passage in many other places—contradicting you and himself—or many testimonies are more credible than one; so that we conclude what we hoped for, namely, that we eat the body of the Lord, substantively, not in shadow. It is obvious, then, that you should flee from these things in every way, because if you diligently turn to the most excellent doctor Augustine, upon whom you depend the most, it is clear that you destroy the pest of this "shadow" error without even drawing a breath.

BERENGARIUS'S OBJECTIONS FROM AUGUSTINE'S LETTER TO BONIFACE ADDRESSED

48. Therefore, now that this calumny has been refuted, let us pass on to what Berengarius objects to from the epistle of St. Augustine to Boniface. It is more than obvious that in this matter he seems to labor more from love of contention than from any reason. For what St. Augustine says: "Just as the sacrament of the body of Christ is in a certain manner the [1465 A] body of Christ, and the sacrament of the blood of Christ is in a certain manner the blood of Christ, so the sacrament of faith is faith,"[78] must not be understood of the sacraments of our altar. For he had been speaking about the sacraments in general. For if the sacraments did not have a certain likeness to those things of which they are sacraments, they would not be sacraments at all. For it is from this likeness, for the most part, that the sacraments receive the names of those things [for which they are named]. Then, descending from the general to the particular, the statement concludes through a simile, saying: "Just as the sacrament of the body of Christ is in a certain manner the body of Christ," etc.,

78. *Letter* 98.9, "Augustinus Episcopo Bonifico" (ed. A. Goldbacher, CSEL 34, 531, lines 6–9 = PL 33: 364): "Sicut ergo secundum . . . fidei fides est."

we can understand with an open mind that this is said about the manna,[79] [1465 B] or also about the bread and wine of Melchisedech,[80] or about another of the ancient sacrifices, which were sacraments of the body and blood of Christ. For by way of figure, they can be called in a certain way the body and blood of Christ,[81] just as Christ is called a rock.[82] And so the man has not sufficiently paid attention to that which he opposes.

49. For even if we should choose to accept that statement from the abundance of statements about the sacraments of our altar, a faithful and ready interpretation is obvious nonetheless. For since our sacraments are substantively [*substantive*] that body which belongs to the Son of God, they are in a certain fashion the figure of that body of which they are sacraments, that is, the Church, which is the body of Christ. For Augustine confirms this in these words in the treatise on John: "And so he wants this food and drink to be understood as the society of the body and his members, that which is [1465 C] the holy Church.[83] The sacrament of this reality, that is, of the unity of the body and blood of Christ, is provided at the Lord's table, in some places daily, in other places with certain intervals of days; and it is taken from the Lord's table."[84] And likewise in a certain sermon on the sacraments:[85] "He who has suffered for us," he says, " has com-

79. Ex 16.15, 31, 33, 35.

80. Gn 14.18.

81. Hurter (*De sacramentis,* 106), injects the textual note here: "*Per figuram corporis et sanguinis Christi.* Puto legendum esse *corpus et sanguis* Christi, vel supplendum, possunt per figuram nominibus corporis et sanguinis Christi appellari."

82. 1 Cor 10.4, Ex 17.6, and Nm 20.11.

83. *In Ioannis Evangelium* 26.15 (ed. R. Willems, CSL 36, 267, line 27), Augustine's text continues: ". . . sancta ecclesia in praedestinatis et vocatis, et iustificatis, et glorificatis sanctis, et fidelibus eius." Augustine, *Tractates on John 11–27,* FC 79, 273.

84. Ibid., (op. cit., 267, line 34). Augustine's text continues: "quibusdam ad vitam, quibusdam ad exitium; res vero ipsa cuius sacramentum est, omni homini ad vitam, nulli ad exitium, quicumque eius particeps fuerit." Augustine, *Tractates on John 11–27,* FC 79, 273.

85. *Sermon* 229, "Ad infantes" (G. Morin, ed., *Miscellanea Agostiniana,* Rome,1931, pp. 29–32). Although the authenticity is doubtful, Fr. Hill's note on this is instructive: "The Maurists only have this sermon as a short fragment,

mended to us in this sacrament his own blood and body, and this is what he even made us ourselves into as well.[86] For we have been made his body, and through his mercy, we are that which we receive."[87] Behold, he has said how the food and drink of the altar are in a certain way the society of the body, which is the Church. Not that food and drink would themselves be the society, but the sacrament of the society. And what we receive, he said, is in some sense ourselves [1465 D] because it is a sacrament of us. So in this way then, Christ's own body is in a certain way through figure that body of Christ of which it is a sacrament, that is, the Church. Nor is there any wonder [at this], since the Lord himself says through the prophet: "With a vestment of justice he has clothed me, like a bridegroom adorned with a crown, and like a bride adorned with her jewels."[88] He calls himself the bridegroom, because he himself is the Bridegroom; and he calls himself the bride, because he himself is, in a certain fashion, that body of his which is the Church, of whom he himself is the sacrament.

50. The similitude that follows commends this understanding to us most aptly. For just as we call the Lord's own body a sacrament of his other body, that is, the Church, so we acknowledge visible baptism as a sacrament of another, that is to say, invisible

---

preserved by Bede and Florus; in fact as a chain of scattered fragments—every other sentence, as it were, from sections 1 and 2. The sermon's authenticity has been questioned; the only solid reason I can surmise for this from the sermon itself is the fact that in section 3 below the preacher refers to the celebrant of the eucharist [*sic*] (himself, presumably) as the *sacerdos,* the high priest: a usage I have never come across before in Augustine's writings. . . . I am hesitantly inclined to share the doubts about the sermon being genuinely that of Augustine's. If it is not, though, then it is one of a very faithful disciple of the master, someone like Caesarius of Arles." *Sermons,* WSA 3/6: 267, n.1.

86. Again, Fr. Hill on this sermon: "This text illustrates very well how Augustine in his eucharistic theology is unequivocally 'realist,' in stating the reality of Christ's presence in the sacrament—'this bread and wine becomes the body and blood of the Lord'; and yet never lingers, as later theology and devotion have done, on that real presence, but goes on immediately to reflect on what the real presence itself means or signifies: namely our unity with him, and in him with each other, in being ourselves the body of Christ." *Sermons,* WSA 3/6: 267, n.3.

87. Cf. "Fragment" of *Sermon* 229, PL 38: 1103.

88. Is 61.10.

baptism. [1466 A] For there exists an exterior baptism, visible water washing flesh; there exists interior baptism, invisible faith in like manner purifying the soul, as the blessed Apostle testifies, who says: "Cleansing their hearts by faith."[89] And again: "And so baptism brings about your salvation, not as the cleansing of a deposit of dirt on the body, but as an appeal to God of a good conscience."[90] And so in like manner, with sufficient agreement, and reasonable faith, we can understand Augustine to have said, "Just as the sacrament of the body of Christ, that is, just as the Son of God's own body is a sacrament of the body of Christ, that is, the Church, so in a certain fashion that body of Christ is the body of which it is a sacrament, that is, the Church." For he himself is the bridegroom, and he himself in a certain sense is also the bride; the same way that the sacrament of faith, which is exterior [1466 B] baptism, stands for that which is a sign of faith, and according to a certain way, is faith. bridegroom + bride

DIFFICULTY OF THE PHYSICAL PRESENCE OF CHRIST IN HEAVEN ADDRESSED

51. Still further, St. Peter offends Berengarius, when he speaks of the Lord as he "whom heaven must hold until the times of the restoration of all things."[91] If heaven should hold him until the end, Berengarius says, then he never leaves heaven so that he might sometimes be present upon the earth. We are of the belief that Christ reigns in heaven; in his opinion, however, he is incarcerated in such a way that even if he should will it, he could not see the miserable earth in his body until the end of time. And Augustine, in the book *De civitate Dei*, says: "Each and every one of the saints will have entered into so great a glory, that wherever the spirit wills to be, there the body would immediately be as well."[92] Berengarius maintains, then, that Christ has come to such great impotence, that he who raised [1466 C] his own body from earth to heaven, cannot return to the earth, even for an

---

89. Acts 15.9.   90. 1 Pt 3.21.
91. Acts 3.21.
92. *De civitate Dei* 22.30 (ed. Dumbart and Kalb, CSL, 48/3, 862, line 19 = PL 41: 802).

hour, until the end of time. O overwhelmingly blind vanity, and
vain blindness! For who, speaking with the common use of language, would fear to say: "For this many months, or for this many
years, he has lived in that city," even if he walked daily out of the
boundaries of the city to his work? In the Gospel it is written
about Anna that she never left the Temple,[93] when nevertheless
bodily necessity would often call her away from it. If for that reason we were to say that Christ bodily descends to the earth daily,
the thought of St. Peter would not oppose us. But far be this
from the prudence of Christians, that we should say that, for
Christ to be sacrificed or eaten upon the earth, it would be necessary for him to depart the heavens for a time. For he is wholly
in heaven while his whole body is truly [1466 D] eaten upon the
earth. And because of the strength of divine power, no one
should judge this thought incredible, both from the above mentioned examples, as well as the elementary proofs of the voice
and the soul.

NECESSITY DERIVED FROM THE SACRAMENTS OF THE ALTAR BEING CALLED "BREAD AND WINE"

52. In fact, who could now hold back laughter after hearing Berengarius interpreting the Lord's words about the sacraments? He says, "This, my body, is necessarily bread, and this cup
is necessarily wine." O most impudent foolishness, obviously not
seeing what he should be saying, or where he is going! For what
is this "necessity," that it should be understood so necessarily to
be bread and wine, when the opposite could be just as reasonably said: "This [hoc], you hear a body implied, now no longer
bread, is my body; and this [hic], you hear a drink implied,[94] now
no longer wine, is the cup of my blood"? Or certainly in this way:
"This [hoc], up until now understood to be bread, [1467 A] from
this time forward is my body, not bread; and this cup, thus far
understood to be wine, from this time forward is my blood, not

93. Lk 2.37.

94. Migne says *potius,* but Hurter believes that the text should read *potus,*
which agrees with the 1529 Freiburg manuscript, published by Ioannes Faber
(heretofore, "Faber edition").

wine." Or certainly in this way, without these "understandings": *hoc* in fact is not a relative pronoun in regard to the aforementioned sayings, but rather a demonstrative one.[95] And therefore the bread and wine, which above were named in the Gospel, are understood here with none of his "necessity."

53. Now what follows distresses me, and I am embarrassed because of it. For who could believe, save that he would show himself as such, that someone could call himself a man and carry on with such puerility and worthless foolishness? But let us see whether or not so great a rationalizer will have arrived anywhere, accomplished anything, or proven something by way of these most "necessary understandings." "It is by this," he says, "that they call the sacraments of the altar 'bread and wine.'"[96] Did that whole effort therefore [1467 B] strain toward this conclusion? Is it to this only that you have so spent yourself, that you should not spare yourself in your old age, and show yourself a most calumnious sophist instead of a glorious disputant, and instead of a skilled craftsman, a most lifeless and inept sewer of rags? For who denies it? Who does not freely confess that the sacraments of the Lord's table are rightly called bread and wine, either because they were first bread and wine, or because once they are substantially changed [*substantialiter transmutata*], they preserve the likeness [*similitudo*] of bread and wine? For so the serpent that was made from a staff is called a staff. In fact, it is written: "Aaron's staff devoured their staffs";[97] that is, the serpent that had been made from Aaron's staff [devoured] their ser-

95. Guitmund's distinction here between the use of the pronoun in the demonstrative, rather than in the relative, sense could be restated in the following way. In the words of consecration, *Hoc est corpus meum,* the pronoun *hoc* indicates demonstratively "this here present before you is my body," as opposed to the relative sense, which would be "this bread present before you, which is my body." Thus Guitmund's realism, as opposed to Berengarius's symbolism, presents an identity between the bread and the body of Christ through the use of the demonstrative pronoun *hoc.*   hoc = realism

96. Both the Migne and Hurter edition read: "Hoc, inquit, ut sacramenta altaris panis *dicatur* et vinum," but the Faber edition says, "Hoc, inquit, ut sacramenta altaris panis *dicant* et vinum," which is how the sentence should read based on its context.

97. Ex 7.12.

pents. And so man, because he is made from it, is often called earth, dust, and clay. [1467 C] So too, because of the similarity, the Apostle says: "The rock was Christ."[98] And in the Psalm [of David][99] it is sung: "I am a worm and not a man,"[100] although he is substantially [*substantialiter*] a man, but only a worm in likeness. And so there are many other examples beyond number. If, therefore, many things, on account of these and other reasons, are rightly called by words that designate far different things, how much more, on account of each of these reasons, can our sacraments, retaining many similarities to the things that they were, although substantially [*substantialiter*] they would hold the truth of the Lord's own body and blood, rightly be called bread and wine?

DIFFICULTY FROM THE COLLECT OF A CERTAIN MASS ADDRESSED

54. Furthermore, we shall now see what objections Berengarius advances on the authority of a prayer of the Church. "The Church," he says, "in a certain Mass prays in this fashion: [1467 D] 'May your sacraments perfect in us, we beseech you, O Lord, what they contain, so that what we do now handle in appearance [*species*], we may receive in true reality.'[101] This prayer then shows that we do not have the true reality, but the appearance [*species*]." Well done, O good analyst, but of what realities are they the appearance and not the reality? You will respond, "Of the body and blood of the Lord." Well. Consider diligently what is said and answer me. What is it that we now handle in appearance? You will reply, "We eat the body of the Lord in appearance and not in substance." Add on the following: "Let us [1468 A] 'receive in true reality.'" Why? Will we eat the body and blood of the Lord truly and substantively in the age to come? Indeed, this is what is prayed: that what we now do in appearance—whatever

98. 1 Cor 10.4.   99. Faber edition only.
100. Ps 21.7.
101. *Corpus orationum,* v. 6, "Orationes in ieiunio mensis septimi, die sabati in XII lectionibus, oratio ad complendum seu post communionem" (ed. B. Wallant, n. 4219, 233 = PL 78: 142D).

it is—we may receive the very same thing in reality. Therefore, if we always eat the body of Christ in shadow in this age, as you fantasize, it remains that we eat it substantially in the next age. But do not think to hide yourself any longer if the way you interpret the aforementioned prayer is absurd and foolish.

55. From the beginning of the prayer, let us diligently examine what the writing wished to say. "May your sacraments perfect in us, we beseech you, O Lord, what they contain." We said above, and we proved in the words of the blessed Apostle Paul, that the divine sacraments designate [1468 B] the unity of the body of Christ which is the Church, and that this is what they contain in signification. Therefore, the Church prays that we may be the one body in Christ, one Church, namely, that which is signified, so that now, that is, when we eat, these sacraments may truly perfect in us the one body of Christ and the one Church which they signify. This, I believe, is a possible understanding and one that is most appropriate for the prayer and most useful for us. The blessed Apostle Paul proves this, and the faith of the whole Church agrees with it. No authority defends the madness of the adversary, however, [1468 C] but rather the whole Church flees from it as a death-giving poison. There is no usefulness for him whatsoever; the prayer itself does not commend his position, but rather an intolerable absurdity which follows his position makes it completely worthless. Who should be hindered in any way, then, by such a bestial, foolish, and totally impossible understanding, when there is a reasonable and proper understanding that should be embraced by all the wise? So you think that this suffices, or do you need more?

Roger

For me, it is more than sufficient, and I marvel at the ruined heretic, prostrate in his own objections and caught in his own snares.

Guitmund

56. Indeed, [1468 D] these are the things from the books of St. Augustine, or from the name of sacrament, or from the prayer just now discussed, that we find that Berengarius is accustomed

to advance as an objection against our faith. If, however, he raises some other objections from St. Augustine, I say, trusting in the power of Christ, that they will be diligently researched, and either will favor us or will not contradict us. Accordingly, let us put an end to this disputation, and we will address those things that remain, if the Lord wills, in another beginning.

THIRD BOOK

RATIONALE OF THE CURRENT WORK

Guitmund

T HIS DISCUSSION has thus far dissolved the arguments that the enemy was trying to advance against the Church from reason and the holy writings. [1469 A] In fact, the stratagems of the enemy would have been thoroughly frustrated, with the help of God, even had we supplied no more than the general custom of the Catholic faith. And this alone should have been enough for you. For only that faith should be held most firmly, even if strongly impugned, which is the Catholic faith. For whoever wishes to be saved—just as the holy Fathers have confirmed and the whole world agrees—must hold the Catholic faith. But if this Catholic faith must be held fast when strongly attacked, how much more so should it not be abandoned when it shows itself invincible in the face of all its challenges? But many more arguments, with the help of God, can still be added to strengthen our position and destroy that of the enemy's. And I know from your entreaties that you desire thirstily that I offer, with God's favor, something from the holy writings—something which would not only more thoroughly destroy the enemy's deceit, but also by its own arguments, show more fully the invincible strength of our position. [1469 B] Therefore, following the line of questioning [that has been adopted thus far], let us first prove that we eat the true body of Christ in his substance, and not in Berengarian shadow, and then the discussion will take care to refute the Bread-Minglers[1] of the body of the Lord.

---

1. Latin: *Impanatores*. Word coined by Guitmund to describe those of the Berengarian party who accept the truth of the Real Presence, yet deny transubstantiation, and hold that the flesh and blood of Christ is somehow "hidden" in

173

PROOF OF THE REAL PRESENCE
FROM ST. AUGUSTINE

2. Since it was said in the beginning of our discussion that
the source of almost all the scandal seems to be from St. Augustine, we should first examine what the same most noble doctor
thinks about the sacrifice of the Church, in his exposition on the
[1469 C] Thirty-Third Psalm. For Augustine, treating how David
was carrying himself in his own hands before Abimelech, says:

> Therefore, brothers, who can understand how this can happen to a
> man? For who is carried in his own hands? A man can be carried in
> the hands of others, but not in his own. How this can be understood
> in the case of David literally, we do not know; however, we do know it in
> the case of Christ. For Christ carried himself in his own hands when he
> said: "This is my body" [Mt 26.26]; for he was holding that very body in
> his hands when he spoke.[2]

O thought most lucid! O thought most trustworthy! O thought
truly most worthy of the most blessed and most excellent doctor
Augustine, from which we in no way should shrink, and [whose
counsel] should be [1469 D] most reverently heeded by all! What
in David, he says, and in other men cannot be found in accordance with the literal sense, is found in Christ. What is that? "For
Christ," he says, "was carried in his own hands, when he handed
over his body, saying: 'This is my body.'" If it is according to the
literal sense, that is, just as the letter sounds, that this is found in
Christ, then what was carried was the body of Christ, in neither a
shadowy nor a figurative fashion, but rather in a substantive one
[substantive]. For if, as it applies to Christ and that which was carried in his own hands, those men would have the pronoun hoc be
understood as according to figure, and [1470 A] not according to
the substance of his body, how then is that found there according to the letter? Is Christ ever, according to the letter, a rock, or
a lion, or a lamb, or a serpent, when he would be all these things

---

the bread and wine, without a change in substance. I have called them "Bread-
Minglers," based on Guitmund's description of them.

2. *Enarrationes in psalmos* 33.1.10 (ed. D. Dekkers, CSL 38, 280–81, lines 1–8
= PL 36: 306). Augustine, *Expositions of the Psalms: 33–50*, trans. M. Boulding,
WSA 3/16 (Hyde Park, NY: New City Press, 2002), 21.

according to figure? By no means. "But we find it in Christ," he says; "how then is it understood in accordance with the literal sense?" It is not possible to construe this statement in any other way; so what he concedes about Christ he denies about David. Therefore, it must not be understood as they would have it, that is, according to figure, but rather, according to substance. I beg every prudent reader, then, to note carefully how effectively all sophistries of those heretics are thus excluded.

3. Therefore, we shall present here, if it pleases, what the adversaries can say about this matter, so that what follows may shine forth more clearly. [1470 C] For when he says: "Christ was being carried in his own hands," and then, "He was holding that very body in his hands"; if our adversaries for their part explain it this way: "'Christ was being carried in his own hands,' that is, 'only the shadow or figure of Christ, not the substance of Christ, was carried in his own hands,' and he carried 'that body,' that is, the shadow or figure of that body, not the substance"; if this, I say, is the way in which they explain it, we can find this same thing in David, this same thing in almost all men. For who among men could not carry some figure of himself in his own hands, in which his substance would not be present (for example, a statue or a picture)? "But this," he says, "we do not find in David himself, and no one is carried in his own hands. In Christ, however," he says, "we find it." Because, [1470 C] he says, that is found in Christ which is not found in David and other men, in the way that [passage] is understood—although they can easily understand that David and the rest of men can carry in their hands some figure of themselves, in which there would be nothing of their substance—it stands most clearly according to Augustine, to be believed without any scruple, therefore, that Christ was not carrying merely a figure or a shadow of himself, as our adversaries say, but in fact the substance of his own body.

4. What will the Shadow-Lovers[3] respond to this? Where, in such great light, will our light-fleers[4] seek a shadow? Behold, the most manifest proofs from Augustine are recited; nothing in

---

3. Latin: *Umbratici.*
4. Latin: *lucifugae.*

them is a stone to stumble on; nothing in them is ambiguous. Let them either defend themselves about these things or stop bringing up Augustine against us; and, as Augustine testifies, let them believe with us [1470 D] in the truth of the Lord's body. But perhaps they had not noticed this text. For if they had carefully considered it, they would not have drawn their heresy from St. Augustine. For whatever they cull from it for themselves, an attentive inspection of it, just as we have said, either makes a case for us, or certainly not against us. In truth, now that we advance this [understanding of the text], it so manifestly destroys them, that, try as they may to avoid it, they can still find no reasoned argument to refute it. Indeed, it is so clear a text, it is so thoroughly cautious, that [1471 A] their garrulity can find no shifty arguments [to contradict it].

5. But I shall now briefly demonstrate the extent of this passage's excellence: it can only be that it was either substantively the body of Christ that Christ was carrying, about which he said: "This is my body," or it was only figuratively. But if only figuratively, they cannot accept those words which preceded it, "because that which is not found in other men is found in Christ"; otherwise, it would be found in others, too. Indeed, every man can carry a figure of himself that would be devoid of his own substance. "But in other men," he says, "it is not found." "No one," he says, "is carried in his own hands." Therefore, it cannot be in figure or shadow, but rather in a substantive way that Christ was carrying the body of Christ.

6. I cannot satisfactorily express how much I delight in these words of St. Augustine, and how much I marvel over that miserable blindness of theirs. [1471 B] For example, from these words it can clearly be shown what the same most blessed man wanted understood, immediately afterward in an exposition on the same Thirty-Third Psalm, where he said: "We must draw near to him to receive his body and blood. They were plunged into darkness in the presence of the Crucified; we are illumined by eating and drinking the Crucified."[5] And again in another place

5. *Enarrationes in psalmos* 33.2.10 (ed. E. Dekkers–J. Fraipont, CSL 38, 288, lines 11–14 = PL 36: 314). Augustine, *Expositions of the Psalms: 33–50,* trans. M. Boulding, WSA 3/16: 31.

he says, "Receive in bread this which hung upon the cross, and in the cup this which flowed from the side of Christ."[6] And in another place: "Believers later drank that which raging men had earlier poured out."[7] Again in another place, which we have already quoted above: "Christ took earth from earth, because flesh comes from the earth; and he received his flesh from the flesh of Mary. He walked here below, in that flesh he walked, and even gave us that same flesh to eat for our salvation."[8] And there is a great number of [1471 C] other passages in many of his books [that speak] in this way. When, therefore, they revere and hold St. Augustine's writings as sacrosanct, even inviolable, what else can hinder them from believing as we do, except perchance their longtime blindness?

PROOF OF THE REAL PRESENCE FROM ST. AMBROSE

7. But you as well, distinguished doctor, most blessed Ambrose, spiritual father of St. Augustine, whom the same most holy man in his books calls holy and blessed, and whose authority (Augustine has testified)[9] as revealer of the martyrs the Apostle Paul commended;[10] a man whom St. Gregory, himself a clearly apostolic man, considered above himself;[11] whose doctrine most blessed

6. *Sermon* 228B.2, "Ad infantes" (PL 46: 827). Augustine: "Hoc agnoscite in pane quod pependit in cruce; hoc in calice, quod manavit ex latere." Guitmund replaces "agnoscite," with "accipite." *Sermons,* WSA 3/6: 262. See also book 2, chapters 44–47, of the present work.

7. *Sermon* 352.2, *De utilitate agendae poenitentiae* 2 (PL 39: 1550). Augustine: "Tunc eis annuntiavit eum colendum quem crucifixerunt, ut ejus jam sanguinem biberent credentes, quem fuderant saevientes." Guitmund: "Hoc biberunt, postea credentes, quod prius fuderant saevientes."

8. *Enarrationes in psalmos* 98.9 (ed. E. Dekkers–I. Fraipont, CSL 39, 1385, lines 21–23 = PL 37: 1264). Guitmund adds "Christus," so that it reads, "Suscepit Christus de terra. . . ." Augustine, *Expositions of the Psalms: 73–98,* WSA 3/18: 474.

9. See *Confessions* 9.7.16, and the finding of the bodies of Sts. Gervase and Protase.

10. According to Hurter, this passage refers to a letter once attributed to Ambrose, where he says that the Apostle Paul appeared to him, and told him of the place where the bodies of certain martyrs could be found. See p. 123, n.1

11. See *Epistle* 48, *Ad Leandrum Episcopum Hispalensem,* PL 77: 497C. On the issue of the valid means of baptism, Ambrose was considered as one who faithfully transmitted the apostolic tradition of the faith.

Benedict judged worthy of reception (as attested to by St. Gregory himself);[12] a man filled with the spirit of the holy prophets;
to whom the glory of the whole Church of Milan [1471 D] has especially attested; and whose meritorious faith the whole world
has reverently embraced (for so many and such great witnesses
would not have lauded you with such great public acclamation if
you had been known to err in the Catholic faith): explain, I say,
what you think about the sacraments of the altar.

8. Certainly you have said in your book *De sacramentis:* "Just as
our Lord Jesus Christ is the true Son of God, not as other men
by way of grace, but a Son by way of nature, as it were, that is,
from the substance of the Father, so it is in the same way that it
is his true flesh that we eat and his true blood that we drink."[13] I
hold, therefore, that you, Ambrose, have said that it is his true
flesh that we eat and his true blood that we drink. But to what
extent is it true? Figuratively or substantively? Teach us, through
the proposed comparison, how we are to understand this as
true: "Just as [1472 A] our Lord Jesus Christ is the true Son of
God," is still not enough. For one can be a son of God, just as
other just men are sons of God through grace, and he himself,
insofar as he is man, can be said to be a true Son of God by
grace, although ineffably greater and more excellent than other
men. You then add, however, what is enough, that is: "Not as
other men through grace, but as a Son by nature, that is, from
the substance of the Father." So it is in this way, then, that you
say that it is his true flesh we eat, and his true blood we drink.
How is it true in this way? It is true, not as the other things,
which, on account of some grace of signification, can be called
the flesh and blood of Christ (just as, for example, through the
grace of a figure, the flesh and blood of the immolated paschal
lamb in Egypt[14] can be called the flesh and blood of Christ; also,
in the same way, [1472 B] the manna and the many other similar
examples), but rather, the flesh and blood of Christ is true flesh

---

12. See *Dialogi* 2.23, PL 66: 177D. Also, a study of the rule of St. Benedict
shows that he drew extensively from the works of Ambrose.

13. Ambrose, *De sacramentis* 6.1 (ed. Faller, CSEL 73, 72, lines 1–4 = PL 16:
453C–454D).

14. Ex 12.5–8.

and blood by way of nature. For the analogy does not fit in any
other way, except that what it denies there, we should deny here;
what it affirms there, we should affirm here. Wherefore, if we follow this similitude so expressly placed, we must confess that what
we receive from the altar is substantially the flesh and blood of
Christ. For if it had been said: "Just as our Lord Jesus Christ is
the true Son of God, so it is his true flesh that we eat, and his
true blood which we drink," it could still be (as it has been said)
an ambiguous thought. For our Lord Jesus Christ, according to
his humanity, is the true Son of God, [1472 C] but by way of grace
as we have said, and not from the substance of the Father.[15] And
in this way it could be said that we receive his true flesh by the
grace of a figure, not by way of the substance of his flesh; and
similarly about the blood. But if the most excellent doctor
thought that, he would not have added anything further. For
why was it necessary to add what would be so evidently contrary
to this sense? The conclusion is now diligently added, however,
which says: "not as other men by way of grace," and lest perchance there remain any little cloud of error, he subjoins: "but a
Son by way of nature." And lest even this should seem obscure,
he expressly states: "that is, from the substance of the Father." All
these conclusions (I say) are most diligently joined [to the state-
ment]: "It is his true flesh that we eat, and his true blood that we
drink," which excludes all the [1472 D] calumnious argumentation of the enemy, and shows the flesh and blood of Christ to be
substantively what we eat and drink. Therefore, if you do not dispute against yourself, O blessed Ambrose, you do not dissent
from the faith. If, however, you do not dissent, it is more beneficial to imitate you than Berengarius.

9. You have plainly seen what the most noble doctor thinks in
this place, without any veil, about the sacraments of the altar.
Now briefly attend to what he also says in another place in the
same book: "Why," he says, "do we use arguments? Let us use his

15. Guitmund's Christological distinction is that the human nature of Christ
enjoys the fullness of grace because of its hypostatic union with the Second Person of the Blessed Trinity, but could not be properly called "of the same substance of the Father," which applies in the proper sense only to the divine nature of Christ.

examples, and by the example of the Incarnation, let us illustrate the truth of the mystery. It is clear that the Virgin conceived contrary to the course of nature. And this body which we
confect [1473 A] is from the Virgin. Why do you seek here the order of nature in the body of Christ, when the Lord Jesus himself
was born of the Virgin beyond the order of nature?"[16] What better statement, I ask, do you seek? What clearer statement? For if
the sacraments of the altar were only a shadow or figure of the
Lord's body, what would happen here beyond the order of nature? For a rock is not beyond the order of nature, but rather
because of the stability of its nature it symbolizes Christ. A lamb
is not beyond the order of nature, but rather it is through its nature, that is, through its innocence, that it, and in a similar way
other things, symbolize Christ. Consequently, if we were to discuss all the testimony from St. Ambrose that could be brought
against Berengarius, it would be tedious, so let us now move on
to other authors.

TESTIMONY OF ST. LEO THE GREAT ON
THE REAL PRESENCE

10. The most holy pope, most ancient Leo, whom all the
Church of God venerates, said in a certain sermon:

And therefore, you should communicate with the Holy Table [1473 B]
in a way in which you have absolutely no doubt about the truth of the
body and blood of Christ. For what is consumed by the mouth is believed by faith. And in vain *Amen* is responded by those who dispute
against that which they receive.[17]

TESTIMONY OF ST. CYRIL OF ALEXANDRIA
ON THE REAL PRESENCE

11. St. Cyril also, together with the two hundred bishops of
the council of Ephesus, which St. Gregory thought should be
held on a par with the Four Evangelists, says thus:

16. Ambrose, *In libro de sacramentis* = *De mysteriis* 9.53 (ed. O. Faller, CSEL 73,
112, lines 45–46 and 51–52 = PL 16: 407A).
17. Leo the Great, *Sermon* 91.3, *De jejunio septimi mensis*, PL 54: 452B.

We approach the spiritual blessings and are sanctified, having been made sharers in the holy body and precious blood of Christ the Redeemer of us all: receiving it, not as ordinary flesh, God forbid, nor as the flesh of a man sanctified and joined to the Word according to a unity of dignity or as one possessing a divine indwelling, but rather as vivifying and made the very own body of the Word himself. For he is by nature life as he exists as God, because he who has united himself to his own flesh is confessed to be vivifying. Therefore, although he says: "Amen, Amen, I say to you, unless you eat the flesh of the Son of Man and drink his blood" [Jn 6.54], we should not think of it as one man from among ourselves (for how could the flesh of a man be vivifying by its own nature?). But as his very own it has been truly made, who for our sake has been made and is called the Son of Man.[18]

And again:

If someone does not confess the flesh of the Lord to be vivifying, and the very flesh of the Word of the Father, but flesh other than his own, joined to him by way of dignity, as if it were a divine indwelling and not vivifying, since it has been made the very flesh of the Word so that it might have the ability to vivify, let such a one be an anathema.[19]

But Berengarius, who did not fear the anathema of those two hundred pontiffs, proposed and added his own anathema, which he professed in an oath with his own mouth at Rome, and in his madness he ran upon his own sword.

PROOF OF THE REAL PRESENCE FROM
ST. GREGORY THE GREAT

12. St. Gregory, too, says in a homily: "And indeed you have learned what the blood of the lamb is, not now by instruction, but by drinking. For the blood that is placed on each of the door posts is now received not only by the mouth of the body, but also by the mouth of the heart."[20] Likewise, in the last book of the *Dialogi* he says:

18. "Cyril's Third Letter Against Nestorius," *Ep. Synodica* (ed. E. Schwartz, *Concilium Universale Ephesinum*, V/1, 240, lines 8–18).

19. "Cyril's Third Letter Against Nestorius," *12 Anathemata*, 11 (ibid., 244, lines 8–12).

20. Gregory the Great, *Homily* 22.9, "On the Gospels," PL 76: 1178B.

This sacrifice alone has the power of saving the soul from eternal death, for it presents to us mystically the death of the Only-begotten Son. [1474 A] Though "he is now risen from the dead and dies no more," and "death no longer has power over him" [Rom 6.9], yet, living himself immortal and incorruptible, he is again immolated for us in the mystery of this holy Sacrifice. Where his body is eaten, there his flesh is distributed among the people for their salvation. His blood no longer stains the hands of the godless, but flows into the mouths of his faithful followers. See, then, how august the Sacrifice that is offered for us, ever reproducing in itself the Passion of the Only-begotten Son for the remission of our sins. For who of the faithful can have any doubt that at the moment of the immolation, at the sound of the priest's voice, the heavens stand open and choirs of angels are present at the mystery of Jesus Christ. There the lowliest is united with the most sublime, earth is joined to heaven, [1474 B] the visible and the invisible somehow merge into one.[21]

For this reason, right here and now, those Shadow-Lovers, whom so many and such great authors oppose by irrefutable authority, should be silent. They should consider again and again not only what in many places St. Jerome, what Isidore, what Bede, but also what all the distinguished, excellent doctors—both Greek and Latin—teach about the body of the Lord, and they should, in yielding to so many and such great doctors, put an end to their error. For we ought not to discuss all of them because of the tedium of a lengthy work, when those which we have discussed cannot be reasonably contradicted.

PROOF OF THE REAL PRESENCE FROM ST. HILARY

13. I wish to draw into the center of the discussion, however, the most blessed Hilary, bishop of Poiters, in his own time almost the only pillar of faith, the teacher of most holy Martin, who was received with the highest devotion by St. Augustine and the rest of the later doctors as well, [1474 C] and by the entire Church of God. For truly I think it would be most agreeable to attend well to what this marvelous disputer thought about the

---

21. *Dialogi* 4.60 (ed. A. De Vogüé, SCh 265, p. 200, line 9, to p. 202, line 24 = PL 77: 425C–428A). *Saint Gregory the Great: Dialogues,* trans. O. J. Zimmerman, FC 39 (New York: Fathers of the Church, Inc., 1959), 272–73 (slightly modified).

Eucharist of the Lord in book eight of the *De Trinitate*.[22] In fact, disputing against the Arians, so as to show that the Father is substantially in the Son, he proved the Son himself to be substantially in us through the Eucharist in this way:

I now ask those who introduce a unity of will between the Father and the Son, whether Christ is in us by the truth of his nature or by the harmony of the will? If the Word has indeed become flesh, and we indeed receive the Word made flesh in the Lord's food, how are we not to believe that he dwells in us by his nature, [1474 D] he who, when he was born as man, has assumed the nature of our flesh that is bound inseparably with himself, and has mingled the nature of his flesh to his eternal nature, in the mystery of the flesh that was to be communicated to us? All of us are one in this manner because the Father is in Christ, and Christ is in us. Therefore, whoever will deny that the Father is not in Christ by his nature [*naturaliter*], let him first deny that he is not in Christ by his nature, or that Christ is not present within him, because the Father in Christ and Christ in us cause us to be one in them. If, therefore, Christ has truly taken the flesh of our body, and that man who was born from Mary is truly Christ, and we truly receive the flesh of his body in the mystery (and we are one, therefore, because the Father is in him and he is in us), how [1475 A] can you assert a unity of will, since the attribute of the nature of the sacrament is the mystery of the perfect unity? We should not talk about the things of God in a human or worldly sense, nor should the perversity of a strange and impious knowledge be extorted from the soundness of the heavenly words by a violent and imprudent manner of teaching. Let us read what has been written, and understand what we have read, and then we shall fulfill the duty of perfect faith. We speak in an absurd and godless manner about the truth of Christ's nature in us—the subject which we are discussing—unless we have learned it from him. He himself declares: "For my flesh is food indeed, and my blood is drink indeed. He who eats my flesh and drinks my blood abides in me and I in him" [Jn 6.56, 57]. He has left no room to raise doubt about the true nature of the body and blood, for according to the statement of the Lord himself as well as our faith, this is indeed flesh and blood. And these [1475 B] things that we eat and drink bring it about that we are in Christ and Christ is in us. Is this not the truth? Those who deny that Jesus Christ is the true God are welcome to regard these words as false. He himself, therefore, is in us through his flesh, and we are in him, while [according to this, that which we are is in God himself]. How deeply we are in him through

22. Hilary of Poitiers, *De Trinitate* 8.13–16 (ed. P. Smulders, CSL 62 A, 325, line 5–328, line 18 = PL 10: 247–49). Guitmund's version varies only slightly from the original, and these variances are noted within the body of the text.

the sacrament of the flesh and blood that has been communicated to
us is evident from his own testimony, when he declares: "And the world
no longer sees me. But you shall see me, for I live, and you shall live.
In that day you shall know that I am in my Father and you in me and I
in you" [Jn 14.19]. If he wished us to understand only a unity of will,
why did he explain, as it were, the steps and the order of unity [1475 C]
that was to be brought about, unless it were that, while he was in the
Father by the nature of the Godhead, we, on the other hand, should be
in him by his corporeal birth, and again that we should believe that he
would dwell in us by the mystery of the sacraments, and thus the perfect unity would be taught by means of the Mediator, since he himself
remains in the Father while we remain in him, and while he remains
in the Father he remains in us, and in this manner we would arrive at
the unity of the Father, since we would also be in the nature of him
[the Son], who is in the nature of him [the Father], while he himself
[the Son] ever remains in us by his nature. He himself thus testifies
how natural is this unity in us: "He who eats my flesh and drinks my
blood, abides in me and I in him" [Jn 6.56]. No one will be in him unless he himself has been in him, while he has assumed and taken upon
himself the flesh of him only who has received his own. [1475 D] Previously, he had already given an explanation of this perfect unity when
he declared: "As the living Father has sent me, and as I live through the
Father, so he who shall eat my flesh shall live through me" [Jn 6.58].
Consequently, he lives through the Father, and, as he lives through the
Father, we live in the same manner through his flesh. Every illustration
is adapted to the nature of our understanding in order that we may
grasp the matter under discussion by means of the example that is set
before us. Accordingly, this is the cause of our life: that we who are carnal have Christ dwelling in us through his flesh, and through him we
shall live in that state in which he lives through the Father. Hence, if
we live through him by his nature according to the flesh, [1476 A] that
is, have received the nature of his flesh, why should he not possess the
Father in himself by his nature according to the Spirit, since he himself
lives through the Father?[23]

HILARY'S 'NATURALITER' MEANS 'SUBSTANTIALITER'

14. I wanted to place here the entire sequence of thought
from the aforementioned book of St. Hilary for this reason: so
that the reasoned, attentive examination of this entire discussion might teach us with unchanging certitude what St. Hilary

23. *Saint Hilary of Poitiers: The Trinity,* trans. S. McKenna, FC 25 (New York:
Fathers of the Church, Inc., 1954), 285–87 (slightly modified).

believes about the truth of the Lord's body that we receive from
the altar. For indeed this marvelous disputer proves that the Father is naturally [*naturaliter*] in the Son, that is, substantially
[*substantialiter*]. For this "naturally" should not be understood in
any other way. For the whole matter against the Arians revolved
on the substantial unity of the Father and the Son. Nor could it
be the case that such an expert disputant would have gone to
such great lengths to prove [that substantial unity], unless it
were in fact the question. And he proves in this way that [1476 B]
naturally, that is substantially, the Son himself is in us. For that
word "naturally" ought not be understood in any other way. For
if it is understood in any other way, the whole disputation itself
wavers. Indeed, how could he prove a substantial unity between
the Father and Christ, if our own unity with Christ were not a
substantial one, since it was adduced to prove the unity between
the Father and the Son? If our own unity with Christ were not
substantial, the Arians could say the same about the Father and
Son's unity, and confirm that it must be understood in this way
by the authority of the very same passage which says: "Every illustration is adapted to the nature of our understanding in order
that we may grasp the matter under discussion by means of the
example that is set before us." Therefore, it stands both with the
disputation's reasoning, and with the cogent authority of this
same man, that "naturally" ought to be understood in place of
"substantially."

Use of tradition to make point about current debate

PROOF OF THE REAL PRESENCE IMPLIED IN HILARY'S
ARGUMENT AGAINST THE ARIANS

15. From this, the preeminent disputant constructs a syllogism this way: If Christ is in us naturally, that is, substantially, not
merely through a harmony of the will, then the Father is in
Christ naturally, that is, substantially, not merely through a harmony of the will. The assumption follows this proposition from
the antecedent in this way: Christ is naturally, that is, substantially in us, not merely through a harmony of the will. Which assumption he, having marvelous expertise in forensic questioning, preferred to place in such a way so as to force the response
by the question, when he says: "I now ask those who introduce a

harmony of the will between the Father and the Son, whether [1476 D] Christ is in us today by the truth of his nature or by a harmony of will?" Then comes the proof of this assumption: "If the Word has indeed become flesh, and we indeed receive the Word made flesh in the Lord's food, how are we not to believe that he dwells in us naturally, he who, when he was born as man, has assumed the nature of our flesh that is bound inseparably to himself, and has mingled the nature of his flesh to his eternal nature (understood as contained under the sacrament), in the flesh that was to be communicated to us?" And all the rest that follows forces that conclusion.   *he dwells in us naturally*

16. And it is almost as if you were asking: How do I know that we receive the Word made flesh in the food of the Lord, or that he joined the nature of his flesh under the sacrament of his flesh that is to be communicated to us? [1477 A] "About the truth," he says, "of the flesh and blood, he has left no room to raise doubts." Why he has left no room for doubt, he subsequently proves, saying: "for according to the statement of the Lord himself as well as our faith, this is indeed flesh and blood." And how it is both the profession of the Lord himself and our faith, that it is both true flesh and true blood, he then demonstrates next by saying: "We should not talk about the things of God in a human or worldly sense, nor should the perversity of a strange and impious knowledge be extorted from the soundness of the heavenly words by a violent and imprudent manner of teaching. Let us read what has been written and understand what we have read, and then we shall fulfill the duty of perfect faith. We speak [1477 B] in an absurd and godless manner about the truth of Christ's nature in us—the subject which we are discussing—unless we have learned it from him. He himself declares: 'For my flesh is food indeed, and my blood is drink indeed. He who eats my flesh and drinks my blood abides in me, and I in him'" [Jn 6.56-57].

Christ declares Jn 6.56

17. Certainly it should be asked here: "Who are those who 'talk about the things of God in a human or worldly sense'?" Are they not those who, having put out the inner lights, rationalize about the heavenly mysteries according to external senses, like men conformed to the present age? Men, I say, who extort impi-

ous understanding from heavenly sayings? Are they those who read what has been written in the way that Hilary prescribes, and just as they read simply, they understand clearly, without any addition of their own? Or are they those who distort and reject the Scripture and what it proclaims, [1477 C] and put in its place certain symbolisms that they have decided upon in their own hearts? Certainly they who simply understand it, just as they have read it, do not distort Scripture, nor do violence to it. Therefore, in St. Hilary's judgment, those who understand the words of the Savior in a perverse and impious way are those who have contempt for a simple understanding, and consequently transform its meaning into a figurative sense, or into whatever else pleases them.   ✗ we should not have contempt for a simple understay

18. After he proved by these words of the Lord that "we truly receive the Word made flesh in the Lord's food," he returns to the minor premise of his syllogism, and shows that Christ is in us not only by harmony, but also substantially, saying: "And these things that we receive bring it about that we are in Christ and Christ is in us. Is this not the truth? Those who deny [1477 D] that Jesus Christ is the true God are welcome to regard these words as false." And to this all the rest are also referred, which up until the conclusion have been inferred. From there, the argument now—for the purpose of a conclusion—faithfully approaches the minor premise (with its own sufficient proof artfully and most briefly repeated in this way): "Hence, if we live through him by his nature according to the flesh, that is, have received the nature of his flesh, why should he not possess the Father in himself by his nature according to the Spirit, since he himself lives through the Father?"

SHADOW-LOVERS REFUTED BY HILARY'S SYLLOGISM

19. Our Shadow-Lovers,[24] therefore, would evade this syllogism of St. Hilary, if they could. Pay attention, O Shadow-Lovers, because the syllogism proves that by the taking-in of this food Christ is substantially within us. When we receive this food, therefore,

24. See n. 3, above.

we receive the substance of Christ. How [1478 A] then is it proved from the fact that "we receive the Word made flesh in the Lord's food," that Christ is substantially in us, if only a shadow of Christ is in this food, and not the substance of Christ? Or how can these elements, eaten and drunk, bring it about that Christ is in us substantively, if he is not in them themselves, save only in shadow? How is it, I say, that, if we receive the Word made flesh in food, as a consequence Christ remains substantially within us? What is the necessity of this proof? How is this a consequence? Indeed, there is no necessity, there is no consequence, if, where there is a figure of some reality, there would consequently be the substance of the same reality. For if I should say to someone: "On this wall is your substance, because your image is there," [1478 B] would he not say that I am insane? But neither would anyone have said, when the lamb of the Law was being consumed, that consequently the substance of Christ would be there, since that paschal lamb is indeed a shadow and figure of Christ. Truly, who would dare to say, when Moses suspended the bronze serpent in the desert,[25] that there the substance of Christ was suspended, since that bronze serpent prefigured the substance of Christ hanging upon the tree?[26] Therefore, if, through Hilary's assertion that Christ is in us substantially, it has been demonstrated that we receive the flesh and blood of Christ in the food of the Lord, which, when they are eaten and drunk, bring it about that Christ is in us, and we are naturally one in Christ, who has assumed fleshly nature, then there is no other result, as we have shown, that can be [1478 C] proved by that except that the substance of the body and blood of Christ is truly in the Lord's food. It is most obvious that this most prudent debater, Hilary, who wished to confirm his assertion this way, believed that we receive the substance of the body and blood of the Lord in the food of the Lord, not the shadow or figure only, as those Shadow-Lovers would wickedly imagine.

20. To put the force of the whole argument on the table as concisely as possible, St. Hilary believed that we receive the Word made flesh either in shadow or substantively. But if he had believed it is in shadow, never would this excellent debater have

25. Nm 21.9.
26. Jn 3.14.

made use of the fact that Christ is substantially in us for his proof, since it would not have profited him. Rather, his enemies would benefit; nor does what he was intending follow in any way from this. On the contrary, both he and any man with a mediocre education [1478 D] could decide quite easily that Christ is not in us substantially. Thus, because this most erudite man made use of it to prove his assertion [about the substantial unity of Father and Son], he did not believe that we ate the nature of Christ's flesh in a shadowy manner, but rather in a substantive one.

AUGUSTINE'S APPROBATION OF HILARY'S TEACHING

21. Indeed, St. Augustine makes reference to this book of St. Hilary with great veneration in his own book, the *De Trinitate*.[27] Therefore, it is obvious that Augustine did not consider it to be an objectionable disputation. It is also obvious, then, that Augustine had the same faith as Hilary. For this reason, therefore, the disputation of the most learned and most blessed Hilary has authority among all the faithful, and the frequent and most foolish quarreling of the Shadow-Lovers should cease.

THE REAL PRESENCE IS PROVEN BY MIRACLES

22. They are rebutted, furthermore, not only by reason of the aforementioned authorities, [1479 A] but also by way of many prominent miracles. If they do not accept miracles, then they declare themselves to be enemies of the Church. For it is miracles, more than anything else, that have propagated and matured the Church. What else is it, then, to deny miracles, than to take away the Church, insofar as she exists herself [by way of a miracle]? For (as someone once said) "by whose art dominion is born, it is retained."[28] For this reason, [they make themselves] enemies of the Church, not sons, if they refuse to accept her

27. Augustine, *De Trinitate* 6.10.11; also 15.3.5.
28. See Sallust, *Catiline Wars* 2; the text reads: "Nam imperium facile iis retinetur, quibus initio partum est."

miracles. What then is more foolish, what is more insane than to deny miracles, when absolutely no created thing would exist without the performance of a miracle? I wish that those of false speech would believe that they do not say anything when they impudently vaunt such things, for the very fact that they can speak, indeed, that they even exist, is only because of a divine miracle!

23. But there are some who reply that they do not reject miracles, yet pompously insist that the books in which these things are read are apocryphal. O iniquitous license! Books that the Church of God for the purpose of building herself up reads, and hands on to be read throughout the whole world, for so long a time, under such great doctors—such books the unspiritual and less learned call apocryphal for no apparent reason, save for the fact that they do not please them. These same men, who freely embrace pagan history, labor to destroy Christian history, which the whole world has embraced. What has pleased the Church, however, and what she has freely accepted, these men obstinately reject simply because it does not please them, and this shows that they are not her peaceful sons, but rather her manifest enemies.

EUCHARISTIC MIRACLES RETOLD

24. Therefore, [1479 C] those who desire to be called sons of the Church do not reject the books which she accepts. For what reason then would any Christian call the *Life* of St. Gregory apocryphal, which was published with Rome as its authority? So many most holy and most learned Roman Pontiffs, with none disagreeing, have up until now approved this book, whose authority so many churches, with all the Christian people agreeing, have accepted and followed until the present time. Indeed, in the same *Life,* it is written that the same most blessed Pope Gregory, with the Roman people present, had withdrawn the particle of the body of the Lord from a certain mother of a family, because she had laughed when she was about to communicate. Then, with the particle replaced upon the altar, and with a common prayer poured out to God [by all], he showed [the

Host] to all the people in the appearance [*species*] of true flesh,
like a finger's width of an ear lobe, for instructing their faith,
both of the matron and also of the people, on the truth of the
Lord's flesh.[29] And when the woman, now more faithful, showed
herself to be filled with trepidation at the thought of receiving
flesh, Gregory, with all the people again offering supplication
for the Lord's mercy upon her, re-offered her the same particle
in the customary appearance of bread.

25. I will briefly mention that miracle read in the *Lives of the
Fathers*[30] (although Berengarius hates it, yet with the Lord's help
it still might be beneficial to others), about an old monk whom
the Abbot Daniel says was simple and in error about the body
of the Lord. When this same monk implored the Lord by many
prayers to remove his doubt, he saw an angel of God [1480 A] over
the altar at the hour of sacrifice, immolating a boy, and the angel
then offered him a particle of the same boy as he approached
for communion. Now newly strengthened in his faith, he was still
terribly afraid to receive, and so after he had poured out many
tears, he then received [the body of the Lord] under the species
of bread. But whom should the deeds of our great father Basil
not move to admiration and praise of the divine goodness?[31] For
in the hands of this same Basil, a Jew (hiding in the midst of the
crowd of people) saw a baby boy being born at the time of sacrifice, and after proclaiming what he saw, accepted baptism because of it.

CONSENSUS OF THE FAITHFUL ON MIRACLES

26. There are many other similar stories that could be told
from our own day, as well as from ancient times, but I shall pass
over them. And for Catholics, a brief mention of miracles suffices; for heretics, however, even several such narratives profit nothing. For these same men tear apart the acts of the Holy Fathers
with a shameless mouth, nor do they love those things written or

29. See Paul the Deacon, *Sancti Gregorii Magni vita* 23, PL 75: 52–53.

30. See Deacon Pelagius, *De vitis Patrum* 5, "Verba seniorum," 18.3, PL 73:
979–80.

31. See Ps.-Amphilochius, *Vita s. Basilii* 7, PL 73: 301–2.

said about them, [1480 B] nor do they even acknowledge that [the tradition of the Holy Fathers] has anything to do with them. But why marvel if Berengarius and his followers despise the histories of the Fathers, when they even contradict the Gospel, and say that the passage where the Lord Jesus came to his disciples despite the "closed doors,"[32] should not be believed. But even in this, what has been narrated by me should prove profitable against them, because, whatever they may quarrel about outwardly, when their conscience turns inward and reflects upon these stories, it is undoubtedly filled with dread and gloom. We [Catholics], however, observe how favorably the world has received these accounts everywhere and for so long a time, for even until now, what the Catholic faith holds about the body of the Lord cannot be hidden. If the most learned and holy popes, erudite and religious abbots, monks, clerics, and all the people of God thought that these accounts were contrary to the right faith, why after so long a time have they not condemned them? Why did they not destroy them? Why did they not forbid them to be read? And those who read them loved them, and, for the edification of the faith, have handed them down to be read up until the present day. In fact, all these have favored them, and not one of them who has either heard or read them has rejected them, nor thought that they were contrary to the orthodox faith that all of them held about the body of the Lord. Consequently, either our Shadow-Lovers agree, having been corrected with all these books, or they should come to the conviction that all those irrefutable witnesses that stand against them should be condemned. Therefore, because they have no further refuge in reason, and such a great cloud of witnesses presses against their foolishness, they should keep absolutely quiet. Let the impiety of the Shadow-Lovers, I say, be perpetually enclosed in silence, [1480 D] when the Catholic truth is made clear by so many distinguished witnesses crying out with such a clear voice. For what sort of man would hesitate to say openly that those men are most foolish and impious who do not fear to corrupt the holy writings for their own pleasure by interpreting them badly, men who consider all the most erudite

32. Jn 20.19.

and venerable authors as of no account in this matter which now
disturbs the Church—a Church which, in the matter of the Arians with its vast enemy host, is known to have had peace when,
through the mouth of Hilary, it defended itself against these very
same Arians with the most rational of arguments? Is it now to be
the case that it be used irrationally to the very great ruin of all
Christians?[33] Now, however, these [same] words have been spoken against the Shadow-Lovers.[34]

REFUTATION OF CONSUBSTANTIATION

27. Now an account should be given against those who have
attacked the Church with reasoned arguments, who, although
they cannot now deny that the substance of the body of Christ
dwells in the Lord's food, yet they do not believe that bread
and wine, through the words of the Savior, are converted into
his flesh and blood. Instead, [1481 A] this group mixes Christ into
the bread and wine, and it is as if by subtle reasoning that they
have founded yet another heresy. In truth, I say, although these
other people are occupied with another error [than that of the
Shadow-Lovers], they are involved in the same error nonethe-

33. Guitmund's argument seems to be this: Hilary accused the Arians of perverting the Scriptures towards their own ends, yet formulated an air-tight argument against them, based on the substantial presence of Christ in the Eucharist,
a substantial presence that the *Umbratici* deny, and that all the Fathers and the
Popes, and eucharistic miracles, support. Therefore, is the Church no less for-
tified against the attacks of the *Umbratici* than she was against the Arians? Is she
supposed to yield to the *Umbratici*, when she did not against the Arians, and if
she yields to the *Umbratici*, what does that say about her position against the Arians, which was articulated by Hilary?

34. This brings to a close Guitmund's disputation against the *Umbratici*, and
henceforward the discussion will be aimed at refuting the *Impanatores*. To counter the former, Guitmund has thus far argued for the truth of the Real Presence, that Christ, with the same body born of Mary, is substantially in the Eucharist. Against the latter, those who hold for the Real Presence without a change
in the elements, he will offer arguments from the Fathers (i.e., from Ambrose
and Faustus of Riez), the liturgical tradition of the Church, and the Scriptures,
that there is a real change in bread and wine that is concomitant with the Real
Presence of Christ in the Eucharist, or to be concise: transubstantiation, as it
was soon to be called.

less. For first of all, they are with those who, as far as they can, contend that nothing of the body and blood of the Lord dwells substantially in the sacraments, but when they are driven from that position (as we have said), they prefer to retreat to this impiety, rather than humbly hold to the honest truth with other men.

28. This, then, is the explanation that they offer for their madness: that through the bread and wine, they say, the flesh of Christ can be eaten and his blood drunk. But what [1481 B] sort of argument is this? For why is it not possible to eat the flesh and drink the blood of the Lord by way of that same flesh and blood, without the aid of another body? For if they fear the horror of flesh and blood, why does the Church's customary answer, given by St. Ambrose in the book *De sacramentis,* not suffice? There it says that the substances [*substantiae*] of things are changed, but, on account of horror, the prior taste, color, and the other accidents [*accidentia*], in so far as they pertain to the senses, are retained. If, however, they respond that it cannot happen [*fieri*] that the color and taste of one body would be retained in another body, we can quickly refute them with [an appeal to] divine power. This, if they were to concede to it, would end the matter. If, however, they should shrink from that, then they should hear what is written: "In all things, whatever the Lord willed, he did, both in heaven and on earth,"[35] as well as the many other arguments that we offer, in a sufficient and abundant response to their blasphemies, arguments that have already appeared in the beginning of this little work.

REASON FOR THE RETENTION OF THE APPEARANCE OF BREAD

29. To clarify the matter by example, they should consider listening attentively to what is read about the manna, that its taste changed to that of any food, according to the wish of him who ate it.[36] And although I should be silent about the causes of the deeper mystery and the most profound wisdom of the divine

35. Ps 134.6.
36. Wis 16.20–21.

counsel, yet, insofar as my insignificant self is allowed to know them, [let me offer the following opinion]: just as then [in the Old Testament] the pleasure of carnal men was indulged, so now [in the Eucharist] the need of weak men is indulged. [In a similar vein] he who removed the disgust by changing the taste of many bodies, now by retaining the taste of one body takes away the horror. Also about the color and the other similar accidents, an account is not difficult to give, [1481 D] since the Lord himself is reported to have shown himself to his disciples in different appearances [*species*]. At one time he showed himself to them in the customary color, at another in the transfigured splendor of the sun and snow;[37] at one time he showed himself as a pilgrim,[38] another time he looked like a gardener;[39] sometimes he would exhibit the outward appearance [*species*] of a servant, and at other times he had the likeness of a teacher.

THE BODY OF CHRIST REMAINS UNDIVIDED

30. But if they take refuge in those reasons which they are accustomed to have in their mouth, that is, that it would seem evil for Christ to be chewed by teeth, for him to be ground by teeth, I think we have sufficiently rendered those arguments null and void in the beginning of this work. For he who could be touched after the Resurrection (as it has been said) with hands and lips, could also be touched with teeth. We deny, however, that the Eucharist can be ground by eating (even if everything that I have [1482 A] said so far does not please Christ, that is, about his body being divided up in a way that brings no harm to him, just as in the case of the voice or the soul, which can be whole in many different places at once).[40] For it happens in this way to hide so

37. Mt 17.2.   38. Lk 24.15.
39. Jn 20.15.

40. See 1.16–17 (1434A). Here Guitmund's point as illustrated in the first book is that even if it does not please Christ that his body, the Eucharist, be divided up and distributed to the faithful as it is illustrated by the example of the voice and the soul that are whole and entire in diverse places at once, nevertheless his body is in no way crushed or ground up. Here is another example where Guitmund uses the words "Eucharist," "Sacraments of the Altar," "Sacraments of the Lord's body and blood," and the "Body and Blood of the Lord"

great a mystery from unbelievers, and provide a useful exercise
of faith for believers. And just as they cannot deny that when a
thousand Masses are celebrated at the same time in diverse places, and because of those diverse places the body of the Lord
seems divided, yet is not at all divided (for although the body is
whole in each of the Masses, it does not seem to be one),[41] similarly, why can they not concede that in one mouth,[42] for the exercise of faith, even though the body of Christ is thought to be
divided, yet he is incapable of being divided nonetheless? In
vain, therefore, do they fear the evil of touching the Lord's body
with the teeth, when [1482 B] this same body can be touched, or
fear breaking the body of the Lord into pieces, when without
any detriment to him it can seem to be divided and ground in
this sacrament, yet remains undivided nonetheless. Why then,
and with what insanity, when these arguments have no force,
and they do not offer any others, do they (as I have said) *impanate* or *invinate* Christ on their own authority? And moreover, the
plan of human redemption certainly demanded that Christ become incarnate, which the prophets predicted would happen,
which Christ demonstrated to have happened, which the apostles preached and the world believed. But no reason demands
that Christ be *impanated* or *invinated* (as we have shown), nor did
the prophets predict it, nor did Christ demonstrate it, nor did

---

interchangeably without any distinction, which illustrates the truth that, in his
mind, namely, Guitmund's, they were all the same reality.

41. Hurter (p. 151, n. 1) says that the "jam non esse unum," refers to "a
unity of presence." He goes on to say that Guitmund is not defending here the
idea that Christ has multiple bodies (*corpus multiplex*), which would be present
in many places at once, but rather, that the same body, which according to substance (*secundum substantiam*) is one, is, by that substantial presence, whole and
entire in many places at once. It should also be noted that Thomas will make a
distinction on this matter between a local presence and a substantial one. What
is implicit in Guitmund, and explicit in Thomas on this, is that Christ is locally
in heaven, and substantially on the altar, and because of this substantial presence, can be whole and entire in the Eucharist in many places at once. Also,
Hurter is of the opinion that *videtur* should be added after *jam non esse unum,*
and then the parenthesis closed—a textual addition that I have followed.

42. Guitmund's point here is that, if a thousand Masses celebrated at the
same time cannot divide the body of Christ, why should the teeth in the mouth
of one communicant do so?

the apostles preach it, nor did the world believe it, save for this small number of heretics.

31. Where did this evil error [1482 C] come from, then, that has so convinced them? The whole world agrees that just as the rational soul and the flesh are one man, so in this way God and man are one Christ. No one dares to say that: God and man, and bread and wine, are one Christ. From where, then, do they derive this new *companation?* Or why does even the Apostle not terrify them, when he says: "If anyone should announce to you anything other than what we have announced to you, let him be anathema."[43] For these men announce Christ *impanated* and *invinated,* but this kind of Christ the apostles have not announced. Hence they incur that anathema by apostolic authority.

32. Indeed, St. Ambrose, in his book *De sacramentis,* discourses at length about these matters, and has taught that the body and blood of the Lord are not hidden in the bread and wine, but instead that the [1482 D] bread and wine are changed [*commutari*] into the body and blood of the Lord, speaking this way: "If, then, there is so great a force in the word of the Lord Jesus, that those things which were not began to be, how much more creative is it that those things which exist be changed into something else?"[44] You hear, therefore, that "they are changed into something else." Also, diligently note that he has not said that they are what they were, but that those things which were (he says), are, but are other than they were. He seems to think this, when he subjoins, "and they are changed into something else," as if he would explain the comparison thus: "If the word of the Lord Jesus brought it about that things which were not should start to be, that is, that things should be from that which they were not, that is, from nothing, how much more creative is it that things which were would exist—that is, they would be those things, that is, the body and blood [1483 A]—from those things that already existed, and not from nothing?" For otherwise this comparison cannot be rightly understood. Those things which were, are the bread and wine, but they are not that which they

---

43. Gal 1.8.

44. *De sacramentis* 4.15 (ed. Faller, CSEL 73, 52, lines 20–23 = PL 16: 441A). Ambrose, *Theological and Dogmatic Works,* FC 44, 302.

were; instead, they have been changed into something else. And this is what he says: "things which were would exist"; and so they would be, but not that they would exist in themselves [*in se*], but instead, they are changed into something else.

33. The same doctor sets forth this understanding in a most obvious way in the same book, saying: "Therefore, we make use of examples great enough to prove that this is not what nature formed but what the benediction consecrated, and that the power of the benediction is greater than that of nature, because even nature itself is changed by the benediction."[45] If, then, [the elements] are not what nature has formed, they are not what they were; that is, they are not bread and wine. From the aforementioned opinion, and this one, it is clearly demonstrated that those things which were, are; that is, [1483 B] the body and blood of Christ have not come from nothing, but from those things which were. They are, however, not what they were, because they are not what nature formed; that is, they are not bread and wine, but they are changed into something else [*in aliud commutantur*], and they are what the benediction has consecrated, that is, the body and blood, because by the benediction, he says, nature itself is changed.

34. And listen further to the doctor of truth:

But if, he says, the words of Elias had such power as to call down fire from heaven [1 Kgs 18.38], will not the words of Christ have power enough to change the nature [*species*] of the elements? You have read about the works of the world: "that he spoke and they were done; he commanded and they were created" [Ps 148.5]. So cannot the words of Christ, which were able to make what was not out of nothing, change those things that are into the things that were not? [1483 C] For it is not of less importance to give things new natures than to change natures [*naturas*].[46]

Again, "But that bread is bread before the words of the sacraments; when the consecration has been added, from the bread it becomes the body of Christ."[47] And again:

(margin note: Ambrose)

---

45. *De mysteriis* 9.50 (ed. Faller, CSEL 73, 110, lines 3–6 = PL 16: 405C). Ambrose, *Theological and Dogmatic Works*, FC 44, 23–24.

46. Ibid., 9.52 (ed. Faller, CSEL 73, 112, lines 38–44 = PL 16: 406C). Ambrose, *Theological and Dogmatic Works*, FC 44, 25.

47. *De sacramentis* 4.4.14 (ed. Faller, CSEL 73, 51–52, lines 6–9 = PL 16:

Before it is consecrated, it is bread; but when Christ's words have been added, it is the body of Christ. Finally hear him as he says: "Take and eat of this all of you"; for "this is my body." And before the words of Christ, the chalice is full of wine and water; when the words of Christ have been added, then blood is effected, which redeemed the people. So behold in what great respects the expression of Christ is able to change all things. Then the Lord Jesus himself testified to us that we receive his body and blood. Should we doubt at all about his faith and testification?[48]

This, then, is the case made by St. Ambrose.

35. St. Eusebius of Emesa, however, [1483 D] says:

Faith should contemplate the truly unique and perfect victim, not the external appearance, nor what the outward vision of men detects, but rather what the internal sight affects. Wherefore, on the merit of heavenly authority, it is confirmed that, "My flesh is true food and my blood is true drink" [Jn 6:56]. Let all ambiguity of infidelity withdraw, when he who is the author of the gift is also the witness of the truth. For the invisible priest by his own word with secret power converts the visible creatures into the substance of his body and blood, saying, "Take and eat, this is my body," and repeating the consecration with, "Take and drink, this is my blood." Therefore, just as by the nod of the Lord's command the heights of heaven and the depths of the sea and the expanse of the earth suddenly existed out of nothing, with equal power, where his might commands, it brings about the reality in the spiritual sacraments. And it ought not seem new and impossible to you that earthly and mortal realities are changed into the substance of Christ; ask yourself who already have been regenerated in Christ;[49] et cetera.

And behold how the most holy Father and excellent doctor, with just a few words, has refuted both heresies. He has destroyed the Bread-Minglers, since Christ in no way whatsoever lies hidden in the bread and wine; rather, visible creatures, that is, the bread and wine, are converted into the substance of the

---

440A): "Panis iste . . . caro Christi." Guitmund uses *corpus* instead of *caro*. Ambrose, *Theological and Dogmatic Works*, FC 44, 302.

48. Ibid. 4.5.23 (ed. Faller, CSEL 73, 56, lines 19–27 = PL 16: 444B): "Antequam consecratur . . . testificatione dubitare?" Ambrose: "Ergo videte quantis generibus potens est sermo Christi." Guitmund uses *disce*, in place of *videte*. Ambrose, *Theological and Dogmatic Works*, FC 44, 305.

49. *Homilia de corpore et sanguine Christi* 17.1–2 (ed. F. Glorie, CSL 101, 196, lines 21–197, line 34 = PL 30: 272B–C). The authorship and date are uncertain, traditionally assigned to Eusebius, Bishop of Emesa (340–60).

body and blood of Christ, and again he says, earthly and mortal things are changed into the substance of Christ. Furthermore, in no small way he dispels the Shadow-Lovers, when he confirms that these things are not converted into just any creature at all, but rather into the substance of the body and blood of Christ.

36. Moreover, [1484 B] he says, "nor should anyone doubt that the principal creatures, at the nod of the power of God and the presence of him, can pass into the nature of the body of the Lord."[50] And again:

When the creatures that are to be blessed by the celestial words are placed upon the sacred altars, before they are consecrated by the invocation of the highest name, the substance which is there is bread and wine; after the words, however, it is the body and blood of Christ. Where, then, is the marvel, if what he was able to create by a word, he can also convert by a word? Now it rather seems as a lesser miracle, if that which is known to have been made from nothing, now that it has been created, can be changed into something better.[51]

What could be clearer? What is more expressive? These people do not understand this, although never at any time could anything be said more clearly by a man.

37. In a certain Spanish missal, which some say St. Isidore dictated, in a certain Mass for the week before Easter, [1484 C] the following can be found:

This, O Lord, is wholly divine; this, O Father, is wholly from heaven; it has changed into the nature of your Son, and is body and blood. It is now not a figure, but truth, now not a mortal creature, but a heavenly nature meant to bestow eternal life on those who eat and an everlasting kingdom on those who drink.[52]

The Lord Jesus himself destroys these Bread-Minglers by the word of his mouth, when, taking the bread, giving thanks, and

50. *Homilia de corpore* 17.8 (ed. Glorie, op. cit., 207, lines 188–90 = PL 30: 275C); Stone, *Eucharist,* 130.

51. *Homilia de corpore* 17.8 (ed. Glorie, op. cit., 207, lines 194 to 208, line 202 = PL 30: 275D); Stone, *Eucharist,* 130–31.

52. The text cited by Guitmund cannot be found in the PL database, nor was Henry Cattaneo able to find it in his paper on Guitmund's patristic sources entitled: "Le fonte patristiche del corporis et sanguinis Christi veritate," *Corpo mistico e teologia trinitaria esegesi biblica fonti patristiche, dialettica ed eucharistia,* CDM 14 (Naples: Edizioni Scientifiche Italiane, 2000), 191.

blessing it, he says: "This is my body." He does not say: "In this my body lies hidden." Neither did he say: "In this wine is my blood," but instead said: "This is my blood." Therefore, the Church of God separates them from herself, when, in the very canon of the Mass, from apostolic tradition she prays in this manner: "Which oblation, [1484 D] O God, we beseech you, that in every way, you deign to bless, accept, ratify, make holy and acceptable, so that for us it may become the body and blood of your most beloved Son, our Lord Jesus Christ."[53] One does not pray that the body and blood might lie hidden within it, or that the body and blood might come into it, but that the oblation itself might become both the body and the blood. By this prayer, Cyprian, Hilary, Ambrose, Augustine, Jerome, Gregory, and all the rest of the ecclesiastical authors, and also those who celebrate Mass with full devotion who likewise assent to this prayer unanimously, strike down our opponents.

38. Indeed, for myself, as I go over this matter of Bread-Mingling again, I cannot express in words how much I marvel, and how I am equally indignant at their audacious stupidity and most insane presumption. For to proceed by human reason [1485 A] against the divine authorities is indeed insane, but to do so without reason is far more insane.[54] And certainly always to rage against God without reason and against reason, can be

53. *Canon Missae, Prex Eucharistica, Textus e variis Liturgiis antiquioribus selecti,* v. 12, ed. A. Hänggi–I. Pahl (Fribourg Suisse: Spicilegium Friburgense, 1968), 433.

54. This doctrine of *impanation,* however, was held by Pope Gelasius I (492–496), in the *Tractatus de duabus naturis adversus Eutychen et Nestorium* (PL 224, sup. 3, 773–74), who compared the change to the Incarnation: "Sacred Scripture, testifying that this Mystery began at the start of the blessed Conception, says; 'Wisdom has built a house for itself' (Prov 9.1), rooted in the solidity of the sevenfold Spirit. This Wisdom ministers to us the food of the Incarnation of Christ through which we are made sharers of the divine nature. Certainly the sacraments of the Body and Blood of Christ that we receive are a divine reality, because of which and through which we 'are made sharers of the divine nature' (2 Pt 1.4). Nevertheless the substance of the bread and wine does not cease to exist . . . [but] by the work of the Holy Spirit they pass over into the divine substance while nevertheless remaining in their own nature." Trans. J. T. O'Connor, *The Hidden Manna: A Theology of the Eucharist* (San Francisco: Ignatius Press, 1988), 72–73.

called the height of insanity. For these men have justified their Shadow-Loving brethren, who are more wretched than the wretched ones. For the Shadow-Lovers cannot go beyond the judgment of the senses, and so can be seen to have erred from their weakness. But these Bread-Minglers derive the causes for their error, neither from the senses, nor from any reason, nor any Scripture; rather, by pride alone they are seen to seethe within, all the while contradicting nature, which they are so accustomed to defend (for one cannot see how in a solid body of bread, another body can lie hidden). Nature contradicts them, [1485 B] I say; the Sacred Scriptures contradict them; no witness of the holy Fathers, no divine oracle, no miracle defends their argument, and with bestial stubbornness they resist solid Catholic piety. And it is for this reason alone: lest they appear conquered by piety. O unfortunate ones, whom piety does not conquer! O most miserable ones, who, while they refuse to be subject to piety, are not ashamed to be the servants of impiety! It would seem most unworthy to respond to their manifest stupidity, save for the fact that their own death does not suffice for them to attain the full measure of their perdition, unless they also lead to perdition whomever they can by their most vile falsehood. And these words are especially directed against them. Nevertheless, may the following disputation, God willing, strike both of the aforementioned heretics together.

39. The very division of the heresies should have been enough for them to see, first and foremost, the falsehood of the argumentation: [1485 C] namely, that at one time they contend that nothing of the flesh and blood is present in the sacraments of God except merely a shadow and figure, while at another time they insist that the substance of flesh and blood is hidden within them. For the apostolic faith, which alone is the true faith, is not divided into affirmation and negation. For the Apostle said: "One Lord, one faith, one baptism."[55] Therefore, the apostolic faith is only one. Their credulity is vain, however, since what it holds in one empty opinion, it is not constrained to hold in another; it is not one, since it is split into both affirmation

---

55. Eph 4.5.

and negation. Hence their empty belief is not the apostolic faith, and thus not the true faith. For this reason then, since they do not have the apostolic faith, they are separated from the apostolic Church, and what the Savior said will apply to them: "Every kingdom divided against itself will be laid waste."[56] To be sure, the Berengarians are divided among themselves, just as we have shown.

40. But perhaps someone might say: "Because [the Berengarians] are few in number, they are not the kingdom." To which I respond: "If they are not the kingdom, they are not the Church of Christ." For the Church of Christ is the kingdom of God, in which God, that is, Christ himself, reigns. But if they are the kingdom, because Truth cannot lie, when they are divided among themselves, they will be laid waste. Truly, the prophet preached about the Catholic Church: "Mount Zion is founded as the fairest height of all the earth";[57] which we see fulfilled in our Church. But the Berengarian's portion is not "founded as the fairest height of all the earth": [1486 A] in fact, not even one little city or one little village is granted to them, so they are not Mount Zion, that is, the Church. The same prophet says: "Sing to the Lord a new song; sing to the Lord, all the earth."[58] Wherefore, St. Augustine in an exposition on this verse ventures to say: "If all the earth is the house of God, anyone in all the earth who does not belong to it is a ruin, not the house."[59] If the Berengarians do belong to all the earth, they are not the house of God, but a ruin. Isaiah says about the Church of Christ: "Raise a glad cry, you barren one who does not bear; break forth in jubilant song, you who were not in labor, for more numerous are the children of the deserted wife than the children of her who has a husband."[60] "She who now has a husband," the Apostle teaches, should be understood as the synagogue of the Jews;[61] and the sterile one is the

56. Lk 11.17.   57. Ps 47.3, 9.
58. Ps 95.1.

59. Augustine, *Enarrationes in psalmos* 95.2 (ed. E. Dekkers–I. Fraipont, CSL 39, 1343, lines 15–16 = PL 37: 1227).

60. Is 54.1.

61. Cf. Gal 4.26, "But the Jerusalem from above is freeborn, and she is our mother."

Church. Therefore, if the Berengarians are the Church of God, [1486 B] let them show us many more sons after such a long time than the Jews have. But this is not the case, as is obvious to everyone. Again, Isaiah on the Church: "Kings," he says, "will be your nurses."[62] And John in the Apocalypse: "The kings," he says, "of the earth will bring their glory to it."[63] But what king of the earth encouraged this Berengarian stupidity? What king of the earth has brought his glory to this [stupidity]? In fact, although some kings at one time agreed with the Arian madness, none, however, have consented to the Berengarian one.

41. God said through [the prophet] Malachi: "From the rising of the sun, even unto its setting, my name is great among the nations; and in every place a pure oblation is sacrificed and offered to my name; for great is my name among the nations, says the Lord of Hosts."[64] Therefore, if the Lord of Hosts says that the oblation [1486 C] that is sacrificed and offered to his name in every place from the rising of the sun unto its setting is pure, then apart from this one there can be no clean oblation. Let Berengarius and his followers realize how unclean their oblation is, which is not offered everywhere, I say, but rather, hardly anywhere. When the prophet Daniel saw the stone cut from the mountain without hands, which struck the statue on its iron and clay feet and broke it into pieces, he explained the vision in this way: it is the Kingdom of God, that is, the Church. He affirms that the four principal kingdoms of the world (that is, those of the Chaldeans, the Medes and the Persians, the Greeks, and the Romans), as the same prophet clearly explains and states later, are to be struck and crushed to pieces in the days of the fourth kingdom, that is, the Roman kingdom, the kingdom of iron, before it ceases to exist. [1486 D] For he says:

In the days of those kingdoms, the God of heaven will set up a kingdom that shall never be destroyed, and his kingdom shall not be delivered up to another people; rather, it shall break into pieces all these kingdoms and put an end to them, and it shall stand forever. That is the meaning of the stone you saw hewn from the mountain without hands put to it, which broke in pieces the iron, tile, bronze, silver, and gold.[65]

62. Is 49.23.   63. Rv 21.24.
64. Mal 1.11.   65. Dn 2.44–45.

42. Indeed, we see with a clearer light that this is about our Church. For the Church herself, when the Roman Empire was still iron, shattered the other kingdoms. And she herself to-day, which no one can deny, has the house of the Savior in the very house of a one-time Roman emperor.[66] For there, through blessed Pope Leo, the Church has promptly damned these Berengarian fictions by his own exhortation.[67] Then she censured him again by this pope, my lord Pope Gregory, who is now reigning,[68] then the Archdeacon of the same Roman See, in the Council of Tours. She graciously received Berengarius himself, so it seemed, corrected and making satisfaction by his own signature.[69] She rebuked him again, however, when he returned to his own vomit, as Pope Nicholas of holy memory acted in the general Council of Rome. And she forced the same Berengarius, before the venerable assembly of the entire world, in approved words,[70] which have been written above and to which many churches had to swear,[71] to abjure the aforementioned insanities by his own mouth, and with his own hands to burn his books, which he had written to defend the same blasphemies. [1487 B] I do not, then, call the little Berengarian nation the four great kingdoms, nor can they be shown to have obtained at any time even one kingdom. Rather, even if they are depicted as having obtained it, his kingdom has now been handed over to another people, that is, our Catholic people. For our people hold the Roman Empire, with all its subjected kingdoms, under the Christian name. Daniel says that the kingdom of the people of God, "shall never be delivered to another people, but rather shall stand forever."[72] The Berengarians, therefore, are not of that kingdom that the

66. Hurter, p. 164, n.1, says that Guitmund is referring here to the Lateran Palace, in which the celebrated Church of the Savior had been dedicated.

67. Pope Leo IX, 1049–1054, Council of Rome in 1050.

68. Pope Gregory VII, 1073–1085. This statement of Guitmund is particularly important for dating the work, since it was obviously written during the pontificate of Gregory before the Council of Rome in 1079. Thus the work must have been written no earlier than 1073 and no later than 1079, and probably in Normandy before Guitmund arrived in Rome.

69. Council of Tours in 1054.

70. "Ego Berengarius" of 1059.

71. Faber prints the text in book one.

72. Dn 2.44.

Bs: of Kingdom of
not of Kingdom
(God), so not
he of
do ✓ *Jo*
✓ ✓ ✓

God of heaven, as it is predicted, will raise up. But if they do
not belong to the kingdom of the God of heaven, then it follows
that they are of the kingdom of the devil. You see plainly, then,
how our [1487 C] Church is confirmed by the testimonies of the
prophets crying out together, but both Berengarian factions are
rejected.

43. About these testimonies, St. Augustine in the last book of
De civitate Dei speaks in this vein against certain philosophers:

Now they may say that we must interpret this belief in another way,
on the ground that if they said the scriptural evidence was nonsense
they would be offering an insult to the God they commend so highly.
But surely they insult him as much, if not more, if they say that the
Scriptures are to be understood otherwise than as the world has believed them; for God himself has approved the belief that the world
would come to hold; he promised this belief, and he has fulfilled that
promise. [. . .] Thus by refusing to believe that God can lie, our philosophers may come to the belief that he will do what he has promised to do; and let them believe in the sense that the world has come
to believe it, since God foretold that the world would believe; he approved that the world should hold this belief; he promised that the
world would believe; and by now he has shown [1487 D] that the world
has come to believe.[73]

Therefore, O Berengarians, if St. Augustine is most clear, as
he usually is, then follow his judgment and believe as the world
believes about the body and blood of the Lord. For if you believe
something else, or the same thing in a different way, your Augustine says to you that you do God a grave injury, because you believe about Christ other than what the world believes, the world,
who would believe as God predicted, praised, promised, and
demonstrated. But if God praised the faith of the world, he has
also condemned your fabrications. For there is with God only
one praiseworthy faith. Therefore, there is binding on you as

73. Augustine, *De civitate Dei* 22.25 (ed. E. Hoffman, CSEL 40/2, 650, line
24 to 651, line 1, and 651 lines 8–12 = PL 41: 793) Guitmund's version omits:
"Utrum enim non potest facere . . . non credendo quod non potest," five lines
in the text (651, lines 2–7) that deal with the Resurrection of Christ. It is clear
in this omission that Guitmund is appropriating the argument of the world's
understanding of what the Resurrection actually meant, with what the world understands the Eucharist to be. Trans. H. Bettenson (New York: Penguin, 1984),
1077.

well what the same St. Augustine has said, in the same last book of *De civitate Dei,* in these words: "If what the world believes is credible, the unbelievers should notice how stubborn they are. [. . .] If it is incredible, how is it that it is believed throughout the whole world?"[74] For this reason, in the judgment of St. Augustine, you are stubborn, because you refuse to believe about the body of Christ what is believed throughout the whole world.

44. Again, St. Augustine says in book four of *De baptismo contra Donatistas:* "What the whole Church holds, not as instituted by councils, but has always held, is rightly believed as having been handed down with apostolic authority."[75] Again, in the seventh book of the same work: "We can assert with the confidence of a secure voice what has been confirmed by the consent of the universal Church, under the governance of our Lord God and Savior Jesus Christ."[76] Therefore, the faith [1488 B] that the universal Church has always held about the body and blood of the Lord, [that same faith] the Church has affirmed by many general councils, and is, therefore, most rightly believed to be handed down by apostolic authority. For if what the Church has always held is the apostolic foundation, and not from councils, how much more should that be believed which the Church has always held, and which (as I have said) has been confirmed by many general councils as handed down by apostolic authority? For indeed, the belief that the bread and wine of the altar of the Lord are substantially changed [*substantialiter commutari*] into the body and blood of the Lord (not as Berengarius deliriously says, that

74. Ibid., 22.5 (ed. E. Hoffman, CSEL 40/2, 588, lines 10–12, 589, lines 15–16 = PL 41: 756). Augustine: "Si rem credibilem crediderunt, videant quam sint stolidi, qui non credunt . . . si autem res incredibilis credita est, etiam hoc utique incredible est, sic creditum esse, quod incredible est." Guitmund: "Si autem res incredibilis est, unde toto terrarum orbe jam credita est?" Trans. by Bettenson, 1027.

75. *De baptismo contra Donatistas,* 4.24.31 (ed. M. Petschenig, CSEL 51, 259, lines 2–4 = PL 43: 174); Guitmund: "Quod universa tenet ecclesia nec conciliis institutum, sed semper retentum est: non nisi auctoritate apostolica traditum rectissime creditur," is an abbreviation of Augustine's text.

76. Ibid., 7.53.102 (op. cit., 373, lines 23–26 = PL 43: 243); Guitmund: "Id autem fiducia securae vocis possumus asserere [adserere], quod in gubernatione Domini Dei nostri et Salvatoris Jesu Christi universalis Ecclesiae consensione roboratum est," is an abbreviation of Augustine's text.

they are only figures and shadows of the body and blood of the Lord, or that Christ is hidden or concealed within them) has been confirmed by the consent of the universal Church. Therefore, that which can be asserted by us with the confidence of a secure voice under the governance of our Lord God and Savior Jesus Christ is that which has been asserted by us.

45. Indeed, [1488 C] if space were duly given, should I choose to discuss the matter with Berengarius himself, since he teaches some people that nothing of the body and blood of Christ is present in the food of the Lord's altar, save only a shadow or a figure, and then to others, as if to satisfy those who seek a more subtle opinion, he responds that the very body of Christ is there, but hidden in the bread, I would ask him what is so displeasing to him in the prior opinion, that to satisfy the more inquisitive he passes over to the other view, or again, what is abhorrent in the latter, that he should return to the former. For by passing on to the second, he rejects the first; by returning to the first, he condemns the second. Thus it happens that, by defending both, he holds neither. Therefore, it follows that, since he hated all the opinions that remain, he knows absolutely nothing of what to believe [1488 D] about these sacraments of the Lord. Furthermore, one thing we know for certain happens: if Berengarius and his followers were ever to be interrogated by learned Catholics about their faith, they would deny in terror what they hold about the body of the Lord, but if they offered their own opinion, they would be unable to defend it. That terrifying sentence of Christ, then, befalls those who deny the true faith about Christ, in which he says: "He who is ashamed of me and my words, of him the Son of Man will be ashamed."[77] And Paul: "If we deny him, he will also deny us."[78] But certainly, if they openly profess their faith and are unable to defend it, if they are the defenders of the true faith [and not we Catholics], where is that which Christ himself has promised to his own, when he said: "I shall give you a mouth and wisdom which all your adversaries will be powerless to resist or refute"?[79] For if they were defending the true faith, [1489 A] there would be someone of them

77. Lk 9.26.   78. 2 Tm 2.12.
79. Lk 21.15.

whom all of their adversaries would be powerless to resist. For indeed, Truth, who has promised this to his own, cannot lie. No one of these can be found whom our Catholics cannot resist: the heresiarch Berengarius has been denounced many times, and by the oath signed in his own hand he is known to have abjured those insane views in general councils. For this reason, it is quite evident that they are in fact not the defenders of the true faith, nor its sons, but rather, enemies of the Church of Christ.

46. If, however, they are the Church of Christ, then either the Church did not begin from Christ, or after a time it ceased to be. It is also most noteworthy, that in this time, before Berengarius raged, these sorts of madness never existed. The Church, however, has existed among the apostles and their disciples from the time of Christ, [1489 B] nor at any time afterward has she ceased to exist. For otherwise the Scripture would lie, as it cries out through the prophets: "And of his kingdom, there will be no end."[80] The archangel Gabriel himself would be lying when he says the same to blessed Mary.[81] Truth himself would be lying when he says: "Behold, I am with you always, until the end of the age."[82] But far be it that Truth could lie, either in his own words or in his great witnesses. The Church of Christ never ceased to be after Christ. Therefore, they are not the Church of Christ. Or, if they lie impudently and say they began from Christ and have persevered until now, let them show, according to Daniel's prophecy, that they have destroyed the four principal kingdoms of the world; let them show that they have filled the earth; let them show that their kingdom has not yielded to another people. [1489 C] But that they cannot do this is sufficiently and abundantly clear to all, since our people possess the kingdoms of the world, and shatter these men with authority and reason. Therefore, our Church was founded by Christ and not by Berengarius, neither did it originate in Tours or Angers, but just as Christ commanded and the prophets predicted: from Jerusalem, from where it shall endure unto eternity. The Berengarian insanity, however, does not belong to the Church of Christ, so let it, in confusion, be forever silent.

80. Cf. Dn 2.44.   81. Lk 1.33.
82. Mt 28.20.

47. Let us now see whether it is possible to complete, in any way, that proposition which we proved so thoroughly in the first book. For we have proved that, if God wills to make this change of bread and wine (which we believe), he does it. Now, however, even the assertion has been sufficiently proved, [1489 D] that is, that God wills to do it. For the Holy Spirit, through the most holy authors who are known to have been his temple, has clearly taught this (as we have shown): the incontrovertible authority of the Old and New Testaments affirmed this, the world universally believed it, and God himself has approved of the Church's faith alone. Undoubtedly then, we must conclude what has been most evidently and necessarily established: God effects a change [*mutatio*] of bread and wine into the substance [*substantia*] of the body and blood of Christ. Therefore, the novel, irrational, false, useless, and most evil inventions of foolish men should be silenced by prudent ones. All of them should yield, I say, to the faith of the Church. For that faith is not new, nor is it the faith of this or that man, but rather of the whole world. That faith alone is rational, [1490 A] alone is true, alone is approved, has been proved in each and every way defensible and invincible, most useful, necessary, most pleasing, and most honest. Where, however, is the *impanation* of Christ read in either the Old or the New Testament? With what reasoning, by what arguments, or what miracles is it defended? What purpose, what use, what honor is there to *impanate* or *invinate* our Lord Christ for no reason? But whether one eats only bread and wine in the figure and shadow of Christ, which they believe, or to consume Christ in the very truth of his substance—who, even if he were a madman, could compare them in respect to usefulness and honor and excellence? For when we believe that we consume the Word of God substantively made flesh in the Lord's food, without any *impanation* or *invination,* nor in shadow, [1490 B] we are filled with the hope that, from the power of the fullness of eternal life abiding in that same food, we will be victorious forever. What is truer than this faith, since it is approved by so many and such great testimonies? What could be thought of as more reasonable than this faith? What, I say, is more useful, more necessary, more honorable than this faith? For when one receives with pure faith, he receives the pure

Christ, and not the *shadow* Christ, or the *impanated* Christ. Rich by the gift of such glory, he should abhor sins all the more with the greatest fear and reverence. With the highest ardor of desire for every form of righteousness he should burn more fervently. Let him strive daily to flee the world, the enemy of his Lord, and now, more certain of his promises in accordance with such a great pledge, more attentively and more ardently, with face unveiled, [1490 C] let him strive to apprehend God, the very source of life, with all his prayers.

48. We have already said many things against them, and there are many that could be said; but, in my estimation, these suffice for pious minds. For what further arguments could they bring against them? It has been sufficiently and clearly shown that their objections, either from rationalizations or from the Scriptures, are no obstacle to our faith, and that those same Scriptures are more supportive of our position [than of theirs]. Since they should realize that their insanities are, individually and all together, thoroughly destroyed by the testimonies of venerable authors and by the prophetic and evangelical witnesses, they should see that our faith is clearly expressed as most firm, most useful, most excellent, and supremely necessary. And what then would be enough for the impious—[1490 D] if, harder than stones, they are struck with the hammers of so many arguments and are still unwilling to yield, and, darker than hell, they cannot be illumined by the great light of the most convincing arguments? Either like prostitutes, they do not know how to blush at their shame, no matter how obvious, or, like demons, they love the madness they have entered upon with such obstinacy that they hate the truth gratuitously and never recover from even the most obvious error. O most miserable men, who should be lamented with an immense shower of tears, if such a great desire for the propagation of fame has so pervaded them that neither the most clear truth, nor the height of their infamy, nor love of eternal life, nor eternal damnation can call them back from their public proclamation of blasphemies. Return, I implore you, "Return to the heart, you deceivers."[83] Why do you die so willingly? This is not

83. Is 46.8.

the type [1491 A] of disputation which should be taken lightly by either side. This disputation is not as it is in school, done for the sake of victory, or as it is in the courts, done for any earthly goods, but done before God, unto eternal and heavenly life: indeed, unending death devours the false side; eternal life, however, crowns the true. Therefore, weigh carefully with a just examination your position and ours; if you have a worthy case against us, produce it; if you do not, be silent. Why will you die willingly? But why should I pursue them further? Now this disputation must come to an end. Yet there is still left a brief word to be said about two remaining propositions, but to prosecute the matter does not call for a long disputation.

DIFFICULTY OF UNWORTHY COMMUNICANTS ADDRESSED

49. Of these two, [1491 B] one affirms that some of the bread and wine is changed [*transmutari*] into the flesh and blood of the Lord, but some, because of unworthy communicants, remains unchanged. The other proposition, however, affirms that all of the bread and wine of the altar is converted into the flesh and blood of the Lord, but when unworthy persons come to Communion, it reverts back again into bread and wine. Those who affirm either one of these ideas, then, are unwilling to have unworthy men capable of participating in the flesh and blood of the Lord. With them, therefore, although the error is different, the cause is nevertheless the same. For they both defend their error with the same arguments: that is, they say that Christ declared: "Whoever eats my flesh and drinks my blood remains in me and I in him."[84] Yet the unworthy do not remain in Christ, [1491 C] nor does Christ remain in them. For they are not able "to serve two masters,"[85] nor at the same time to be a member of Christ and of the devil. They say, then, that they do not eat the flesh of Christ, or drink his blood. And they even strive to claim the example, found in the *Vitae patrum*, of a certain old man who had a vision of an angel withdrawing the body of the Lord from

---

84. Jn 6.56.   85. Mt 6.24.

unworthy recipients, to whom, upon approaching for the purpose of receiving Communion, the angel gives coal in place of Communion.[86] If then, they say, such people do not receive the flesh and blood of the Lord, it must be the case that what they receive has either not changed [*mutatum*], or it has reverted back into its prior nature. And their reasoning up to this point must, with God's help, be refuted now.

50. And, in fact, of the first example it should be noted that it offers them nothing; in fact it greatly repudiates their opinion. For if [1491 D] bread to be offered to the unworthy should remain unchanged, what does the coal given to them, rather than bread, mean? But if all the unworthy are feeding on coal, are not all the worthy truly feeding on the flesh and blood of the Lord? Therefore, nothing of the bread remains unchanged. Rather, if the flesh and blood were changed into coal for the unworthy as these approached, then they were not changed into bread and wine; for coal is neither bread nor wine. Therefore, in this example, their opinion (as I have said) is more damaged than illustrated. For us, however, this example is in no way seen as contradictory. For in his eyes, it could be that the appearances of flesh and blood, in which Communion was offered to the just, are withdrawn from the unjust, and, for the purpose of showing their iniquity, the same flesh and blood are offered to them [1492 A] in the appearance of coal. For certainly it does not always happen this way (as I have already said), but so that the evil of the sins to be corrected would be revealed through the angel to the old monk who was present, the flesh and blood could be withdrawn by the angel in truth, and coal brought in from elsewhere in a moment and administered. Therefore, either one of these scenarios could have come about in a way that is consonant with our faith.

51. Let us now attend to the words of the Lord where it is said: "He who eats my flesh and drinks my blood remains in me, and I in him." In explaining these words, we put forward not our interpretation, but rather that of St. Augustine, from the book *De verbis Domini*. "For," he says, "these words should not be

---

86. See 2.19 of this work and n. 23 on Rufinus of Aquileia.

understood to apply universally, but only in a certain way, namely, in this way: he who eats the flesh and drinks the blood of
Christ [1492 B] remains in Christ, and Christ in him; he who eats
worthily eats that way."[87] "For he who eats and drinks unworthily
eats and drinks judgment unto himself."[88] Therefore, if everyone who eats and drinks unworthily eats and drinks judgment
unto himself, it must necessarily be understood that only he
who eats in another way, that is, worthily, remains in Christ, and
Christ in him. For the purpose of this comparison, then, the
one who eats unworthily should not be considered to be eating,
but rather, as much as he can, to be treading upon it with contempt. He eats then, and does not eat. He eats corporally, but
does not eat spiritually, that is, not in that sense, not with that
moral disposition, not with that charity, so that he does not eat
worthily.

52. Those words of the Lord are to be received in a similar
way, when he says: "Anyone who will have sinned against the
Holy Spirit will not be forgiven in this age, nor in the age to
come."[89] Now these words are not true unless they mean some
special way of sinning; otherwise, everyone who sins against the
Son sins against the Holy Spirit. For no one can offend the Son
unless he also offends the Holy Spirit. But "anyone who speaks
against the Son," the Lord says, "it will be forgiven him."[90] Therefore, one who sins against the Holy Spirit will also be forgiven.
What could be the reason that is offered here, then, unless one
is to understand that there is a special kind of sin against the
Holy Spirit which would be so grave that, in comparison with it,
the other sins cannot be said to be sins against the Holy Spirit?
This statement, too, is similar: "He who believes and is baptized
will be saved."[91] And this one: "Whoever calls upon the name of
the Lord will be saved."[92] For not all who believe have also been

---

87. *Sermon* 71.17, *De verbis Evangelii Matthaei 12:32,* PL 38: 453.

88. 1 Cor 11.29.

89. Mt 12.32, Vulgate: "Qui autem dixerit contra Spiritum Sanctum non remittetur ei neque in hoc saeculo neque in futuro." Guitmund: "Qui peccaverit
in Spiritum sanctum, non remittetur. . . ."

90. Ibid.   91. Mk 16.16.

92. Jl 2.32.

baptized, neither will all who call upon [1492 D] the name of the Lord be saved; but only those who believe with good morals and call worthily upon the name of the Lord will be saved. And many other statements of this sort are found in the Sacred Scriptures, which cannot be competently understood except conditionally.

53. So the topic concerning which this discussion was begun should be interpreted in this way: "He who eats my flesh and drinks my blood *worthily* remains in me, and I in him." As for the fact that the unworthy, who do not remain in Christ nor Christ in them, eat the same flesh and drink the same blood, hear the same St. Augustine, in book five of *De baptismo contra Donatistas,* where he says:

Just as Judas, to whom the Lord gave a morsel, prepared a place within himself for the devil, [1493 A] not by receiving anything evil, but by receiving it in an evil way; so it is that whoever receives the sacrament of the Lord unworthily, does not make the sacrament evil, since he himself is evil, nor will he have received nothing because he does not receive unto salvation. For it was no less the body and blood of the Lord for those of whom the Apostle said: "He who eats and drinks unworthily, eats and drinks judgment unto himself" [1 Cor 11.29].[93]

These words are Augustine's. Therefore, since both the worthy and the unworthy eat the same flesh, but with diverse minds, and drink the same blood of the Lord, and since the Gospel statement says, "whoever eats my flesh and drinks my blood remains in me, and I in him," according to the Apostle and St. Augustine, following the pattern of many other such sentences [1493 B] competently understood, it offers them nothing; moreover, the previously adjoined example of the old man wholly detracts from their position. Therefore, since the case presented in this document cannot be found deficient in the entirety of its argumentation, this novel invention should cease among Christian men from now on, lest, if they should teach another position, then they themselves should incur that apostolic curse that declares: "If anyone should announce to you anything other than that which you have received, a curse be upon him."[94]

93. Augustine, *De baptismo contra Donatistas* 5.8.9 (ed. M. Petschenig, CSEL 51, 270, lines 6–13 = PL 43: 181).
94. Gal 1.8.

54. For what purpose is served if no unworthy person receives the body of the Lord, and consequently a portion of bread remains unchanged—that is, on account of the unworthy? Since no one would dare to call himself worthy, because Scripture says: "Man does not know whether he is worthy of love or hatred in this life,"[95] and neither would he dare to enter into judgment about another, for it is written: "Praise no man in his life, for man sees the outward appearance; God, [1493 C] however, sees the heart":[96] it would then follow that no one would dare to confess confidently that it is the body of the Lord that either he or the whole people receives. But if no one will dare to confess it confidently, then the priest rashly affirms, "This is the body of Christ," [and] rashly the people respond *Amen,* which means, "it is true," since they simply would not know what it is, because they are all ignorant of everyone's merits, their own and everyone else's. But may heaven forbid that the religious confession of the whole Church be altogether reprehensible. Let each one believe and say confidently, even if he confesses himself to be unworthy, that what he receives is the body of Christ.

55. Assume that a most unworthy priest celebrates Mass, and he alone receives the whole of what has been consecrated. If what that unworthy priest was going to receive remained unchanged because he was going to receive the whole of it—then nothing of the bread and wine [1493 D] would change into the flesh and blood of Christ. But if, on account of his unworthiness, nothing of bread and wine was changed, the iniquity of the priest would then have proved stronger than the words of the Lord and Savior (heaven forbid!), and even the faith of the Church would be false, which believes that by way of both good and bad ministers the words of the Lord work [*operari*] equally. But heaven forbid that it should be believed by all the faithful that the iniquity of a man could weaken the words of the Savior! Far be it that the faith of the Church be false, which alone before God is praiseworthy, and which believes that the words of Christ are equally efficacious through good and evil ministers! Hence, what an unworthy priest was going to receive did not remain unchanged because of him.

95. Eccl 9.1.
96. Sir 11.30.

Since he receives the whole of that which has been consecrated, the most unworthy priest eats and drinks the flesh and blood of Christ. But if this is the case—or rather, because it is the case—falsely is part of the bread and wine said to remain unchanged on account of the unworthy. Therefore, let human suspicion of this sort be forever silent, and let us hold only what is commended to us in the very canon of the Mass. For there it is so written: "Which oblation, you O God, we beseech that in every way, you deign to bless, accept, ratify, make holy and acceptable, so that for us it may become the body and blood of your most beloved Son."[97] It does not say here that part of it becomes his body and blood. Nor did our Lord Jesus Christ, when he said: "Eat of this all of you," add: "for part of it is my body"; but rather only: "For this is my body."

56. What man, with even an average level of understanding, would not shudder just to hear that strange notion, namely, that the flesh and blood of the Lord turns back into bread and wine on account of the unworthy? The flesh and blood of the Lord are indeed incorruptible. But what is incorruptible is neither corrupt nor can be corrupted. And to destroy its own essence and to return into corruptible bread and corruptible wine is indeed a great corruption. Hence, the flesh and blood of the Lord cannot now be changed back into bread and wine. Therefore, this error, too, should be buried in eternal silence. Both of these groups should take care not to bring a profane fire to the divine altar,[98] lest they perish before the Lord. Let them take care not to transgress the borders of their fathers, which they set up for them.[99] Indeed, there is "much food," as Solomon says, "in the fields of the fathers; but some is harvested unjustly."[100] But the

97. *Canon Missae, Prex Eucharistica, Textus e variis Liturgiis antiquioribus selecti*, v. 12, ed. A. Hänggi–I. Pahl (Fribourg Suisse: Spicilegium Friburgense, 1968), 433.

98. See Lv 10.1–2: "During this time Aaron's sons Nadab and Abihu took their censers and, strewing incense on the fire they had put in them, they offered up before the Lord profane fire, such as he had not authorized. Fire therefore came forth from the Lord's presence and consumed them, so that they died in his presence."

99. See Prv 22.28: "Remove not the ancient landmark which your fathers set up."

100. Prv 13.23.

foods of this sort of teaching cannot be found in the fields of the fathers. Therefore, they have been harvested unjustly.

Roger

Inasmuch as I can judge, I see that you have carried out everything with the soundest of reasoning.

Guitmund

57. Consequently, let us briefly demonstrate what our whole discourse has accomplished. Because our sacrifice can neither be only the shadow or figure of the flesh and blood of Christ, nor does Christ conceal himself, *impanated* in the bread, as Berengarius maintains [1494 D], nor does the truth tolerate the idea that the substance of bread and wine is changed in part [*ex parte*], and in part persists unchanged, nor that it is right to believe that after the change it reverts back into that which it was, or that it is changed into anything else, it stands to reason, then, that this only, with the help of God, would be pure and solid faith: that all of that bread and all of that wine of the altar of the Lord are therefore substantially [*substantialiter*], by way of divine consecration, changed [*commutentur*] into the flesh and blood of Christ. Afterwards, therefore, they can be absolutely nothing other than, from now unto eternity, the flesh and blood of our Savior, the Lord God Jesus Christ, to whom we offer eternal thanks for so great a grace. Who reigns with God the Father, and the Holy Spirit, forever and ever. Amen.

INDICES

GENERAL INDEX

accidents, 9, 19, 20, 124, 125, 136, 194, 195

Ambrose, St., xiii, 18, 47–50, 51n42, 59, 67, 68n94, 70n98, 77, 78, 80, 83, 84n174, 120, 124, 129, 177–80, 193, 194, 197, 198n45, 199, 201

appearance, 6, 8–11, 14, 16, 17, 18, 20, 51, 53–57, 64, 66, 75–77, 104, 130, 131, 133, 136, 142, 157, 159, 161, 170, 191, 194, 195, 199, 213, 216; *see* species

atteri, 12, 13, 14, 16, 33, 96, 99, 100, 101–3, 117

Augustine, St., xi, xiii, 30, 42–47, 52–55, 57, 58, 63–65, 70–72, 73n113, 76–80, 81n161, 82, 84–86, 95, 96, 107n33, 108, 112n48, 113n50, 115n53, 118, 120, 124, 137, 142, 144, 145–49, 154, 155n60, 157–65, 167, 171, 172, 174–77, 182, 189, 201, 203, 206, 207, 213, 215

Berengarius, xiii, 3–5, 8, 12, 21, 27, 29, 31, 33–35, 38–43, 46–48, 51–55, 58–60, 91–98, 128, 129, 131, 133, 135–37, 140–44, 158, 160–62, 164, 167–71, 179–81, 191, 192, 204, 205, 207, 218

body of Christ, 7, 8, 10–16, 20, 34, 42, 49, 51, 52, 55, 56, 59, 61, 65, 67–69, 71, 73, 75–77, 80, 84, 86, 87, 93, 102, 104n27, 105, 106, 108, 109n36, 110, 116, 121, 125n84, 134–36, 141, 143, 144, 151, 156, 157, 164, 165–67, 169, 171, 173, 174, 176, 180, 193, 195, 196, 198, 199, 207, 208, 216; body of the

Lord, 5, 6, 10, 12, 43, 49, 54, 64–66, 84, 100, 106, 110, 118n61, 130, 134, 137, 138, 141, 142, 146, 147, 149, 151, 154–56, 164, 170, 173, 182, 190, 191, 192, 196, 200, 208, 212, 216; born of Mary, 4, 159n65, 193n34; crushed by teeth, 13, 100, 104, 195n40, 204; incorruptible, 61, 116, 132; undivided, 14, 15, 105, 106, 107, 116, 195, 196

Bread-Minglers, 173, 174n1, 199, 200; *see Impanatores*

change, accidental, 18, 19, 20; four causes and generations, 121–27; substantial, 4, 6, 8, 18, 19, 20, 21, 33, 34, 97n13, 117, 124, 125n82, 169, 170, 207, 218

Communion, Holy, 12, 37, 94, 95

commutari, 7, 19, 21, 47, 126, 197, 207

conversion (of elements), 4, 6, 10, 21, 35, 49

converti, 4, 7, 21, 34, 81

Council of 1059, 3, 4, 12, 13, 23n94, 33n9, 205n70

Council of 1079, xv, 3, 4, 5, 11, 20, 21, 34n11, 205n68

Council of Tours, 38, 205

Cyril of Alexandria, xiii, 63, 64n80, 180, 181n18

dissipari, 12, 14, 16, 96, 109n36

elements, 4, 6, 8, 9, 10, 18, 21, 49, 51, 68, 97, 126, 135, 188, 193n34, 198

essence, 5–7, 9, 10, 11, 41, 45, 46, 50, 66, 76, 133, 136, 159, 217

INDEX OF HOLY SCRIPTURE